TO SHOW
ANOTHER WAY

TO SHOW ANOTHER WAY

*How to Learn, Heal, and Serve
at a Time of Crisis on Planet Earth*

BY SUSAN S. TROUT, PhD

THREE ROSES PRESS • ALEXANDRIA VIRGINIA

Susan S. Trout: *To Show Another Way:*
How to Learn, Heal, and Serve at a Time of Crisis on Planet Earth

Portions of this book were first published in *Born to Serve:*
The Evolution of the Soul Through Service, The Awakened Leader:
Leadership as a Classroom of the Soul; and *The Clarion Call:*
Leadership and Group Life in the Aquarian Era.
Others were first published in Susan Trout's blog and in newsletters
of the Institute for the Advancement of Service.

Published by Three Roses Press, P.O. Box 320245, Alexandria, VA 22320
Printed in the United States of America
Signature Book Printing, www.sbpbooks.com

ISBN-13: 978-1-7340102-0-6
Library of Congress Control Number: 2020901297
Cover and book design by Jane Perini
Thunder Mountain Design & Communications
Photo by Maggie Scobie

Be mindful
when you have an opportunity
to show another way.

Message from Masters
when asked what we could do to help
restore Light, Love, and Power on Earth.
Source Unknown.

To all
who, by word or example,
show another way
to learn, heal, and serve
at this time of crisis
on Planet Earth

TABLE OF CONTENTS

INTRODUCTION

Never forget that you are one of a kind.
Never forget that if there weren't any need for you
in all your uniqueness to be on this earth,
you wouldn't be here in the first place.

~ BUCKMINSTER FULLER

These are delicate times on Planet Earth. Rather than facing and resolving the numerous crises that exist throughout the world, there is a strong impulse to bury our heads in the sand. We are overwhelmed by what is already part of our reality, what the future is likely to bring, and what urgent actions must be taken to bring about the healing of our planet. Denial is humanity's defense against recognizing the truth of what has become a life-and-death actuality. It is the human way to think only of our own needs, ignoring unpleasant facts and willfully remaining ignorant.

Many of us have pondered and prayed for clarity regarding our personal responsibility in solving rather than perpetuating the upheavals humanity is currently experiencing. Whatever is ours to do on Earth at this time must honor the wisdom of our hearts, the nature of our minds, and the stamina of our bodies. My own prayers for clarity regarding the Institute's and my responsibility were answered on April 1, 2019.

April 1 is an auspicious day in the history of the Institute for the Advancement of Service, the spiritual-educational nonprofit organization I cofounded 40 years ago. (For more information on the Institute, see the back of this book.) On April 1 in 1997, I received the Dalai Lama's foreword to my book, *Born to Serve: The Evolution of the Soul Through Service*, in the mail. Earlier that year I had a dream in which the Dalai Lama asked me about the book's focus. I sensed he wanted me to ask him to write its foreword.

Unsure of what action, if any, to take, I asked a Buddhist monk about the meaning of my dream. He immediately responded, "You must do it! You must do it—you must ask him to write the foreword!" I contacted a colleague who personally knew the Dalai Lama and asked her to relay my request to him. She did so and he agreed. On April 1, 1997, the day before *Born to Serve* went to press, the foreword arrived from Dharamshala, India.

April 1, 2019, proved to be another momentous day for the Institute. On this particular day, I noticed a dramatic change in a large photograph of Swami Muktananda in the Institute's meditation room. Swami Muktananda is the founder of the Siddha Yoga Path in Ganeshpuri, India. Soon after I acquired the picture in 2010, I noticed that his mouth was moving constantly—as though he were chanting. To my surprise, **his picture changed dramatically on April 1, 2019**. On that day and for many days after, he chanted in the picture with *gusto,* his body swaying back and forth. He was so alive I thought he would jump out of the picture! His eyes glistened and Light filled his face.

The instant Swami Muktananda's picture changed, I knew that I would write a book that supported and guided people during our current crisis on Planet Earth. The book would view Earth as a school and explore what we, its "students," learn from what it teaches us. Concise and easily applied universal teachings would offer practical suggestions and the kind of encouragement and direction so many people are searching for as we wrestle with how to save our planet. The book, *To Show Another Way*, was born on April 1 and was completed three months later.

To Show Another Way

Years ago, I read an unpublished book dictated by a group of Masters from the higher realms. The Masters shared that many souls were asking them what they could do, as part of humanity, to help restore Light and Love on Earth NOW—during these dangerous, unpredictable, and transitional times. The Masters response to their inquiry was this:

Be mindful when you have an opportunity to show another way.

Reading this message affected me profoundly. The Masters did not specifically state to whom we were to show another way. When I read the Masters' message, I understood that, not only are we **to show another way** to others, *we must first show another way to* *ourselves—AND we must show another way to care for our Home, Planet Earth.* All that I have subsequently written about and taught at the Institute has been inspired by this message.

For years, few people responded to my verbal and written expressions of the Masters' message. I recognized that the dramatic shift in Muktananda's picture, together with the ongoing love and assistance of his successor, Swami Chidvilasananda, was energizing the Masters' message. I was being given the strength and wisdom to write a book about **showing another way** to live and be during this unstable time on Planet Earth.

To Show Another Way is intended to be a loving and supportive companion that can comfort and guide those currently experiencing intense insecurity, fear, and pain. The book's teachings respond to the sincere wish I have heard expressed by many people to develop inner strength for themselves and to help others do the same. As one of the teachings in this book explicitly states, in the face of these challenges, even the strong must be made stronger (see Chapter Six, "The Strong Must Be Made Stronger").

It is important to be gentle with yourself as you work with the teachings in this book. Learning **to show another way** is like learning a new language—it requires sustained effort, steadfastness of purpose, and, most importantly, *patience* as we learn to see, speak, listen, and act differently in service to ourselves, others, and Planet Earth. Although some of the ideas in this book may not be new to you, applying them consistently is a spiritual path in itself. If you can view the process of your learning through the eyes of the heart, you will speed your progress and lighten your way. You can, in other words, **show yourself another way** to learn through patience, gentleness, and love.

I often ask myself, "What if people who believed in my potential and opened doors for me throughout my life had not been there **to show me another way?"** Many people have helped me transform an experience—whether it was a challenge, misjudgment, or trauma—into learning, healing, and service. Some have pulled me back from the brink of disaster and literally saved my life. Why wouldn't we want to do this for others and for ourselves as well?

The responsibility of parents and teachers to show their children and students another way to learn and relate to one another is fundamental. Parents are responsible for guiding their child's developing psyche, teaching the child about civility, tolerance, patience, and self-worth. Teachers are responsible for assuring their students do not suffer school trauma, which occurs when ineffective teaching methods are used and when children are bullied because they have learning or social challenges.

We might note here the contribution to the emotional and social wellbeing of young children by the great educator Fred Rogers in his preschool television series, "Mister Rogers' Neighborhood." His pioneering TV show taught children about tolerance, sharing, and self-worth, addressing such topics as the death of a family pet, sibling rivalry, and divorce. Rogers himself had a difficult childhood, one in which he was shy, ill, and often taunted and bullied for being overweight. He is an excellent example of someone who learned and healed from his own personal traumas to go on **to show another way** to the many young children who learned from his gentle, accepting manner and profound teachings.

This book's universal teachings can potentially transform each life event into learning, healing, and service, helping humanity—and all of nature—restore Light and Love on Earth. Individuals and members of various groups, including families, communities, workplaces, states, and countries are searching for responsible ways to live on Planet Earth.

Showing another way to ourselves and others
is the ultimate purpose of Earth as a school.

Earth as a School

We are spiritual beings having a physical experience on Earth. As such, the purpose of being on Earth is to learn, heal, and help others. We share the gifts of what we have learned and healed in our life by **showing others another way** to care for themselves and for our Home. We are not meant to view what happens in our life as an excuse to harm ourselves, others, or Planet Earth.

To show another way does not only mean being shown *positive* ways. We may view some of our early life circumstances and perhaps even later ones as damaging to our wellbeing and assume we have not been **shown another way**. Know that traumatic life experiences at any age can show us what **not** to be or do for ourselves or for others. We can transform our negative life experiences into positive teachings, recognizing that we have, indeed, been **shown another way.** This knowledge and awareness can support us in **showing another way** to others who have experienced life in a similar way.

Earth as a school offers opportunities to learn what it means to be human and to help others and our planet. We are on Planet Earth to

- identify and heal our mental, emotional, and spiritual wounds,
- care for our physical body,
- learn specific lessons unique to us that we came to Earth in order to learn,
- share what we have learned and healed through our behavior, words, and service to others,
- see the bigger picture of what gifts Earth offers to humanity,
- honor and care for Earth's wellbeing, and
- experience the presence of the Divine in ourselves, others, and Planet Earth.

We waste our life on Earth when we fail to learn from our mistakes, failures, grievances, and challenges, as well as from our successes, gifts, and talents. We squander what we have learned if we do not, in some way, apply what we know and extend the gifts of our learning to help others and the planet.

I have identified several universal teachings of Earth as a school which make up the substance of this book. This curriculum has been developed, taught, and used at the Institute for the past forty years. It includes teachings and practices involving spirituality, psychology and neuropsychology, metaphysics, physical and mental health, communication skills, true leadership, and group consciousness.

Topics of the curriculum of Earth as a school as developed at the Institute include teachings and practices in the following twelve subject areas:

- Seeing the Bigger Picture of Life on Earth
- Taking Humanity's Next Evolutionary Leap
- Honoring Commitment and Self-Responsibility
- Knowing What Really Matters in Life
- Helping Nature Heal
- Radiating Light

- ◆ Living Our Destiny
- ◆ Engaging in Personal Healing
- ◆ Joining Heart and Mind
- ◆ Loving Our Will
- ◆ Receiving the Gift of Spirituality
- ◆ Serving Others and the Planet

This curriculum is explored in depth in *The Soul of Service Trilogy*, a series of books I wrote between 1997 and 2009, which constitutes the Institute's fundamental teachings. *The Trilogy* includes *Born to Serve: The Evolution of the Soul through Service* (1997), *The Awakened Leader: Leadership as a Classroom of the Soul* (2005), and *The Clarion Call: Leadership and Group Life in the Aquarian Era* (2009). *To Show Another Way* can be considered a distillation of *The Trilogy*'s teachings that have been revised, amplified, and assembled to address the unique needs on our planet at this specific time in the destiny of our world.

The teachings in *To Show Another Way* offer ways to successfully participate in the curriculum of Earth as a school. They provide insight, comfort, healing, and approaches to personal growth and service that are especially relevant during the current crisis on Planet Earth. To engage with these teachings is to take profound action. When we commit to **showing another way** to ourselves and others, especially at this time—when it is both particularly challenging and crucially necessary to do so to save our own lives and the life of our Home—we take the first step toward our ultimate destiny as human beings: to evolve as souls by extending the gifts of our learning in service to others.

Our greatest glory is not in never falling,
but in rising every time we fall.

~ Confucius

HOW TO WORK WITH THIS BOOK

True humility is staying teachable
regardless of how much we already know.

~ Anonymous

Preparing to Work with the Teachings of This Book

Taking the following two inventories before beginning to work with the teachings in *To Show Another Way* will introduce you to the spirit and intention of this book.

1. **Make a list of people or events in your life that you recognize as having shown you another way.** Typically, we are shown another way when we are not expecting it. Being shown another way often comes as a surprise. Its power can enhance, expand, redirect, or even save our life. We typically never forget receiving this unexpected and treasured gift. **This list should reveal both positive and negative ways you have been shown another way. As you make your list, consider negative circumstances as well as positive ones.**

   One positive example of how I was **shown another way** was when I was a freshman in college. I had begun focusing on extracurricular activities—that is to say, *parties*—at the expense of using my time for my studies. At one of the parties, a young man I did not know suddenly walked up to me and said, "You don't belong here. Your life is about something far more important and you need to pay attention to that. Don't waste your life." I felt the truth of what he was saying as, indeed, I was trying to learn how to be a "social butterfly" so I would fit in with my peers. There have been many people throughout my life who have made comments that suggested I was off-purpose with what I came on Earth to be and do. Always, I took such comments seriously, and with a sense of gratitude, became more conscious of how I spent my time and made more appropriate choices.

My experience at the party was an example of how we can be shown another way through a *positive* experience. **We can also be shown another way when someone treats us in a way that has a negative influence on our life.** In some cases, we might live many years with only negative experiences of being shown another way before we realize that these experiences are actually revealing another way for us to live our life. Most of us have had experiences with harsh, hurtful or abusive people and events. Although they may not at first seem to have done so, these people and events also **showed us another way:** they showed us the *opposite* way to be treated, to treat others, and to live our life. When we are treated with cruelty or unkindness, we are being shown there is also another way to choose to speak, to interact, to live, to *be.* For this reason, **your list should include both the positive and negative circumstances of how you have been shown another way.**

2. **Make a list of people or groups who have told you that you have shown them another way,** sometimes many years after the event. It is common not to be aware of what you said or did at the time and therefore have no memory of it. If so, you will probably respond, "I said (or did) that? I don't remember doing so." **When this is true, it is likely your intent to show another way was pure, inspired, and appropriate to the person or situation.**

For example, a person whom I counseled during a crisis in her life nearly 30 years ago recently said to me, "I am here on Earth today because you saved my life many years ago. I had decided to end my life at the time and, because of the way you related to me, I didn't follow through with my plan." In fact, several people have told me that I saved their lives and I have no memory of when or how I did that.

How to Work with the Teachings

To Show Another Way has 12 chapters. Each chapter has four teachings and there is a total of 48 teachings in the book. The teachings present a variety of approaches for **showing another way** to ourselves and others. I have lived these teachings and taught them to thousands of people for more than 55 years, and they have been tested and proven to be relevant in people's lives. They are universal teachings—true and applicable for anyone, regardless of age, occupation, level of education, stage of life, spiritual orientation, or lifestyle. Because they are timeless, they will always be pertinent regardless of when you choose to work with them in your life. At the same time the teachings are timeless, they are also time-*ly*. I wrote them to address the needs of people across the globe trying to makes sense of and learn to live in a world that is dangerously imploding—both literally and figuratively.

One way to work with *To Show Another Way* is to focus on one teaching a week over the course of a year. At the end of each teaching, you are offered ways to apply it in your life. You may wish to dedicate a personal journal to recording your responses, experiences, reflections, and insights when engaging with the applications.

Although the book has been structured as a year-long study, with the teachings progressing from introductory to more advanced, you might choose instead to focus on a certain teaching or topic that addresses a current and urgent need. In the Appendices, a Table by Topics is provided to help you locate teachings that address each of the book's 12 subject areas. A Table of Practices is also offered for easy access to the various practices, such as meditations and prayers, included throughout the book.

Another way to work with *To Show Another Way* is to participate in a Support Circle that studies and applies its teachings. A guide with suggestions on how to structure a Support Circle, including information on the group's purpose, agenda, practices, communication guidelines, and healthy group boundaries, is also included at the back of the book.

Your responses to the self-inquiry questions at the end of each teaching will help you identify what weakens your inner strength and what makes you stronger. The questions encourage you to take a fresh, honest, nonjudgmental look at how successful you are in **showing another way to yourself and to others**. Self-inquiry questions can assist you in identifying life patterns that either help or hinder specific aspects of your physical, mental, emotional, and spiritual strength. Self-inquiry also strengthens your **commitment** to practice the teachings.

The Power of Commitment: Guiding Principles

There are a hundred valid reasons why something can't be done,
but only one reason, commitment, why it can.

~ JONATHAN LOCKWOOD HUIE

To benefit fully from Planet Earth as a school—a classroom of life—we need to embrace the power of commitment. When we consistently practice commitment, we discover that taking action and gaining results becomes easier and makes us stronger. Commitment is a process, the result not of waving a magic wand but of patience and practice. I invite you to make a personal commitment to fully engage in the teachings of *To Show Another Way*, knowing that Earth's school gifts us with unique opportunities to learn, heal, and serve.

Commitment can be absent or inconsistent under certain circumstances, including when we feel forced into something, when we feel obligated, when our actions don't match our beliefs, when we are working so hard that we are burned out and always unhappy, or when making a commitment feels like an impossible burden. If we fear making a commitment, it may be because we have a fear of the unknown, have anxiety about possible failure, or have concerns of not having sufficient time to meet both work and personal commitments.

Here are 14 guiding principles that strengthen the power of commitment within us:

1. Commitment connects our values, intentions, and actions.

2. Passion is the fire from within that motivates us and allows commitment to blossom.

3. Persistence and patience are qualities of the will that enable us to manifest our commitment long after the initial excitement is gone and when it is not easy. (To develop and strengthen the will, see Chapter Eight.)

4. When we commit fully to engaging in the process that will manifest an idea, the outcomes will be what they are meant to be. If we commit merely to the outcome and ignore the process, we have sabotaged both.

5. Commitment means keeping our word and involves congruency between intent, words, and action.

6. Commitment asks us to be authentic—who we are matches how we are being.

7. Commitment and vision are inexplicably tied together. When we expand our vision while deepening our commitment, we can produce powerful results.

8. Commitment inspires us to be and do our best.

9. While commitment lives in the declaration and words, evidence of commitment lives in the actions we take and do not take.

10. We choose to create what we want when we surrender to our commitment.

11. We *show* our commitment, over and over, in our actions. If our actions do not match our commitment, we simply *are not* committed to it. We may have a belief, a hunch, a preference, a desire, but not a commitment.

12. Commitment can be fulfilling an unpleasant obligation that is freely chosen. An example of this would be taking a teaching post at an impoverished school where the working conditions are poor, salaries are low, and supplies are not available.

13. Commitment is larger than just us and can involve creating a better world, not for just ourselves but for generations to come.

14. When we make a choice, we simultaneously make a commitment to that choice and accept responsibility for the outcome of that choice.

*When you're interested in doing something, you do it only
when it's convenient. When you're committed to something,
you accept no excuses, only results.*

~ KENNETH BLANCHARD

Until One Is Committed…

Scottish mountaineer and writer, W. H. Murray (1913-1996), joined the British Army at the start of World War II and was captured in Egypt in June 1942. He spent three years in prisoner of war camps in Europe, where he wrote a book entitled *Mountaineering in Scotland* entirely on toilet paper, the only paper he had available. After the Nazi guards found and destroyed the manuscript, Murray started the book again. At the time, because his health had degenerated from the poor diet in the camps, he believed he would never climb again. The likelihood was also strong that the guards would find the new manuscript. Yet, to the astonishment of his fellow prisoners, Murray persisted. The second manuscript survived and was finally published in 1947.

Murray's intrepid determination in the face of such adversity reflects the heart and soul of commitment. He went on to write several more books on the subject of mountaineering. In one of these, *The Scottish Himalayan Expedition* (1951), he penned some of the most frequently quoted lines about commitment in the English language—about what happens when we don't have it, and what happens when we do.

Asked by a friend and fellow mountaineer to help plan a Scottish expedition to the yet un-climbed Garhwal peaks in the Himalayas, Murray contemplated the multiple difficulties the team faced in planning the trip, let alone carrying it out. These included the team's inexperience in Himalayan mountaineering, their inability to speak the language of the region, the unavailability of maps, the quantities of food and gear that would be required to be prepared, and the little time available to plan the expedition. The problems seemed insurmountable, and Murray despaired that "nothing had been done" at the eight-week point at which he had been brought on to help organize the mission.

His famous quotation on commitment follows. I have placed his words on the page as a poem in order to honor their power and emphasize their wisdom:

[W]hen I said that nothing had been done I erred in one important matter. We had definitely committed ourselves and were halfway out of our ruts. We had put down our passage money—booked a sailing to Bombay. This may sound too simple, but is great in consequence.

> Until one is committed
> There is hesitancy, the chance to draw back,
> Always ineffectiveness.
> Concerning all acts of initiative (and creation),
> There is one elementary truth,
> The ignorance of which kills countless ideas
> And splendid plans:
>
> That the moment one definitely commits oneself,
> Then Providence moves too.
> All sorts of things occur to help one
> that would never otherwise have occurred.
> A whole stream of events issues from the decision,
> Raising in one's favour all manner
> Of unforeseen incidents and meetings
> And material assistance,
> Which no man could have dreamt would have come his way.
>
> I have learned a deep respect
> For one of Goethe's couplets:
> "Whatever you can do, or dream you can, begin it.
> Boldness has genius, power, and magic in it."

Take the Hand of Tomorrow for the Yesterday Is No More

*Many things about tomorrow I don't seem to understand
but I know who holds tomorrow and I know who holds my hand.*

~ AUTHOR UNKNOWN

We stand precariously at the midpoint of the transition from the Piscean Era to the Aquarian Era—what was "the yesterday" and what will be "the tomorrow." No longer having a foothold in the past, we step onto uncharted land. Old organizational structures and belief systems collapse around us as new ones emerge. Our beloved Planet Earth is in crisis and calls on humanity to rescue it from extreme ecological and spiritual distress. Conflicts between the old and new and the known and unknown arise. We struggle to adjust to change and develop new models of living on our planet before we do it further harm. We know we are connected in a meaningful way to one another and to all Earth's animate and inanimate reality. We are not isolated from one another in the world nor are we separated from the Divine. The more we align with our connectedness, the more we experience help from God, Goddess, All That Is—and the more we are mindful when we have an opportunity **to show another way.**

Piscean "yesterday" that is no more	Aquarian "hand of tomorrow" that shows another way
Competition	Cooperation
Hierarchical decisions	Shared decisions
Separation from leader and one another	Partnership with leader and one another
Territorial priorities	Global priorities
Homogeneity	Diversity
Self-discovery	Group discovery
Personal vision	Shared vision
Individual needs	Group needs
Outer authority	Inner authority
Problem solving by addressing effects	Problem solving by addressing cause
Separation of spirituality and science	Integration of spirituality and science
Brotherhood	Brotherhood and Sisterhood; humanity
Superiority of masculine energy	Equality of masculine and feminine energy
Disregard and abuse of Planet Earth	Care and respect for Planet Earth

Take the Hand of Tomorrow

As individuals, leaders, groups, and countries, we take the hand of tomorrow when we

- ◆ are mindful when we have an opportunity **to show another way** to be in the world,
- ◆ welcome the emerging consciousness of the Aquarian era,
- ◆ know the feminine heart is united with the masculine mind,
- ◆ deepen and unify our inner life,
- ◆ transform our organizations and communities as awakened leaders and groups so that we can truly support our members and those we serve,
- ◆ go beyond focusing on self-transformation by dedicating our life to serving humanity and Planet Earth,

◆ harvest the good from where we have been and welcome change, calling on the wisdom of the Universe to help us with the practical application of that awareness, and

◆ deepen our collective understanding of what wants to emerge in the world.

A Clarion Call to Action

As we take a step through the Aquarian doorway, we hear a clarion call to action. We feel the urgency of the planetary transformation and the need to seek creative ways to participate. We choose between the old and the new and between what was and what will be. We move beyond religiosity into spirituality. We practice cooperation and learn how to live as one global family. We are mindful when we have an opportunity **to show another way**. *We take the hand of tomorrow for the yesterday is no more.*

You have to take ownership and leadership of tomorrow.
For that to be possible, you have to strengthen your capacity
and widen your vision as a global citizen.

~ BAN KI-MOON, DEPUTY CHAIR OF THE ELDERS

To Show Another Way: Applications

Journal on two or more of the following questions to deepen your understanding of this teaching and make it practical in your own life. It is essential to be specific as you respond in order to go deeper in your awareness and understanding.

◆ In what ways can I **show others another way** to "take the hand of tomorrow?"

◆ What is my next step in practicing group cooperation?

◆ If I don't already have a meaningful connection with nature, how can I develop one?

◆ How am I preparing for challenges that presently exist and for those yet to come?

◆ If what is true for the world at large is true for me, in what way am I a microcosm of the macrocosm?

Start Where You Stand

Wherever you stand, be the soul of that place.
Your bright gaze will kindle this old shadow world
To blaze up once again with the fire of faith.

~ RUMI

In the previous teaching, we focused on where humanity stands as it transitions from the Piscean to the Aquarian Era. In this teaching, we'll explore where we, as individuals, stand in various aspects of our personal and interpersonal life.

Starting where we stand doesn't mean we are where we want to be or that we even like where we stand. Rather, starting where we stand asks us to be honest about where we are in our life—what we already know versus what we have to learn, when we do or don't live our spiritual ideals, and how open we are to think, live, and act in a more genuine way.

For example, we may realize that where we now stand is in overwhelm, anxiety, and fear, recognizing we have limited tools to work with our various issues. We may have already been introduced to approaches we can use—perhaps in a book we've read or a speech we've heard or from a healing workshop we've attended. How many times have we gathered physical, emotional, or spiritual methods and never used them or tested their relevance in our life? Perhaps we now want to take a stand of a different sort, a stand to *drop our resistance* to **being shown another way.** Perhaps we are ready to make a genuine effort to be the person we are destined to be.

Start Where You Stand: An Example

Some years ago, a peace march was organized in New York City on the day the United Nations was debating whether to pass a resolution on disarmament. Thich Nhất Hanh, the Zen Buddhist monk and peace activist, joined fifty of his multinational, multicultural friends and marched holding a banner that read, "Reverence for Life." They decided to walk down the streets of Manhattan in the style of a walking meditation. Thich Nhất Hanh writes in his book, *Creating True Peace*:

> Groups of young people around us were marching quickly, almost running, and shouting slogans like "Disarmament now! Down with nuclear weapons!" Our group did not say anything; we just walked slowly and peacefully. We learned later that, because of our way of walking, we slowed 300,000 people behind us. Throughout the long walk, there were groups behind us shouting, "Can't you walk faster?" trying to pass us. When they went by us, they would look back in frustration at this cluster of people who were moving so slowly. But then a curious thing happened. As they watched us, they changed their attitude, quieted down, and began to walk more slowly themselves. **It became a true peace walk.** People still remember this walk because of the small group in the "March for Peace" who actually practiced peace with every step they took.

Thich Nhất Hanh's choice to use a walking meditation as a tool is an example of what it means to **start where you stand**. His decision is also an example of **showing another way**. It was not the number of miles he and his group walked or the speed of their step that expressed their stand. Rather, they used what they knew and knew where they stood. **They used the tool of mindfulness as their way of conveying their stand for peace, and their mindfulness worked to show another way** to the other peace activists. The frustrated and impatient marchers, whose tools were shouting slogans and running, were using the tools *they* had. Thanks to Thich Nhất Hanh's example, they soon found better tools to use.

Exploring Where We Stand Today

Understanding how to start where we stand invites us to identify where we are NOW in our life: our philosophy of life and how we view our purpose, mission, personal vision, and shared vision—the vision we share with the groups with which we are involved. Periodically reflecting on the following questions helps us identify where we stand:

- ◆ What is my philosophy of life?
- ◆ Why am I here? (purpose)
- ◆ What am I to do while I am here? (mission)
- ◆ Where do I want to go while I'm here—what do I want to reach for? (vision)
- ◆ Whom am I to go with—who shares my vision? (shared vision)

We can also explore starting where we stand in specific settings or aspects of our life that may or may not reflect our philosophy, purpose, mission, and vision, such as

- ◆ events and relationships in our daily life, including present challenges and/or opportunities,
- ◆ relationships with a coworker, parent, family member, friend, and so forth,
- ◆ the status of our fulfilled and unfulfilled dreams,
- ◆ the nature of our work in the world,
- ◆ special interests and projects,
- ◆ elected membership in groups or committees, and/or
- ◆ beliefs and actions as a citizen of our community and country.

A gap typically occurs between where we stand now in our life and where we wish to stand in the near or far future. This gap creates what learning organizational expert, Peter Senge, calls *creative tension.*

Creative Tension

Energy is created between our current reality and our vision of what we wish to become. An energy generates a force within us called "creative tension." This energy keeps both our vision and a clear picture of our current reality before us. This is **not** the same as emotional tension, anxiety, or stress due to discouragement, hopelessness, or worry. There is no emotional tension in creative tension. If we equate emotional tension with creative tension, we will have a tendency to lower our vision as a way to reduce our emotional tension. The price for doing this is abandoning the vision of what we really want.

Creative tension is the recognition that, at this time, our current reality does not match our vision. At the same time, the gap between our vision and our current reality provides the very energy source needed to take action. We can use the energy of the gap to generate change and make the gap smaller between our vision and our current reality.

Peter Senge writes: "Failure is, simply, a shortfall, evidence of the gap between vision and current reality. Failure is an opportunity for learning—about inaccurate pictures of current reality, about strategies that didn't work as expected, about the clarity of the vision. Failures are not about our unworthiness or powerlessness." His explanation **shows us another way** to view the gap between where we are and where we want to be.

Living Life Completely and Well

Starting where we stand in various aspects of our life invites us to welcome **the journey of living life completely and well**. Such a journey requires that we welcome creative tension into our life. Creative tension allows us to identify our current reality and thus where we have yet to go. To do this we can practice becoming aware that, if we do this or that, our vision will be closer to realization.

Instead of feeling victimized, resentful, or bitter, we have a choice to be responsible for our feelings and reactions and to learn from them. When we choose to learn from our life experiences, the quality of our relationship with ourselves and others changes. We deepen our compassion for those in pain, whether they are of the human, animal, or plant kingdoms. When we live life completely and well, we learn from our experiences, attain a pure heart, and have a quiet mind—we learn, grow and serve at this time of crisis on Planet Earth. When we start where we stand and honor the creative tension between our vision and our current reality, we live a soul-inspired life.

A mistake is an event,
the full benefit of which
has not yet been turned to your advantage.

~ ED LAND, INVENTOR

To Show Another Way: Applications

1. Apply the teaching of "Start Where You Stand" to a current situation or aspect of your life in which you're seeking guidance about your next step. The situation or aspect of your life that you select can be personal or involve the health and well-being of your workplace, home, city, state, country, or Planet Earth.

   Use the above sections "Exploring Where I Stand Today" and "Creative Tension" as guides for your exploration.

2. Consider the following question through contemplation or journaling: How is my example of "Exploring Where I Stand Today" **showing me another way?**

What Really Matters

We cannot change the world as it is,
but by opening ourselves to the world as it is,
we may find that gentleness, decency and bravery are available –
not only to us but to all human beings.

~ CHÖGYAM TRUNGPA, TIBETAN BUDDHIST MASTER

Have you noticed that truth, when clearly stated, is typically short, to the point, and has a universal appeal? This is true for the following six teachings. If practiced daily, these truths can literally transform our personal life and the life of Planet Earth. Why? Because they tell us *what really matters,* using universal language that speaks to the soul of humanity.

Showing Another Way

Ask yourself this question: "What if people who believed in my potential and opened doors for me throughout my life had not been there **to show me another way?"**

Many people have helped us transform an experience, challenge, misjudgment, or trauma into learning, healing, and service by saying or doing the right thing at the right time in the right way. Some have literally saved our life or rescued us from a wrong and possibly dangerous decision. *What really matters* **is that we help others in the same way.**

A Devotional Life

Our soul is on earth to experience human life and to learn spiritual lessons that the school of Earth offers—unconditional love, forgiveness, compassion, peace, serenity… and how to care for the health and wellbeing of our home, Planet Earth. To live a devotional life is progressively to surrender ourselves to our Divinity in all that we think, say, and do. In this state we are willing channels through which powerful Love and Light energies can flow and enrich our personal life, relationships, and chosen service on behalf of Mother Earth.

What really matters is that we commit to the human actions that underpin the integrity of life on Planet Earth: prayer—meditation—alignment with Soul—service.

Humility

We are humble when we recognize we are not on Earth to discover how important we are but rather to learn to live a meaningful life and make a difference in the lives of others. *What really matters* is allowing humility to teach us regardless of how much we think we already know and understand.

Forgiveness

Forgiveness allows us to stand free of any guilt associated with our negative feelings and actions about our life. Through forgiveness, we achieve a genuine acceptance of ourselves and others. We become healers of that which we ourselves have been healed. When we have healed a particular grievance within ourselves, we naturally and effortlessly extend "the gift of lilies" to those we believe harmed us, and choose to use what we have learned from our life to help others and our planet. (See Chapter Three Teaching Four for an extended teaching on forgiveness as "the gift of lilies.")

Partnering with Planet Earth

Planet Earth and all living things, including animals and plants, are in grave distress due to humanity's exploitation, abuse, and misuse of her lands, seas, and sky. *What really matters* is that every human being becomes responsible for healing and preserving the planet, moving beyond focusing only on self-transformation to becoming Earth's loving and knowledgeable partner.

Spiritual Awareness and Selfless Service

Service is life itself, giving and receiving in every encounter, whether that encounter is with other people, animals, a cause, the material world, or oneself. Selfless service is giving *what really matters*—the right thing in the right amount for the right reason and at the right time. Our service extends Light and Love into the world through prayer, meditation, and action.

> *The only way to survive the level of turmoil we are facing in the world is to pursue life in a different way.*
>
> ~ JAMES REDFIELD

To Show Another Way: Applications

Describe how practicing the six teachings on *what really matters* can potentially transform your life:

- ◆ Showing Another Way
- ◆ A Devotional Life
- ◆ Humility
- ◆ True Forgiveness
- ◆ Partnering with Planet Earth
- ◆ Spiritual Awareness and Selfless Service

S.O.S. ~ Pray for Planet Earth

The Earth needs our prayers and practice, the light of our spiritual aspiration.
Her cry is both for our hands and hearts, for our love and care.
This is a calling to those who are awake to bring together heaven and earth,
spirit and matter, to remember that every step is sacred.

~ LLEWELLYN VAUGHAN-LEE

Alarm bells are ringing. Our beloved planet is experiencing extreme ecological and spiritual distress. The resilience and regenerative ability of Earth's ecosystem is no longer sustainable. Organisms—all living things—and their environments are unable to play their distinctive role in the interconnected ecosystem of relationships. The air, land, and water are toxic, poisoning what we eat, drink, and breathe, causing birth defects and life-threatening diseases. The dire consequences of global warming, natural disasters, and the destruction of land, sea, animals, and insects, are ignored by governments with no political will. Human relationships at home and abroad have become increasingly divisive and rigidly rooted in discrimination, polarity thinking, prejudice, fear, and a separation of the "haves" and "have-nots." Violence, rage, and severe depression abound.

Earth's S.O.S. ~ *Save Our Souls*

To stop the speed of coming disaster, Planet Earth has put out an S.O.S.—a call for humanity to *Save Our Souls.* **Earth's S.O.S. asks that we design and put into practice** *a* **new story about how to live life with integrity on Planet Earth.** This new story will enable us to acknowledge our interconnectedness and to *live* it. For the good of all, we will recognize and engage our spiritual relationship with our planet. **One primary way we can live this story is by** *praying for Earth.* With **love and prayer,** we will transform our energies, from dark to light and from separation to unity. We answer the S.O.S. by aligning with our Soul and joining with humanity to create this new story—**to show another way** for ourselves, our countries, and our planet.

In his 2019 book, *Including the Earth in Our Prayers,* renowned Sufi teacher Llewellyn Vaughan-Lee writes that, "Earth is dying, species are depleted, oceans are full of plastic, as our cultures seem caught in divisiveness." Earth, who has "nourished us with Her endless generosity, whom we have raped and desecrated, is unbalanced, sick, and needs our care and attention." To survive, Vaughan-Lee contends, **humanity must immediately make a major change in its mindset by moving beyond focusing on self-transformation and by no longer denying that we are starving the Soul of the World of its spiritual energy—of Love and Light—energy that it needs for regeneration and evolution.** With a mindset of Love and Light, humanity can take action and dedicate itself to being of service to life and to Earth's Divinity.

How can we **show another way** during the uncertainty of our times? **We can keep the sacred alive with a commitment to pray for our planet daily.** We can use the opportunity this challenge of uncertainty presents by *changing our mindset.* In addition to praying for our planet, we can seek out practical ways to engage in ecology. We can plant healthy mental, emotional, and spiritual seeds within ourselves and our families. We can nurture these seeds and see what they can do with their own power over time.

How to Pray for Planet Earth

Praying for Planet Earth extends Love and Light to its entirety—inviting individuals, countries, nations, and nature (plants, animals, all living creatures, together with earth, air, land, sky, and sea) to receive Love and Light from the Divine.

Step One: Place one or both hands over your heart. In silence, visualize Planet Earth and feel its spiritual presence in your heart. You may wish to express directly to Mother Earth your deep concern for Her health and wellbeing.

Step Two: From your heart, say this prayer as many times as you wish:

> **"As part of humanity, I pray that Planet Earth receive Divine Love and Light for its highest possible evolution."**

This Buddhist prayer does not focus on what we think the planet needs, such as better government, cooperation among countries, or an improved economy. **Rather, the prayer invites Love and Light to support and guide Planet Earth's highest possible evolution at this time.**

Bringing the Prayer into Reality

After saying the prayer, we must take some sort of appropriate **action** that **shows another way**. His Holiness the Dalai Lama highlighted this need during a talk he gave to a small group a few years ago in Dharamsala, India. When asked, "Is praying for peace in the world helpful?" he responded:

> Praying for peace [or Love and Light] is good, but if that's all you do, it's a waste of time and may be counterproductive. If you walk away from such prayers feeling that you've done your part, you're deceiving yourself.

In other words, **after you pray you must *show another way* by taking appropriate actions every day to support bringing that prayer into reality.**

What actions can we personally take that **show another way** to help Planet Earth receive Divine Love and Light for its highest possible evolution? We each must reflect on what that might be for us. For example, we might decide to focus on helping nature by reducing our family's household wastefulness by more than half in the next six months. We could become active in some ecological group or committee in our community. We might volunteer at an animal shelter. We could decide to listen from our heart when communicating with others about the needs of Planet Earth. Our actions must be practical, integrous, and something we commit to doing. Small actions can lead to further actions, as well as inspire others to take action themselves. Enacted in the right spirit, any action brings us into alignment with our Soul—and this in turn serves the planet and all its inhabitants.

After regularly using the prayer, "As part of humanity, I pray that Planet Earth receive Divine Love and Light for its highest possible evolution," you will discover that you can easily connect your heart to the planet in prayer. Decide when and what amount of time you wish to spend offering prayers of Love and Light to Planet Earth. Honor that commitment.

Most importantly, call on your inner strength to handle the uncertainty of our time. Do your best not to harm and add further pain to Planet Earth. Know your life will be enriched and filled with meaning and grace when you make a commitment to answer the urgent S.O.S. from our beloved Home.

An Offering of True Service

Praying for Planet Earth is an expression of offering True Service. True Service turns the beneficial energy of our inward growth back out to flower in the external world. It supports health and wellbeing on all levels of participation—self, family, leadership, group, country, and planet. True Service is alive within us when we take any action that **shows another way** to protect our planet and all of her inhabitants, sentient and insentient.

To have a sense of empowerment and possibilities for True Service related to healing the planet, follow Theodore Roosevelt's advice to "keep your eyes on the stars and your feet on the ground." Begin NOW to live "the new story" of interdependence and sacred ecology—to *Save Our Souls* and save our beloved Planet Earth.

In spite of the fog of human brokenness and violence enshrouding the world,
the Light is always there as well.
We are the sun whose radiance can burn away the fog.
All it takes is for us to choose to be that sun, to be that Light,
and to act from that choice.

~ DAVID SPANGLER

To Show Another Way: Applications

Journal on one or more of the following questions using specific examples:

1. In what way did this teaching expand my understanding and application of "being mindful when I have an opportunity **to show another way"?**

2. How I might begin to live "the new story" of interdependence and sacred ecology on Planet Earth by **showing another way?**

3. What actions have I taken since I've begun saying the Prayer for Planet Earth: "As part of humanity, I pray that Planet Earth receive Divine Love and Light for its highest possible evolution"?

On the Wings of an Eagle

If I had the wings of an eagle
I would soar to the heights of the sky
To look down on the beauty of life itself
And the marvels of creation from on high

~ RICHARD MORIARTY

You may have noticed that the phrase, "the bigger picture," has become more prevalent in our language over the last several years. This phrase often weaves itself throughout conversations and writings of those drawn to an expanded—even an *evolutionary*—perspective of life. When we heed the call to see a bigger picture, we accept the invitation to explore what it means for ourselves, for others, and for the world at large.

A call to see the bigger picture is a call to rise above the daily fray of events, whether personal or global. In our personal life, we may face physical and mental health challenges, financial uncertainty, broken relationships, lack of education, and loneliness. Living in an unstable world adds to our distress—a world blanketed with natural disasters, wars, economic insecurity, misused technology, political upheavals, terrorism, pandemics, and threats of global destruction from climate collapse.

Eagle Consciousness

Once we choose to see the bigger picture, we expand our search for a higher consciousness that exists beyond our present comprehension of the world and our linear, black-and-white thinking. We begin to seek answers to far-reaching questions that **show us another way** to see the world, such as:

- ◆ What is the greatest need in our world today?
- ◆ How do we connect with our inner strength?
- ◆ What is the highest service we can extend to humanity?
- ◆ How do we learn to stretch our perception and see the bigger picture of our personal life, of our work, of our place on the planet, and of our Universe?

These questions remind me of what a colleague recently said to me: **"To learn to see the bigger picture, we must fly on the wings of an eagle."** In other words, to learn to see the bigger picture, we need **to be shown another way** to view the world. We must consciously rise above events and view the totality of their patterns, their energies, and their truths. We must move into more of the air element and out of the density of the earth element. We must move out of the cave of the bear into the sky of the eagle.

The eagle symbolizes high ideals, loftiness, clear insight, dignity, wisdom, and the highest place we can reach. The eagle is strength, height, authority, pride, victory, release from bondage, contemplation, inspiration, ascension, and the element of air. Mythically thought to be able to fly up to the sun and gaze unwaveringly upon it, the eagle represents the spiritual principle in humanity that soars heavenwards. Developing eagle consciousness would not be a small attainment in one's life.

Cultivating the metaphor of eagle consciousness is a powerful way to see the bigger picture of our personal life, our community, our nation, our world—and the Home where it resides, Planet Earth. On the wings of an eagle, we fly high and soar. We utilize the air element to carry us above to a place that frees us from our personality entanglements. In this place we see the greater good of all, where all differences have a win-win resolution. We see events and patterns of events; we see cause and the effect of cause.

The Bigger Picture of Service

Few of us are able to consciously and consistently see the bigger picture. To do so requires that we practice **showing ourselves another way**—readjusting our thought processes, letting go of old belief systems, and embracing a new reality. Seeing the bigger picture punctures our illusions of what we believe to be true. We learn the true meaning of the phrase, "things are not as they appear to be." Truth revealed by the bigger picture comforts us. Contrary to being fearful of what we may not know, seeing the truth of what's so can gift us with healing, relief, and serenity.

Seeing the bigger picture has a learning curve. If developing eagle consciousness is our heart-centered goal, we need to learn how and when to shift our awareness from small to large, from constraint to expansiveness, and from limitation to previously un-imaginable possibilities. Our compassionate actions will arise naturally when we see the bigger picture of service, serving others by giving the right amount of the right thing for the right reason and at the right time.

The eagle does not escape the storm.
The eagle simply uses the storm to lift it higher.
It spreads its mighty wings and rises
on the winds that bring the storm.

~ JACK WHITE

To Show Another Way: Applications

Choose one or both of the following to explore "the bigger picture" in your life:

1. Place the focus of your attention in your heart. Silently observe an interaction between two people. Use eagle consciousness by centering your awareness on "moving out of the cave of the bear into the sky of the eagle."

   Ask yourself: What impact did using eagle consciousness have on how I experienced and interpreted this interaction? On how I was **shown another way**? Be specific.

2. Fly on the wings of an eagle when you listen to or watch the news. Ask yourself these questions in relation to two or three news items:

What patterns, energies and truths emerged for me as I viewed the news from the perspective of the bigger picture? What is the larger truth "behind" the words? Behind the nonverbal language of news reporters and those being reported on? How was I **shown another way** to listen to or watch the news?

Be a Cathedral Builder

Mankind was never so happily inspired as when it made a cathedral.

~ Robert Louis Stevenson

A s "residents" of Planet Earth, we have access to a unique personal quality that enables us to stand strong when facing extremely challenging circumstances. That quality? The ability to see the bigger picture. In fact, the idiom we use to describe the opposite—when we "can't see the forest for the trees"—has been around for hundreds of years. It reportedly first appeared in 1546 in a collection of proverbs by the English writer John Heywood. "The bigger picture," on the other hand, did not become part of common usage in our language until 1904.

Seeing the Bigger Picture

On the website "The Happy Manager," created by Phil Higson and Anthony Sturgess, British authors of *Uncommon Leadership: How to Build Competitive Advantage by Thinking Differently*, Higson and Sturgess illustrate the power of seeing the bigger picture by means of the classic short story of the three stonecutters. Their version of the story, a popular metaphor in management circles, is as follows:

> One day a traveler, walking along a lane, came across three stonecutters working in a quarry. Each was busy cutting a block of stone. Interested to find out

what they were working on, he asked the first stonecutter what he was doing. "I am making a living." Still no wiser the traveler turned to the second stonecutter who kept on hammering while he asked him what he was doing. "I am doing the best job of stone-cutting in the entire country," he said as he cut his block of stone to make sure that it was square and that the dimensions were uniform so that it would fit exactly in its place in a wall. A bit closer to finding out what the stonecutters were working on but still unclear, the traveler turned to the third stonecutter. He seemed to be the happiest of the three and, when asked what he was doing, replied: **"I am building a cathedral."**

The Happy Manager, relating the story to leadership, explains that the first stonecutter saw his work simply as a means of earning a living, while the second stonecutter was focused on his individual performance, not on collaborating with the other workers. The third stonecutter was happy in his work because he saw the bigger picture of what this work would become.

Cathedral Thinkers

The Happy Manager brings in a further interpretation of the story from management guru Peter Drucker. Drucker describes the third stonecutter as having a vision—but notes that having a vision is not enough. The Happy Manager expands upon Drucker's interpretation by noting what is essential is that we **show another way:**

> … to show that vision, to share it, and to inspire others to understand and work towards it. The third stonecutter becomes a leader when his view of his work is shared by his workmates—when none of them says they're simply doing their job.

The Happy Manager applies a concept from Peter Senge, founder of the Society for Organizational Learning, to further explore the way we can view the third stonecutter's process. The Happy Manager applies Senge's principle—"the responsibility of a leader is not just to share a vision but to *build a shared vision*"—to produce a new response from the third stonecutter. In this iteration of the story, the third stonecutter is now building St. Paul's Cathedral in London, and his response is:

> "I am helping Sir Christopher Wren build a magnificent cathedral to the glory of God."

Here, the stonecutter's personal vision opens up into a shared vision—shared not only with the master architect (Christopher Wren) whose plans he is fulfilling, but also with all those who will come to worship at this house of God. Finally, the Happy Manager quotes Charles Handy's *The Hungry Spirit:* "We may not need any more cathedrals but we do need *cathedral thinkers,* people who can think beyond their own lifetimes." In other words, we need cathedral thinkers **to show us another way** to see the bigger picture.

Seeing the Forest AND the Trees

To show another way, we must first see the bigger picture by stepping back to see the entire perspective, situation, or issue. It's easy to get lost in the weeds with our heads down. To see beyond the details, we need to look up and focus on understanding larger principles, truths, and plans. We lose perspective when we are too heavily invested in a particular view or too fixated on a particular approach—that is, when we can't see past the end of our nose, when we can't see straight, when we can't see our hand in front of our face—and when we can't see the forest for the trees. When we are in the midst of critical situations, we can't often see just how critical those situations are.

The most fundamental situation where we need to see the bigger picture is in Planet Earth's dire need for restoration and balance. Without this expanded view, we aren't able to understand the larger cause of the collapse of our planet and thus will be unable to find our way to the solutions for its renewal. The situation has become critical and we must act NOW. We can't **show another way** to others or to our planet until we see the bigger picture of their situation and identify what their souls need. If we are too focused on the details, we can't see the forest for the trees—and we can't see that what we are really doing is building a cathedral.

When the vast cathedral of our being
becomes a sanctuary for all creation,
we become the face of God.

~ JONATHAN LOCKWOOD HUIE, SELF-DESCRIBED
"PHILOSOPHER OF HAPPINESS"

To Show Another Way: Applications

Respond to one or more of the following inquiry questions:

1. Based on the stonecutter story:

   ◆ In what way am I like the first stonecutter? The second? The third? In what way do I exemplify the way Peter Drucker views the third stonecutter? In what way am I the stonecutter who is building St. Paul's Cathedral in London?

   ◆ How did the story of the stonecutters **show me another way** to approach my work in the world, whatever I consider that to be?

   ◆ How can anyone be a cathedral builder, regardless of his or her work or role in the world—such as a parent, child, brother, sister, spouse, teacher, laborer, cook, bus driver, and so forth?

2. Recall a past or current meeting or gathering in which you observed yourself, a fellow worker, or a member of a group (family, work group, friends) focus on the details and lose sight of the bigger picture—when you or they couldn't see the forest for the trees. Ask yourself, "How might I gently **show another way** in this situation? What might I say or do?"

Humanity's Next Evolutionary Leap

We have an obligation not only to love each other,
but also in our love to make ourselves as lovable as possible
so that it is easy for our sisters and brothers to love us.

~ WILLIAM OF ST. THIERRY

Humanity is in the process of transitioning from the third and fourth dimensional Piscean Era to the fifth dimension of the Aquarian Era. What does this mean for us, individually and as a species? During this global paradigm shift, we have an opportunity to move through and beyond the energies in which we currently reside and take a quantum leap into the edges of another dimension of being—where we manifest a completely different way of living in our world, on our planet, even in our own bodies.

An in-depth exploration of the information in this teaching can be found in my 2009 book, *The Clarion Call: Leadership and Group Life in the Aquarian Era*, which describes the energetic nature of this progression and addresses the anticipated gifts, challenges, crises, and needs of the midpoint years (2008-2025) of the five-hundred-year transition from the Piscean to the Aquarian Era. Here, I offer a brief synopsis of the realities of the third, fourth, and fifth dimensions, how they manifest in the Piscean and Aquarian eras, and offer an Aquarian metaphor of leadership. The purpose of this introductory teaching is **to show another way** to view what is currently happening on our planet and to invite you to use this information to learn, grow, and serve others who are struggling to understand what is happening in our world.

The Timeline of the Global Paradigm Shift

Although there has been much said and written about "the Shift" currently happening on our planet, I regularly encounter individuals who are not aware of what this Shift entails and what it means for us and for our world. Subtle fifth dimensional Aquarian energies first appeared on Planet Earth around the year 1760. Predictions suggest that, by the year 2260, Piscean energies will have yielded to Aquarian energies. The Aquarian Era, like all other astrological eras, will span 2,120 years. Although we know the basic nature of Aquarian energy and some ways it could manifest, much is unknown as to exactly what will emerge during the transition and throughout this new era. What we do know is that a crisis of great proportions is occurring, as predicted, between 2008 and 2025 as we shed the old Piscean ways of the world and welcome the new Aquarian energies. **It is during the peak—the most unstable years—of the transitional period, between 2008 and 2025, that we must especially focus on being mindful to show ourselves and others another way.**

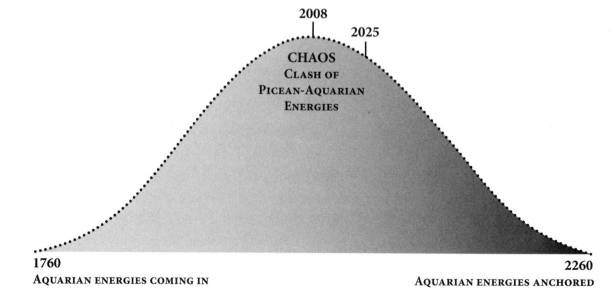

2008

2025

CHAOS
CLASH OF
PICEAN-AQUARIAN
ENERGIES

1760
AQUARIAN ENERGIES COMING IN

2260
AQUARIAN ENERGIES ANCHORED

The Piscean Era

Third dimensional reality is perceived through our physical senses. Our senses tell us that we are separate from everything—from people, animals, plants, stones—indeed, from all things animate or inanimate. Because third dimensional thinking is dualistic, we perceive things as good or bad, right or wrong, black or white, and react accordingly. Conflicts are viewed as reflecting "just the way life is" and that things are only going to get worse. It is a reality of illusions, of limits and fears, and the material world is viewed as the only reality.

Fourth dimensional reality is more focused on caring for ourselves, other people, and the planet. New possibilities begin to emerge, such as developments in personal growth and spirituality. However, in this dimension we get caught up in needing to be special and having strong views and judgments about those who don't act the way we do. In the later phases of the fourth dimension, we live with more of an awareness of love, care, compassion, forgiveness, and inner peace. However, we remain caught in dualistic thinking of right-wrong.

Only **the power of the heart** can usher us out of the third and fourth dimensions and into fifth dimensional understanding. Our conflicts and stress increase when we use only our head; it is our heart that accelerates our evolution into the fifth dimension. When we use the intelligence of our heart, we manage our physical, mental, and emotional wellbeing and develop intuition and knowingness.

The Aquarian Era

In **fifth dimensional reality**, we choose between faith and knowing and between religiosity and spirituality. We are called to practice cooperation and are motivated to manifest the Aquarian values of partnership and group consciousness. We are guided by intuition and non-dualistic thinking. Our actions are energy-efficient and we perceive all as light and energy. We know it is our responsibility to manage these energies and our actions in an effective way.

Key to fifth dimensional reality is its promise that our world will be imbued with an energy that unites **masculine mind** (clarity, order, practicality, knowledge, and words) with **feminine heart** (cooperation, beauty, synthesis, connectedness, poetry, art, and tenderness). In this way, we not only deepen and unify our inner life, we harvest the good from where we have been and call on the wisdom of the Universe to help us with the practical application of that knowledge. We deepen our understanding of what wants to emerge in the world, moving out of the personal into the collective and out of duality into wholeness.

Aquarian Leaders: The Brilliants

Many people feel they were born with a destiny to help others during this transition by **showing another way** to live on Planet Earth. They know the unique assignment they are to carry out during the early years of the Aquarian Era and have already positioned themselves to play critical roles. I refer to these people and groups as *brilliants*. The term "brilliant" is defined as both a gem and as a specific cut shape for gems—the preferred one for diamonds. The many facets of the brilliant amplify and enhance the light they reflect.

The brilliant can serve as an Aquarian metaphor, representing the Soul through which Light pours from Divine Source. The Soul reflects the Light and, in turn, radiates it out into the world. This Divine Light radiating from the brilliants invites us to take the necessary quantum leap across the edge into the fifth dimension, where we are destined to learn how to live as one global family.

May the hearts of humanity heed the clarion call to join in the Light of the brilliants.

An ancient clarion call — will be the trumpet we hear
as we leave the third dimensional Piscean world
and enter the fifth dimension of the Aquarian Era.

~ FROM *THE CLARION CALL*

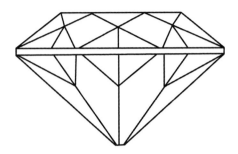

To Show Another Way: Applications

Respond to two or three of the following questions:

1. In what ways do I see myself continuing to reside in the third and fourth dimensions?

2. What aspects of fifth dimensional reality are beginning to appear in my life?

    ◆ In my workplace?
    ◆ In my family?
    ◆ In my community?
    ◆ In my country?
    ◆ On our planet?

3. How might I **show another way** to those who appear "stuck" in a Piscean approach to life?

Synchronicity ~ Expect a Miracle

The more we can slow everything down—
and wait for a synchronistic event
to show us the way—
the easier life is to handle.

~ JAMES REDFIELD

I was late for work one morning and in my haste, I drove quickly down a ramp that merges onto a main highway. Just as I was about to merge, I saw a chipmunk starting to run across the road in front of me. I slammed on the brakes and screamed at the chipmunk, "Get back where you belong!" I had stopped my car at the exact moment a large truck was speeding past me—the exact moment I would have been merging onto the highway. My car shook from the rumble of the truck. The chipmunk scampered back to the city park he had come from. The synchronistic encounter with the chipmunk had saved my life—a miracle! I was so moved by this experience that I wrote to *Washington Post* columnist John Kelly about it. He found the story compelling enough to publish it in his column.

Being Helped by Invisible Hands

Referred to as "mysterious or magical coincidences," synchronistic events occur at the right time, in the right way, and for the right reason. Mythologist Joseph Campbell calls synchronistic encounters "being helped by invisible hands." Sent by our Higher Consciousness, Soul, Guardian Angel, Solar Angel, Higher Self, God-Goddess-All-That-Is, synchronicities are vitally important messages delivered to us by a person, event, dream, or insight. Synchronicity, the flow of unexpected events that occurs in our life, **shows us another way** to live on Planet Earth.

Synchronistic events have a unique energy that sets them apart from typical conversation and from day-to-day events. This energy is often described as uplifting, reassuring, nurturing, clarifying, and "just what I needed." As evidenced by my chipmunk story, synchronistic experiences can be lifesaving when they protect us from danger or stop us from making a potentially harmful decision. Synchronistic events are person- or group-specific—they are tailor-made for us individually or for our group. It's impossible to receive someone else's synchronistic message.

For example, a person you meet at a party shares that she had to withdraw from college because she had not persisted in her schoolwork, when, at the exact time, you are in danger of the same thing happening to you. This meeting inspires you to rededicate yourself to your college studies. Or, a person mentions how much a particular health professional helped her and you realize that health professional sounds exactly like the kind you've been seeking. Perhaps you have a dream that offers insight and advice about a troubled relationship. Or, you're serving on a board that is struggling to work together and receive a synchronistic email from a professional organization you didn't even know existed that specifically offers support and best practices for board development. Synchronicities are everywhere when we know how to look for them.

Welcoming Synchronicity

We have to **SLOW DOWN** *if we wish to notice and benefit from the flow of synchronistic events in our life.* It's easy to feel overwhelmed by problems and demands coming at us at lightning speed. The more we slow things down—and await synchronistic events **to show us another way**—the easier it is to feel guided, protected, and supported in all aspects of life. The more we notice and acknowledge synchronistic events, the more they take place. All that we need to remember is that synchronicity will happen—and then await its arrival. We can expect synchronicities to become a common occurrence in our life. Slowing down and staying alert are essential if we wish to benefit from them when they happen. Staying in the flow of synchronicity will lead us forward.

If we ignore synchronicity and only use our free will, we risk going off course and missing opportunities. The more we are aware that synchronicity is an inherent part of our life on Earth, the more we will experience our life as meaningful, on purpose, and joyful.

The following behaviors open the door for synchronistic events to appear in our life:

◆ holding an intention to be of service to humanity and Planet Earth,

◆ telling helpful truths—truths that have no agenda and are not harmful to ourselves or others; truths that have no twists, no investments, and no projections towards ourselves or others, and

◆ being honest with ourselves—honesty without an agenda is uplifting, clarifying, and healing; it is the antidote to lying to ourselves or others.

Another Synchronicity

Soon after writing the points above about telling helpful truths and being honest with ourselves, I checked my email—a common source of synchronistically received information. A message from Mark Hyman, a functional medicine physician, was waiting in my in-box. It was titled: "Why We All Lie, How It Messes Up Our Lives, and How to Fix It." This was the synchronistic theme of his message:

When we address the lies we tell ourselves and others,
connect with our personal integrity,
and embrace the spirit we're often keeping locked away,
some amazing things can happen.
Spiritual health is something that's often forgotten in an effort to become well.

~ Mark Hyman

To Show Another Way: Applications

Choose one or both of the following to explore or practice in relation to this teaching:

1. Recall past synchronistic events that **showed you another way** by shifting the focus of your life or dramatically changing your view about someone or something. Describe the impact these events had on your life at the time and subsequently.

2. Observe your thoughts and words, noting when you may be lying. If you catch yourself lying, maintain your integrity by making the correction immediately.

   Lying takes many forms, including

   ◆ not keeping my agreements, saying I will do something and not following through,
   ◆ exaggerating,
   ◆ taking all the credit for something, not acknowledging the participation of others,
   ◆ omitting relevant information,
   ◆ believing my point of view or memory is the only valid one, discounting the views and memories of others, and
   ◆ not writing down appointments and thus "forgetting" them.

Let the Elephant Pass By

One moment of patience may ward off great disaster.
One moment of impatience may ruin a whole life.

~ CHINESE PROVERB

Elephants first came thundering into my life in a way I never could have imagined. I was a college freshman at a private university in Indiana. One of the optional physical education courses I chose to take was modern dance. I had not previously known about this kind of dance, as I came from a small farming community where such things were unheard of, let alone taught. I was eager and excited as I entered the gymnasium for the first class. The instructor began by asking each of us, one by one, to go to the front of the class and "act out" an object or thing. When it was my turn, I stood in front of the class, bent down, put my hands together, and gradually raised my arms above my head as a way of acting out how a seed grows and becomes a flowering plant. As the flower, with my arms raised skyward, I looked up and welcomed the warmth of the sun. I was delighted that I had chosen to express the growth of such a delicate, living object.

Immediately, my fellow classmates laughed and shouted with certainty, "She's an elephant!" My memory of the remaining days in the class are blurred. From that day forward I carried the belief that I was not capable of ever dancing beautifully and elegantly. I've never forgotten the day I was told I was an elephant.

Elephant Blessings

Not until I went to India to stay at an ashram many years later did elephants re-enter my life in a very unusual way. When I entered the ashram grounds, I noticed a number of marble statues of gods and goddesses. I was immediately drawn to a large statue of a being with a human body and an elephant head. I'm a little embarrassed to tell you this—but I immediately fell in love with this being! I soon learned this was Ganesha, the esteemed Hindu God who helps people remove obstacles and overcome sadness. To me, Ganesha was alive—a living presence—and was to become a beloved lifelong teacher, helper, and friend. The Elephant-God became a healing symbol for me, even more so after learning that elephants symbolize the strength of our True Self.

Let us move forward some twenty years. I am lying on a table receiving an acupuncture treatment. I am there because I have severe pain that has lingered for months. While on the table, I move into a place of silence where no pain exists. Suddenly, I "see" myself pushing the rear of an elephant to get him out of my way. I believe he is blocking my path. I push with great effort but to no avail. And then—a pleasant, booming voice says to me, "Let the elephant pass by!" Instantly, I stop pushing and recognize that this statement is not just a literal suggestion to stop pushing the elephant, but an important personal message of wisdom: let the pain pass in its own healing time.

Pushing the Elephant

How many times in our life have we used our will to force something to happen because we wanted it *now* rather than in its own natural timing? We are impatient as we push through ideas, push the speed of our work, push other people to do things our way and in our timing. We push our spouses and families to change and do our bidding because *we* are uncomfortable. Most of all, we push ourselves to have instant gratification and instant results. We push ourselves to deaden the pain, thrashing about in all forms of addictions.

We hang on to our beliefs and desires and react with anger and fear when others don't fulfill our wishes. We don't accept or love ourselves, believing we are not worthy, confident, or competent. Examples abound of stressful lives that result from remaining attached to worn-out beliefs and repeating automatic behaviors. The end result of this approach is typically a breakdown of some aspect of our body, mind, or spirit. Human beings are not intended to live anxious, defeating lives.

A Happy Ending

Everyone, and I do mean *everyone,* young and old, with whom I have shared my elephant story has instantly understood the depth of its meaning. Each recognized that to live life completely and well—physically, emotionally, mentally, and spiritually—it is essential to "let the elephant pass by" and welcome **being shown another way.**

Ah… my college elephant story had a happy ending after all!

A gentle hand may lead
even an elephant by a hair.

~ IRANIAN PROVERB

To Show Another Way: Applications

Choose at least one application to explore or practice in relation to this teaching:

1. Select a situation in your life in which you did not "let the elephant pass by" and thereby endlessly obsessed on the event. How might this teaching **show you another way** to view the situation?

2. Practice saying "Let the elephant pass by!" as a mantra when you find yourself reacting instead of responding, forcing instead of letting be, or rejecting rather than learning from a life experience.

3. What animal story do you have in your life that has served **to show you another way?**

Healing from Kabooms

Gracious words are like a honeycomb,
sweetness to the soul and health to the body.

~ PROVERBS 16:24

KABOOM! We experience an emotionally explosive event that shatters our current reality. Or, KABOOM! We go through an incident that moves us so deeply it dramatically shifts our inner reality to a more loving and expansive one. In either case, we make a choice. We either choose not to make changes in our life (outer *or* inner) and thus remain the same, or we choose to wake up and modify our life so it's different from what it was. If we choose to wake up, we will not be the same person we were before our kaboom.

Having a "WOW" effect, a kaboom immediately gets our attention because it has a distinctive voice, sound, feeling, quality, or visual image. It can either be loud and dramatic or quiet and subtle. A kaboom can motivate us to change how we live our life, to challenge what we believe to be true or not true, and to examine how we relate to humanity and the planet. The number and type of events that can trigger a kaboom are endless. For example, we can experience a kaboom from an upheaval or trauma, perhaps a cancer scare, an emergency surgery, the death of a child or partner, an accident, a painful illness, or an unkind comment from a long-time friend. A kaboom can also come from an inspiring book, an insight, a healing experience, kind words from another, or an experience of unconditional love from a pet.

Kabooms are unexpected, coming out of left field. Our reactions to kabooms are typically strong and irrational. The intense emotions they provoke in us can be overwhelming. We rant and rave, sob with abandonment, cry tears of joy, or feel a peaceful glow in our heart. Regardless of what form a kaboom takes, it can potentially strip away a negative belief, a haphazard way of life, or a relationship that no longer serves our physical, mental, emotional, or spiritual wellbeing.

What Wants to Emerge

For many, waking up after a kaboom is followed by a major shift in their physical, psychological and/or spiritual development. Kabooms **show us another way** to live our life and relate to others. Parts of us have been in denial or asleep. We might have been unaware of the forces that were inhibiting, restricting, and distorting our motivations. Are we replaying a past, negative event? Do we have a Dr. Jekyll and Mr. Hyde within us? What needs to be awakened in us so we can choose a life of joy, unconditional acceptance, honesty, and integrity? Are we ready to forgive by learning from our painful experiences? What philosophy of life is trying to emerge? What is the hidden masterpiece within us that wants desperately to be revealed?

Lila, a student in one of my classes, shared a kaboom experience with me that can occur in the lives of those helping someone who has serious challenges. After many years as a recovering alcoholic and participant in two twelve-step programs, Lila agreed to be a twelve-step sponsor for Phyllis. Phyllis' substance abuse had left her homeless and out of work. Lila proceeded to help Phyllis in every way she could. She offered her room and board in her own home and supported her in finding a job by helping her select the proper clothes, typing her resume, and driving her to interviews. She accompanied Phyllis to twelve-step meetings and provided an immediate presence whenever Phyllis had a crisis. Lila felt fulfilled, and Phyllis began getting her life in order.

One day about six months into their relationship, during a discussion of Phyllis' progress, Lila experienced a kaboom. Phyllis suddenly blew up at her, calling Lila manipulative, controlling, and poisonous. Lila was devastated. Only after intense self-examination was she able to learn from this experience, realizing that her service to Phyllis came from her own need to be nurtured and affirmed. By trying to "fix" Phyllis, Lila had projected her loneliness and lack of self-love, self-appreciation, and self-worth onto her. As long as Phyllis accepted the projection, Lila felt fulfilled—her needs were met. Lila used this kaboom to examine her motivation for serving others and to make a major shift in how she related to those seeking help.

Kabooms Wake Us Up

I experienced a different kind of kaboom when I was getting my doctorate degree at Northwestern University. Because of intense anxiety about my ability to succeed, I was seriously considering leaving the program. Unexpectedly, a person I had worked with in Alaska contacted me, saying she was immediately flying to Chicago to meet with me about something very important. When we met, she asked if I was thinking about dropping out of the doctoral program. Her question surprised me, as I had told no one I had been thinking of this very thing. When I said "Yes," she said, "You are **not** to do that. You need to complete your degree in order to accomplish what you came on Earth to do." With her message delivered, she immediately flew back to Alaska. Her unexpected directive woke me up. I recognized the truth of her comment and continued my studies.

Waking up clears our mind and opens our heart because it clarifies our motivations, our wishes, and the decisions we make as a result of them. Waking up helps us define how we want to be, what we want to do, and what actions we want to take to bring about a change in our life. **Kabooms always show us another way.** Waking up is healing because it brings new understandings and purpose to our life. *It focuses our attention on what really matters.* Most of us experience many kabooms in our life. Our challenge is to welcome the potential transformation that can come with each one of them. Our life becomes a series of kabooms that again and again transform our reality from what was so to what is true now.

Kabooms Are Waking Up the World

In an earlier teaching in this book, "Humanity's Next Evolutionary Leap," I write about the current transition from the third and fourth dimensions of the Piscean Era to the fifth dimension of the Aquarian Era. We are in the midst of a major evolutionary challenge on our planet. Old organizational structures and belief systems are collapsing. Global warming is threating our planet's survival. The planet—not only humans and animals, but all of nature, and even Mother Earth herself—is experiencing intense fear and stress about an unknown future.

The good news is that masses of people are viewing their kabooms as wake-up calls that **show them another way** to live on Planet Earth. The following are some of the shifts that are occurring on our planet as kabooms wake people up to Aquarian values:

- ♦ from competition to cooperation,
- ♦ from territorial priorities to global priorities,
- ♦ from being head-focused to being heart-centered,
- ♦ from individual needs to group needs,
- ♦ from superiority of masculine energy to partnership of masculine and feminine energies, and
- ♦ from separation to unity.

What can we do to support our waking up? Keep life simple. Take one day at a time, one experience at a time. Make a choice to change one thing every day. Persevere. Don't give up. Be patient. Don't waste time worrying or giving power to fear. Trust. **Use each life experience as an opportunity to choose another way.** Serve others by **showing them another way** through your actions.

There is one ultimate purpose for recognizing and learning from the kabooms in our life: to remember to sing the song of Divine Light and Love to ourselves, others, and Planet Earth.

In the middle of every difficulty lies opportunity.

~ ALBERT EINSTEIN

To Show Another Way: Applications

Journal on the following questions:

1. What past or recent kabooms do I particularly treasure because they redirected my life by **showing me another—**and better—**way?**

2. How have I supported others experiencing kabooms in their lives by **showing them another way?**

Beyond Hope and Fear

*It is not hope **or** fear.*
They are not exclusive—
nor do you experience one or the other.
Rather, fear is underneath hope.

~ TENZIN WANGYAL RINPOCHE

Some time ago, I had what Swiss psychoanalyst Carl Jung calls a numinous dream. Jung defines the numinous experience as an inner or outer occurrence that conveys something essential about ourselves that our unconscious wants us to know. Numinous events explain an aspect of spiritual wisdom that we need to actualize in our life. They connect us with sacred knowledge. There is always a feeling of fascination about a numinous event.

Numinous experiences feel mysterious. They carry a spiritual message from the Divine and often communicate a message that can seem terrifying. Regardless of the nature of a numinous dream or experience, we will feel driven to uncover its spiritual meaning.

In my numinous dream, I am doing my best to hide from a man I believed to be dangerous. As often happens in dreams with such a theme, the man finds my hiding place. He walks up to me and orders me to eat two poisonous leaves.

Immediately, and with an air of absolute conviction, I look at him, unafraid and determined. I proclaim, "NO! I want to live my life completely and well!" He turns and walks away.

Two Poisons/Two Questions

After contemplating the dream's meaning, I identified two numinous questions: what are the two poisons in my life? and, what does it mean to live my life completely and well? I spent nearly three years seeking answers to my questions—from books, from people, and from contemplation. Yet I failed to uncover the hidden truths of these two fundamental questions.

And then... a synchronistic event occurred. I decided to attend a retreat led by a Tibetan Buddhist teacher, Tenzin Wangyal Rinpoche. Imagine my excitement when I discovered that the topic of the retreat addressed obstacles to spiritual growth.

In a talk at the retreat, Rinpoche defined living life fully as cultivating an inner refuge into which we release our obstacles and then engage in creative actions that serve ourselves and others. I raised my hand and shared my poison leaves dream, asking him if he could identify the two poisons in my life. Without skipping a beat, he answered, "Hope and fear." Fear, he explained, drives our motivation for "hoping this" and "hoping that." For example, if I say I "hope" I have the inner strength, motivation, competence, and confidence to live my life completely and well, I am saying this because I'm fearful that it won't happen. Rinpoche's explanation resonated with me deeply.

So—the two poisons in my life had been identified. Now, what was I to do about them? There appeared to be two major next steps: (1) find a place within myself—an inner refuge—where I could align with my Higher Self and release the two poisonous, and thus dangerous, obstacles in my life, and (2) take action that turned the poisons into smoke.

The Inner Refuge

Our inner refuge is a sacred place within our heart. We connect to our inner refuge when we meditate and align with our Higher Self. We receive spiritual guidance and insights when in this sacred place. We can also release negative thoughts and feelings in our inner refuge.

In our inner refuge, **we are shown another way.** We recognize that we have the ability to be self-responsible for what poisons our life and welcome what will dissolve the poison. In this space, we can draw on our inner strength and confidence to tend to our physical, mental, emotional, and spiritual wellbeing.

We can also choose to learn from our pain. Instead of feeling victimized, resentful, or bitter, we know we have a choice to be responsible for our feelings and reactions and to learn from them. When we choose to learn from our life experiences, we are not only **being shown another way,** we can share our learning by **showing another way** to help others. Pain can teach us another way to learn, grow, and serve.

Teachings about Hope and Fear

Soon after attending the retreat, I developed a severe case of shingles. I had "hoped" I had managed a recent anxiety concerning the sale of some property, which required finding and moving to a new location and redefining my work responsibilities. Yes, these actions are all listed at the top of the stress charts. The shingles delivered the message that, indeed, this stress proved to be too much for my immune system.

Looking at my shingles experience from a perspective of hope and fear, I told myself: "I *hope* my shingles pain is short-lived and I'll be well in a couple of weeks… I *hope* the treatment from my Western physician cures the problem in a short time… I *hope* I can bypass the nerve pain people tell me can sometimes last for years… I *hope* I can keep up with my work responsibilities… I *hope* there's a magic bullet that will cure the pain immediately…" Reader, you get the point. Perhaps you can even hear your own "hopeful" thinking in my self-talk.

Beneath each of these "hopes" was *fear*—*fear* and thus doubt that any of these hopes would come true, *fear* and doubt that the pain would ever go away, *fear* and doubt that I could find a healing approach that worked, *fear* and doubt that I would be able to continue working, *fear* and doubt that I could discover what approach was best for my healing, and so forth. On the one hand, I "hoped" I wouldn't experience the relentless pain that had no remedy. On the other hand, I "feared" and thus doubted my pain would ever go away.

A Turning Point: Becoming Self-Responsible

One day, following several months of medical appointments with my internist, she said to me, "There is nothing more I can do to help you, so you won't need to make another appointment." I was devastated and felt adrift. I realized how much I had hoped my problem could be resolved with a magic pill or treatment from Western medicine. Fear that a simple solution didn't exist was beneath this hope.

Soon after leaving the doctor's office I had a powerful insight: I *do* have the ability to be self-responsible for my pain and to search for solutions that meet my needs. I *can* draw on my inner strength, competence, and confidence to design a holistic healing program. Soon, I selected a medical intuitive, a Qigong healer, and a chiropractor as helpers, and learned Buddhist breathing practices. I increased my meditation time and wrote in my journal, dialoguing with my pain and with my heart, the area where my nerve pain was located.

In the process of becoming self-responsible for my own healing, several teachings emerged that **showed me another way** to work with my pain:

◆ Instead of choosing hope and feeling victimized, resentful, or bitter, I could choose to be responsible for my feelings and reactions and to become aware of what the pain was teaching me.

◆ My pain revealed how much the two poison leaves, hope and fear, had kept me from living my life completely and well.

◆ When I chose to learn from my experience and to allow solutions to emerge from within, the quality of my relationship with my problems and challenges changed.

◆ My pain served to deepen my compassion for those in pain, whether their pain is physical, emotional, mental, or spiritual, and whether those in pain are of the human, animal, or plant kingdom.

I discovered that my pain totally disappeared whenever I was engaged in a meaningful action, whether I was doing my spiritual practices, helping another person, engaging in my work, talking to a friend, taking a walk in nature, or otherwise participating in the world with a loving manner. I discovered that the antidote to my pain was to my live my life completely and well, without hope and without fear. **My pain had shown me another way.**

The pain you feel today is the strength you feel tomorrow.

~ ANONYMOUS

To Show Another Way: Applications

Respond to one or both of the following suggestions:

1. Select a *recent* experience in your life regarding which you felt "hope." Repeat the following phrase several times until you identify the "fear" that lies beneath "hope":

   "On the one hand, I *hope*_____; on the other hand, I *fear*
   _____."

   Journal on your insights and note any learnings. Ask yourself: If I could see my experience from a perspective other than hope and fear, what would that be?

2. Recall and describe a numinous dream that you sense has the potential to awaken a spiritual truth within you. Ask yourself the following questions:

   ♦ In what way have I recognized the spiritual meaning of the dream in my life?

   ♦ In what way did the dream **show me another way** and thus refocus my life?

Forgiveness ~ The Gift of Lilies

Darkness cannot drive out darkness; only light can do that.
Hate cannot drive out hate; only love can do that.

~ Martin Luther King, Jr.

To live our life completely and well requires that we understand the conscious and unconscious nature of our human psyche. If we choose to live a life of peace, love, and service, we need to make a commitment to learn how to have a healthy mind, body, and spirit. Until we learn to observe ourselves with detachment, we remain largely unaware of our inner motivations and the impact we have on ourselves and others. Unconscious motivations, often accompanied by neglect of our physical, mental, emotional, and spiritual health, impact our personal life and our relationships with others.

To become authentic, competent, and confident, we must understand and honor one another. Without this mutual understanding and respect, we feel separate and isolated from family members, coworkers and the rest of humanity. If we are to live self-responsibly, we must address our obstacles to embracing life by engaging in inner work, removing personality blockages, working with our shadow tendencies, and withdrawing our projections.

The Shadow of Our Psyche

Like the unseen portion of an iceberg that exists underwater, 90 percent of our energies operate at an unconscious level. These energies form what is known as our shadow. To fully commit to living a soul-inspired life, we need to address obstacles in the deep layers of the iceberg by dissolving the energetic blocks that interfere with having a healthy mind, body, and spirit.

The deepest layer of our unconscious shadow rests in the shadow of our family and of other childhood relationships, such as those with a relative, teacher, or caregiver. We are often unaware that we carry our experiences, unresolved issues, and attitudes about early relationships in our unconscious. For example, those of us who experienced unhealthy boundaries in our family of origin are likely to develop codependent relationships with others as we grow up and into adulthood.

Projection

Projection is the process by which we impose our shadow onto someone or something outside ourselves. Through projection, we give away those qualities, positive and negative, that we don't want to accept in ourselves. When we project, we impose our will on someone or something by imposing our beliefs and ideas. By imposing our will, we disempower the person imposed upon while serving our own needs—rather than giving, we take. When we have a strong emotional reaction to someone or something, we are projecting onto that person or thing what we do not acknowledge in ourselves.

We tend to react negatively to the behavior or appearance of another person who reminds us, often unconsciously, of a family member with whom we've had conflict. We project an interpretation onto this person because the person reminds us of a parent or sibling towards whom we still have unfinished business. Therefore, when we are triggered by or judge someone, it is important to ask ourselves, "Who does this person remind me of?"

Forgiveness as the Gift of Lilies

When we forgive others, we extend the loving energy of "the gift of lilies." We see them as persons in their own right with opportunities to learn from their own life challenges. We see that they are no different from ourselves—searching for love, value, and purpose in their lives and making many mistakes along the way. To forgive another, we must first see that our triggers identify what we need to forgive in ourselves. Forgiveness is the willingness to learn from our triggers and mistakes and to share what we've learned to help others. Through forgiveness, we achieve a genuine acceptance of ourselves and others—**we show another way.**

Whenever we do not forgive, we extend the negative energy of "a crown of thorns" to those toward whom we have a grievance. In a sense, we keep them in prison and stand guard to insure they stay there. In fact, we are both in prison! When we offer a person a crown of thorns, we see the person who has triggered us as wrong, bad, or intentionally hurtful.

Forgiveness does not mean that we deny what has happened. Denial is always unhealthy and leads only to the festering of our wounds. Forgiveness does not imply that criminals should be allowed to go free or that someone who has harmed us physically or psychologically should be allowed to continue to do so. That is just as damaging psychologically and spiritually to the other person as it is to ourselves. Further, the inability to forgive a frailty in another person indicates that we have the same negative condition existing in us. If we forgive that weakness in another, the act of forgiveness serves as an antidote to our own weakness. It is also true that, if we forgive a weakness in ourselves, it is easier to forgive another of that same weakness.

Forgiveness as a Process

Forgiveness does not assume a certain action is taken—it is a process rather than an action. The process of forgiveness opens our heart and invites in compassion, which results in the mind letting go of grievances. When we have compassion for another person, we have compassion for ourselves. We can imagine ourselves back to a time before we developed a grievance against the person and re-experience holding that person in our heart. By reconnecting to our original, innocent love, we can easily forgive the person in the present moment. The moment we release the grievances we hold, we free ourselves.

Most of all, forgiveness is grace in action. Grace does not come from without, from above, from elsewhere—it comes from within us. When we welcome grace into our life, grievances fall away, the veil lifts, and our heart opens. Our heart and mind come into alignment and our feelings match our thoughts. Grace is the energy of forgiveness, an energy that melts away our grievances and pain and opens the space for another way to view the event. Grace is the source of the experience of forgiveness. It is a gift we give to ourselves.

A True Story of the Meaning of Forgiveness

When Martha sat across from me in a workshop I was leading and began her process, I was impressed with how calmly and confidently she stated her need to do grief work relating to the death of her sixteen-year-old daughter. I did not know that what was about to unfold was the most profound example of forgiveness I had ever heard.

Eighteen years before, Martha's daughter, June, had been brutally murdered by a man in their hometown. The family expressed their rage through verbal attacks and multi-million-dollar lawsuits against the assailant and the legal system. For fourteen years, members of the family drained all their energy by hating the killer. They wanted revenge for the grief and horror he had brought into their lives. Even though they won a civil case against the murderer and were awarded over a million dollars, they felt no peace.

One day, ten years after June's death, Martha's son handed her a book he had been reading, *A Course in Miracles*. The book, he said, had brought him peace. Martha was comforted by the book's teaching that forgiveness doesn't deny what has happened. The *Course* teaches that what is needed is the willingness to search for a truth that lies beyond the situation. The truth she discovered was that she wanted to be free of the rage that was killing her and her family. To be free meant she needed to forgive her daughter's killer. She and her husband decided to visit him in prison.

What took place in their encounter with the man who killed their daughter was something very unexpected. As Martha and her husband faced him, they saw his humanness, his pain, and his grief. They felt not hatred and revenge, but great compassion and love toward him. The three of them hugged and sobbed out the pain for the tragedy that they shared. Martha felt released from her hatred for the first time since her daughter died. She and her husband decided to periodically visit the man. In the course of time the three of them talked openly about what had happened and why.

By the time that Martha came to my workshop, she was ready to complete another part of her grieving process by focusing on the healing needed within the family unit. She recognized that, over time, she had been extremely successful in teaching her children to hate. As a result, they continued to suffer. In the workshop, she made a commitment then and there to reverse her prior teaching.

Martha's story teaches us the true meaning of forgiveness. Forgiveness occurred because the people involved, the "victims," opened their hearts. Martha was able to see that the murderer was no different than herself, a person searching for love and value in a life filled with challenges.

Martha subsequently shared her healing with others by becoming a counselor in a crime victim/witness program helping those personally affected by crime.

Extending Our Healing in Service to Others

The spiritual law of extension ensures that we naturally become healers of that which we ourselves have been healed. For example, a person healed of grief about being betrayed extends the possibility of healing for others who have been betrayed. Said in another way, when we have healed a particular grievance within ourselves, such as betrayal, we naturally and effortlessly extend the gift of lilies to the one who betrayed us as well as to others, in general, who have been betrayed.

It is vital to recognize that **forgiveness is not something we have to do—it is something we have to BE.** To let ourselves and those to whom we've given the crown of thorns out of prison, **we must** *be* **forgiving**. True forgiveness gifts us with a conscious awareness of our inner spiritual reality. We are blessed by the angels for having done so.

Out beyond ideas of wrongdoing and rightdoing,
there is a field. I'll meet you there.

~ RUMI

Extending the Gift of Lilies ~ A Guided Visualization

Directions: Sit in a quiet, pleasant place where you will not be disturbed. Practice the guided visualization silently in your mind. There is no need to speak to the person to whom you are offering the gift of forgiveness. If you do the visualization with a pure intention, the person will receive the loving energy of your gift without any words being spoken. (Note: You can also extend the gift of lilies to groups, organizations, countries, etc.)

Visualization:

Take three deep breaths.

Center your awareness in your heart. Go to the next step only after you feel ready to view the person in the spirit of the gift of lilies as described in this teaching.

Picture the person to whom you wish to extend the gift of lilies in front of you.

Hold the lilies in your hand.

Look in the person's eyes, gently offering them the gift of lilies—the gift of love, the gift of understanding.

The gift of lilies is accepted. You and the person gently bow to one another.

Both of you now continue your life's journeys.

Reflection:

Respond to these two questions:

1. Note how you felt before and after you extended the gift of lilies. Ask yourself: What insights do I now have about my relationship to this person (group, organization, country)?

2. Ask yourself: In what way does this visualization **show me another way** about forgiveness?

Am I in My Right Place?

The will is meant to guide you to your right place
and will do so if allowed to.

~ Ceanne DeRohan

S arah, a woman with many talents and a generous heart, said to me, "I am over-whelmed, my life is meaningless, and my health is in shambles. I don't know what to do." Sarah's concerns are akin to our own. We are overwhelmed by distractions, such as the invasive impact of technology, the prevalence of polarized media, and the multiple warnings about the destruction of our climate and environment. We worry about how we are going to make a living, pay our expenses, find uncontaminated food, and maintain a healthy body. We procrastinate, neglect our health, and feel exhausted. Most of all, we fret about the absence of enthusiasm, energy, joy, and purpose in our life.

"Sarah," I asked, "Do you feel you are in your right place?" "What is THAT?" she shrieked. After remaining silent for a few moments, she spoke again, this time in a calm, quiet voice. "I assumed I was. But maybe I'm not because I'm so miserable."

Finding and Recognizing Our Right Place

The process of finding our right place not only has many variations from person to person, it often takes years—even a lifetime—to discover. Typically, **we have many next right places before we find our ultimate right place**. Most of us have a variety of jobs and experiences that serve as stepping stones that prepare us for our ultimate right place. These stepping stones provide us with certain experiences, skills, and competencies that we need to prepare us for our ultimate right place. For example, beginning in high school, I worked in multiple professional and volunteer settings in the U.S. and abroad. At the age of 40, I found my ultimate right place—as an author and director of a nonprofit organization that provides psychological and spiritual support to people of all faiths at this time of crisis on our planet.

What characterizes right places? How can they be described and defined? How can right places provide opportunities to make a difference in today's world? How can right places **show another way**?

First, *right places exist in every aspect of our life.* We have right places in our home. Right places can be a favorite route we choose for driving our kids to school or the grocery store we select for doing our weekly shopping. Our geographic location, our workplace, and our relationships can all signify we are in our right place. Individuals, groups, nationalities, nature, pets, and natural resources all have their own right places.

Second, *we are in our right place if it meets our needs and **shows us another way** to respond selflessly to the needs of others.* This encompasses a wide range of work settings, including businesses, schools, medical facilities, public and private service organizations, and so forth. We have a responsibility to seek and find our right place in order to evolve as souls and serve others during the extraordinary challenges facing us as we transition the evolutionary cycle from the end of Piscean Era to the first steps of the Aquarian. (For more on this transition, see "Humanity's Next Evolutionary Leap" in Chapter Two.) We know we are in our right place if we are able spontaneously to give the right amount of the right thing for the right reason and at the right time. When we serve in this way, the supply of what we have to give to all sentient beings and to our planet is unlimited.

Third, *finding and recognizing our right place is a matter of the heart.* It is our heart that recognizes our right place because the heart is where Spirit (Divine Source) and Will (Divine Will) unite. Our reasoning brain plays a role but it is not the final decider. In *Right Use of Will*, Ceanne DeRohan writes, "The path of bringing the balance of Spirit and Will into your Heart will show you what is right for you, and you will be able to recognize the perfection of it as you move along." Synchronistic events often play a key role in discovering both our next and ultimate right place. (For more on finding synchronicity in the everyday, see "Synchronicity ~ Expect a Miracle" in Chapter Two.)

Fourth, *we are in our right place if it is made visible in our life*—often by just such synchronistic events. Synchronistic events are unexpected and are sent by the Divine to support us, clarify our thinking, point us in a particular direction, or stop us from doing something that is not in alignment with our life purpose. They **show us another way** by offering information about or direction for finding our next or ultimate right place. Our life purpose and mission become visible to us in our right place. When we are in our right place, we are able to answer these questions:

- ◆ Why am I here?
- ◆ How am I to be?
- ◆ What am I to do?
- ◆ Who am I to do this with?
- ◆ Where am I to go?"

Fifth, *we are in our next or ultimate right place if we are being **shown another way*** to

- ◆ learn, grow, and contribute to the greater good of others,
- ◆ feel positive, valuable, and accepted, knowing our life is meaningful,
- ◆ see the truth beyond appearances,
- ◆ have abundant energy,
- ◆ be open to learning from our mistakes and accept the challenges that appear,
- ◆ focus our attention away from the negative and towards the more positive aspects of life, and
- ◆ emanate enthusiasm, selfless service, compassion, and joy, even during the hardest of times.

Do you remember Sarah? After she listened carefully to my explanation of a right place, she responded, "Now I see the cause of my misery. I am not in my right place."

We will naturally create an outer reality—a right place—
that matches the inner balance of Spirit and Will in our heart.

~ CEANNE DEROHAN

To Show Another Way: Applications

Finding one's right place—next or ultimate—must be explored over time. Taking a week, a month, or longer, contemplate the following questions:

1. Am I in my next right place or my ultimate right place?

2. How do I understand each of the five characteristics that are typical of next or ultimate right places?

   ◆ Right places exist in every aspect of our life.
   ◆ Right places meet our needs and encourage us to respond selflessly to the needs of others.
   ◆ Right places are recognized as a matter of the heart.
   ◆ Right places are made visible in our life.
   ◆ Right places **show us another way** to be in the world.

3. What, if any, changes in my life would I like to make after considering these five aspects of finding one's right place?

The Jewel Within

When man finds his real Self,
he becomes aware of the fact that in every man there is a jewel,
a real Self, and this knowledge makes him love and respect everyone.
He is ready to sacrifice himself to help others find their own jewel
and live according to the level of that awareness.

~ TORKOM SARAYDARIAN

Too many of us fail to recognize and accept that we are a treasured human being. We hide our Light under a bushel. This belief, dear ones, is "old hat." The time has come to put on a new hat that reminds us there is a Jewel within each of us. For individuals, this Jewel is our Soul. For a group, it is the Group Soul. This Jewel enables us to consciously and deliberately receive guidance from the Divine and extend Light and Love into the world. The Jewel helps us to live a purposeful and joy-filled life and help others do the same.

A Quest for the Jewel

Ageless wisdom teacher Torkom Saraydarian, in his book *Cosmos in Man,* tells a story about his personal quest for the Jewel. While traveling from country to country, he met a 114-year-old man who lived in a one-room hut in the middle of a forest. When he asked the man about his search for something real that was eternal—a Jewel—and that would bring him joy, the man told him these truths:

> There is a Presence that is the path leading to the Jewel. The shortest way to find that Presence is to watch, to observe your behavior, your emotional and mental actions, reactions, and activities. You must always remind yourself that these activities do not originate in your real Self, but have two different origins.
>
> One originates in your lower vehicles mechanically. The other comes from a higher source, which is your Guardian. If you practice observation enough, you will discriminate between these two. One is mostly selfish, negative, separating, materialistic, narrow, and limiting. The other is selfless, joy-giving, courageous, fearless, sacrificial, all-embracing, group-conscious, spiritual, progressive, enlightening, and leading to service, dedication, and gratitude.
>
> Once you are able to discriminate between these two, the next step will be to tune yourself to the higher one, and express the impressions that you receive from that Inner Presence, which will eventually lead you to your Self, to the Jewel.

Saraydarian writes that a release of old beliefs and a welcoming of the Jewel Within will potentially emerge in the next few years. This Jewel will **show us another way** by bringing us new and creative innovations with vitality and clarity.

When we tune ourselves to our Inner Presence, we experience a greater awareness of our real Self, our Soul. Being aware of the presence of our Soul becomes a reality when we engage in selfless service. We are **shown another way** to be in the world.

The following Soul Alignment meditation will guide you to an experience of the Jewel Within. Allow it to help you find your own Jewel. Once you discover it—in everything you are and do, let it shine, shine, SHINE.

Soul Alignment Meditation (The Jewel Within)

Purpose: To align with our Soul (the Jewel Within)—the spiritual principle and the guiding Light toward which the human soul is consciously or unconsciously evolving.

Our Soul's function is to protect, guide, teach, and inspire.

When to Align: Aligning with our Soul can be done at any time. Doing so is especially helpful at the beginning of the day or before any activity in which we wish to have support and guidance. Conversing with our Soul is helpful when we have a problem about which we seek insight and resolution.

Directions: The Jewel Within is located within our auric field—the energy field which surrounds our body. The human *soul* (lower case "s") is located in the heart. Therefore, in the meditation, the words "heart" and "human soul" are used interchangeably. Each individual's Soul (capital "S"—the Jewel Within) is located about eight inches above the head.

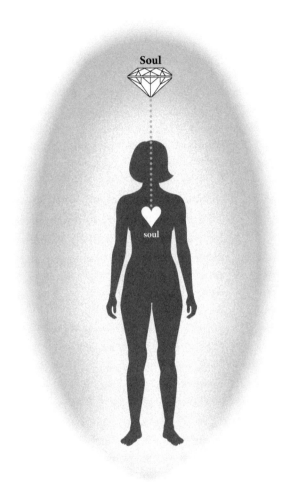

Sit in a comfortable position when doing the meditation and in a quiet place where you will not be interrupted. ***Pause at least 10 seconds between each step.***

1. Take three deep breaths to calm your physical body. (pause)

2. Take three deep breaths to calm your emotional body. (pause)

3. Take three deep breaths to calm your mental body. (pause)

4. Focus your awareness in your heart.

5. Visualize a line of energy extending from your heart down to the heart of the Mother of the Earth.

6. Visualize a line of energy from your heart to your Soul, located above your head.

7. Visualize the energy extending from your Soul to Divine Source.

8. In silence, hold this alignment from the heart of the Mother of the Earth to Divine Source. See the energy of Source moving down the alignment to the heart of the Mother of the Earth and then back again to Source, creating a circuit (circular movement) of energy carrying Divine Will to all levels of manifestation. Sit in silence and meditate (20 minutes is recommended).

Live in a way that you can increase the health,
happiness, prosperity, love, and light of others.

~ TORKOM SARAYDARIAN

To Show Another Way: Applications

Establish a daily practice to align with your Soul (your Jewel Within), especially every morning and/or evening. Reflect on these questions:

◆ Does being aware of the Jewel Within shift the priorities in my life?
◆ Is this awareness changing how I relate or communicate with others?
◆ How does the Jewel Within teach me **to show another way** to myself and others?

The Power of Intention

As a man thinketh in this heart, so is he.

~ JAMES ALLEN

An intention is an aim or focus that guides our action. It can be likened to a laser beam pointed in a specific direction to accomplish a certain result. In order that it achieve its desired purpose or goal, the laser beam must be precisely directed. With such precision, the beam's energy is concentrated in the right amount for the right reason and in the right way to attain the desired result. We have witnessed how the power of precisely placed laser beams has dramatically changed our culture in the industries of medicine, science, and agriculture, among others.

The Energetic Field of Intention

Like a laser beam, our intentions have tremendous power and predictable outcomes. If we want to shift the quality of our inner and outer life, we must first look at what energizes that shift. The energetic source of change is found in the nature of our intentions. Early nineteenth-century writer and pioneer of the self-help movement, James Allen, wrote numerous inspirational books. In his best-known book, *As a Man Thinketh*, he writes:

A person's mind may be likened to a garden, which may be intelligently cultivated or allowed to run wild; but whether cultivated or neglected, it must and will bring forth. If no useful seeds are put into it, then an abundance of useless weed-seeds will fall therein and will continue to produce their kind.

Every thought-seed sown or allowed to fall into the mind and to take root there produces its own blossoming sooner or later into action, and bearing its own fruitage of opportunity and circumstance… [N]othing can come from corn but corn, nothing from nettles but nettles.

We understand this law in the natural world and work with it; but few understand it in the mental and moral world. Suffering is always the effect of wrong thought in some direction… [A]s we alter our thoughts towards things and other people, things and other people will alter towards us. We imagine that thought can be kept secret, but it cannot; it rapidly crystallizes into habit, and habit solidifies into circumstance.

Intention-setting is at the heart of our psychological wellbeing and spiritual development. Intentions are not isolated events; rather, our intentions interconnect within the vast matrix of our life—within the energetic structure of our own mind-body-spirit and within the energetic network of our relationships with other people, with other things— indeed, with everything there is. Meditation teacher Sharon Salzberg writes about the way our intentions resonate within the matrix of our life in her book, *Lovingkindness*:

The vibrational tone of any intention, the motivation behind our speech and action, reflects the kind of seed we are planting in any moment… [T]he seed is planted in a field. The result, the fruit, depends not only on the potential of that one seed, but also upon all the variable factors of the field. All of our intentions interconnect; they modify and influence one another.

The field, with its vast interconnectedness—it is connected to everything in the Universe—typically cooperates by first helping us remove obstacles to the fulfillment of our intention, thereby **showing us another way**. Hidden aspects of ourselves may suddenly reveal themselves. These obstacles take many forms, including resistance to change, self-critical thoughts, and sabotaging behaviors. Doing shadow-work by asking self-inquiry questions about our motivations is especially helpful when obstacles emerge. Synchronicities (helpful and meaningful-seeming coincidences) may also occur more often when we consciously work to carry out our intentions.

Although working with personal intentions is not always a smooth process, it can lead to a more empowered, contented, and fulfilling state of being. When we direct the laser beam of our intention directly upon achieving the highest physical, mental, emotional, and spiritual goals for our life, we honor our life purpose and realize the development of our soul.

Into your hands will be placed the exact results of your thoughts.

~ JAMES ALLEN

To Show Another Way: Applications

Respond to one or more of the following questions:

1. As I reflect on my willingness to set intentions and honor them by following through:

   ◆ What might my obstacles be when I say I am going to do something but I don't keep my word?

   ◆ How can I **show myself another way** so that I maintain the integrity of keeping my word?

   ◆ What are my intentions regarding applying the teachings in this book that address some of my personal concerns?

2. What are some examples of how the closing quote of this teaching deepens my understanding of certain experiences in my life? *Into your hands will be placed the exact results of your thoughts.*

3. What intentions do I wish to create about **showing myself another way** at this time in my life?

The Power of Integrity

A pessimist sees the difficulty in every opportunity;
an optimist sees the opportunity in every difficulty.

~ Winston Churchill

Regardless of what we do in the world, an inner awareness and evaluation of our purpose and motivation are essential to maintaining the integrity of our service to others. If we choose to dedicate our life to service, we might ask ourselves these questions:

- ◆ What is my purpose for doing this?
- ◆ Who am I doing this for?
- ◆ How am I **showing another way** for myself? for others?

As you read the following two stories, consider how these questions can be applied. These stories teach us how we can make a beneficial difference in the world because they **show another way** to be and serve with intentionality and compassion.

Making a Difference

A young boy on vacation goes for a walk on the beach. Up ahead he notices an old man stooping down to pick up a starfish. He sees the old man fling the starfish back into the sea. The boy runs to catch up to the old man and asks him, "What are you doing?"

The old man answers, "The stranded starfish will die unless they are returned to the water."

The boy says, "But the beach goes on for miles and miles. There are millions of starfish. How can what you're doing make any difference at all?"

The old man looks at the starfish in his hand and then, with a mighty heave, throws it into the safety of the waves. He then turns to the boy and says, "It makes a lot of difference to that one."

Love Is the Answer

A newly ordained priest at a parish in Washington, D.C. was assigned to drive a van that daily brought soup to a group of homeless men who lived beneath a bridge. For the first three days that the priest delivered the soup, he thought, "It's good that I can help these poor, unfortunate people."

On the fourth day, he drove up to where the men were living and started dishing out the soup. As he handed the men their bowls of soup, they angrily threw the soup back at him and yelled, "We are not dogs!" The young priest was shattered. Yet in that instant he knew he had been viewing the homeless men as helpless, needy, and inferior.

From that day on, the priest changed his approach, treating the men as equals and friends and helping them in ways they wished to be helped. The men grew to love and honor the priest and he served them for many years. When he died, droves of homeless men came to his funeral and expressed their deep respect and appreciation for what he gave them… **integrity.**

The story of the priest is an example of the consequence of thinking that serving others means doing something FOR them rather than learning something FROM them. The priest was being served by those he thought he was serving. Most importantly, he learned that it is not what we do that matters but the love with which we do it.

It doesn't matter what you do in the world
as long as you come from the heart.

~ ALEXANDER LURIA, NEUROPSYCHOLOGIST

To Show Another Way: Applications

Respond to one of the following suggestions:

1. Write a short story about a time when you were told you had made a significant difference in someone's life by **showing that person another way**. Note whether your heart received this.

    After completing your story, consider the role integrity plays in the actions of your main characters.

2. Write a short story about a time someone made a significant difference in your life by **showing you another way**. Note if the person was aware that he or she had empowered you in some significant way, perhaps redirecting your life, alerting you to a wrong decision, or even saving your life.

Destiny ~ Our Life's Masterpiece

*The two most important days in your life are the day you are born
and the day you find out why.*

~ MARK TWAIN

I am on a train traveling from London to Wales, where I am scheduled to give a workshop on inner healing. Gazing out the window, I am comforted by the beauty of the plush green- and brown-speckled rolling hills. I am thinking about the healing workshops I have just led in Belfast, Paris, and London. I ponder the depth of emotional pain I witnessed in the group members that resulted from the trauma of physical and emotional neglect and abuse. The psyche can withstand considerable ill treatment, but there comes a point when it shatters. At that moment, because we can no longer withstand the pain, we spiral into despair. As I reflect upon this, I become aware of how fortunate I am to have healed so much of my own mental anguish. I see how the despair I experienced in my life gradually transformed into inner strength and taught me how to help those in similar circumstances. I am also aware that I continued to have a persistent, in-the-bones desire for inner peace and for living life completely and well.

As the train speeds toward Wales, I know a vital aspect of my destiny has emerged—namely, that I am destined to honor the mind-body-spirit's need for wholeness by helping others reintegrate their fractured psyches, one gentle step at a time. My entire life has been, up to this point, focused on discovering how the psyche functions, how it can be wounded, and how it can be mended. My clinical training in communication disorders and neuropsychology has prepared me well, but my major understanding of the human psyche has come from observing my own healing and the healing of others.

Following this experience and, over time, another aspect of my destiny began to unfold: to view service as both an evolution of the soul and as the means to happiness for individuals, leaders, groups, and organizations. I noticed my heart sang whenever I had the opportunity to put into practice and share what I had learned about soul-inspired service, leadership, group life, and organizational design. I recognized that competency in these areas required considerable knowledge, skill, hands-on experience, and a commitment to learn from my mistakes. We cannot give away what we don't have ourselves.

What Helps Our Destiny to Emerge

Synchronistic opportunities, both major and minor, have supported this destiny and have helped me learn how **to show another way** to others. Three such opportunities were particularly significant: **First**, I was offered the chance to cofound and chair a holistic-clinical university training program in brain disorders. **Second**, I was invited to cofound and lead a community service organization that trained adults and teens to serve those seeking emotional and spiritual support. In both university and community settings, I designed trainings that required helpers to care for their physical, mental, emotional, and spiritual health by engaging in inner work and spiritual development. Another element of both programs was that participants willingly extended the gifts of their healing in service to others. **Third**, I was inspired and financially supported to share these teachings by writing *The Soul and Service Trilogy*.

Emerging destinies require hard work, perseverance, humility, determination, and discernment. They also depend upon the recognition that certain decisions, made using our free will, can take us off purpose and away from our destiny. I discovered that the driving force of my destiny was a deep desire for inner peace. Regardless of what happened in my outer life, I wanted my inner life to remain calm and wisdom-oriented. Undeniably, the journey of our destiny involves learning not only from smooth sailing in calm waters, but also from braving battering winds that can drive us off course.

Ten Attributes of Destiny

Certain attributes are characteristic of our destiny. Those who wish to move toward their destiny and recognize its emerging steps may be guided and supported by these attributes.

1. Destiny exists as an unrealized potential within us that persists in its yearning to be fulfilled.

2. We have a personal destiny and a spiritual destiny. Our personal destiny uses the unique qualities and inclinations of our personality and its free will to make choices in the world, searching outside ourselves for our right "to be." Spiritual destiny occurs when we turn inward and begin the journey of the spiritual evolution of our soul.

3. Free will is the freedom to say yes or no—and to say either of these absolutely, partially, or conditionally—if our destiny is to be fulfilled on our own terms.

4. We may experience challenges in attracting the right environment to live out our soul's destiny.

5. The seeds of our destiny begin to form in childhood. Our destiny can be seen in how we played as children, our personality traits, what books we chose to read, what values our parents espoused, what activities we liked or disliked, and what we announced we wanted to be when we grew up.

6. There are as many different destinies as there are people on earth.

7. We need not be famous or successful in worldly terms to claim a destiny. The fulfillment of our destiny may be as a medic, farmer, firefighter, parent, banker, actor, teacher, caretaker of animals, scientist, activist, hermit, construction worker, or any other role.

8. Following our destiny does not mean we know every twist and turn in the road or that we are always able to avoid barriers blocking our progress at certain junctures in our journey.

9. Destiny emerges through synchronicity. Synchronicity, or the flow of unexpected events, is a signal of our destiny unfolding. Synchronistic events lead us forward by giving us experiences that guide us, awaken us, and alert us to how we can live a fulfilling and meaningful life. Synchronicities often **show us another way.**

10. When we say yes to our destiny, we sense an inner certainty that we can and will complete the task assigned to us, knowing it matches our abilities and talents.

Living Our Destiny

Destiny emerges, one amazing step at a time, as precious seeds planted in the present for future sprouting. When we live our destiny, it becomes an expression of both **being shown another way** and of **showing another way** to others. Every soul longs to discover its destiny. The overarching destiny of our soul's existence, which is the overarching destiny of *all* humans, is to remember that the world is sacred and to discover what it means to be a human being. At the time of our death, we are blessed if we can authentically say, "I have lived. I have loved and been loved. **I have been shown another way by others and I have shown others another way. I have said *yes* to my destiny.**"

> *I don't know what your destiny will be,*
> *but one thing I know:*
> *the only ones among you who will be really happy*
> *are those who have sought and found how to serve.*
>
> ~ Albert Schweitzer

To Show Another Way: Applications

Imagine a trusted family member, friend, or colleague describing your destiny in a eulogy.

1. How might they describe your destiny and its fulfillment?

2. What would you especially want them to acknowledge about your destiny?

If We Build It...

You never change things by fighting the existing reality.
To change something
BUILD A NEW MODEL
that makes the existing model obsolete.

~ BUCKMINSTER FULLER

Some time ago, when I first read Buckminster Fuller's "build a new model" quotation, I was reminded of the popular 1989 movie, *Field of Dreams*. Many of us resonated with that movie's inspiring message just as we have with Fuller's innovative philosophy and inventions. The quote and the film suggested to me important similarities between Buckminster Fuller, an American visionary, designer, architect, poet, author, and inventor, and the *Field of Dreams* character "Shoeless" Joe Jackson, based on the infamous "Black Sox" member from the 1919 Chicago White Sox team who, together with seven of his teammates, was accused of throwing the World Series. Both the "Shoeless" Joe of the film and Buckminster Fuller, each in his unique way, are examples of **showing another way**.

Throughout his life, Fuller (1895-1983) was concerned with the question, "Does humanity have a chance to survive lastingly and successfully on Planet Earth, and if so, how?" *Field of Dreams* "Shoeless" Joe—who experiences redemption in the film—was concerned with a similar question: "How can people be reminded that all that was once good can be good again?" Just as Fuller advocated that humanity will survive on Earth if we change reality by building new models, "Shoeless" Joe advised an Iowa farmer that he could escape foreclosure if he shifted his intention from scarcity to abundance: "**If we build it [a new model], they [those we are to serve] will come**."

Becoming a Change Agent

Fuller and the 1919 White Sox team of the film are examples of change agents. The word "agent" comes from the Latin *agere,* meaning to drive, lead, act, and do. A change agent is capable of producing an effect that can inspire and motivate individuals and groups. A change agent is an active principle, a means by which a guiding intelligence asks timely questions and achieves a result. Change agents Buckminster Fuller and the White Sox team of *Field of Dreams* practiced this principle and served humanity **by showing another way.**

Our world is in global shock and is in critical need of change agents. The dependency of the old is crumbling; rising from the rubble is the interdependence of global economics, government, science, education, family, environment, medicine, and health. Existing institutional models don't meet our needs and so have become obsolete. The well-worn band-aid approach can no longer prop up what once was. To survive, we must change—by reaching deep into our compassionate hearts and creative minds. **We must BUILD NEW MODELS for being in the world by developing and practicing purposeful interconnectedness—in essence, we must practice group consciousness.**

Interconnectedness and Cooperation

A group is a collection of people who try to reach a common goal through cooperation, perseverance, and selfless motive. Whether our group is a family, a company, an organization, or a nation, we can add our unique contribution to the pool of new models. We can be part of the solution rather than part of the problem. Once these new models are in place, we will experience our interconnectedness as a greater humanity. We will discover what it means to be truly in the world together. We will live a life that causes as little damage as possible to ourselves and to others.

Torkom Saraydarian, teacher of Ageless Wisdom, writes, "In learning the true meaning of group consciousness, we stop seeing ourselves as separate beings, separate from all others, and begin to see our link to all of humanity, to Nature and Cosmos." In the process of this realization, we learn the science and art of cooperation. People everywhere are finally realizing that having cooperation and being in group consciousness are the true and only keys to our survival as a species. Such people are **showing another way.**

The Institute for the Advancement of Service—the organization I cofounded and where I serve as Executive Director—is one group among many whose purpose is building a new model and thus **showing another way.** At the Institute, our purpose is to create a model for soul-inspired service, leadership, and group life within a holographic learning organization that meets the needs of our changing world. We have been evolving this model for more than forty years. The Institute is one response to Fuller's question about how to live lastingly and successfully on Planet Earth, and one expression of "Shoeless" Joe's dream of goodness—"If we build it [a new model], they [those we serve] will come."

What is *your* response to Fuller's question? To "Shoeless" Joe's dream? Will you join Bucky Fuller and "Shoeless" Joe—as well as the Institute and countless other groups and individuals—in **showing the world another way?**

Never forget that you are one of a kind.
Never forget that if there weren't any need for you
In all your uniqueness to be on this earth,
You wouldn't be here in the first place.

~ BUCKMINSTER FULLER

To Show Another Way: Applications

In the spirit of the quote by Buckminster Fuller at the beginning of this teaching, respond to two or more of the following questions:

1. How have I, personally, been **shown another way** by someone who has built a new model?

2. How have I personally built a new model and **shown someone or a group another way**?

3. Does my workplace, community, state, and/or country function according to an old model? If so, what new models would I like us to build?

4. Have my friends, relatives, teachers, and colleagues shown me old models? If so, what new models would I like us to build?

Destiny as a Celestial Speed-Up

There are winds of destiny that blow when we least expect them.
Sometimes they gust with the fury of a hurricane,
sometimes they barely fan one's cheek.
But the winds cannot be denied,
bringing as they often do a future that is impossible to ignore.

~ NICHOLAS SPARKS

Are you among those who have recently stepped into that part of the mind that observes and takes the pulse of worldly activity around you? If so, you recognize that

- many people, including you, are living lives of markedly greater intensity and speed, with more internal and external upheaval,
- there are abundant opportunities to confront, clarify, and heal personal, interpersonal, and global issues,
- you can no longer postpone working on your own personal growth and healing,
- it is of crucial importance both to serve humankind in some way and to support the healing and wellbeing of our planet, and
- there is a vital need to focus on service by **showing yourself and others another way** to live on Planet Earth.

If these things are true for you, then you have chosen to take full advantage of this unique time in humanity's history, when our planet is transitioning to a higher vibrational level of spirituality and human existence. (For more on the transition from the Piscean to the Aquarian Era currently taking place on our planet, see "Humanity's Next Evolutionary Leap" in Chapter Two.) During a transition such as this, we can *expect the unexpected*. In such circumstances, it is fundamental that we stay connected to our true essence and, as the Masters have told us, "have faith—everything is all right."

How can we use the "celestial speed-up" of unexpected shifts in our inner and outer worlds to serve the evolutionary process that is our destiny—for ourselves, for others, and for Planet Earth at this unique time in the history of our world?

Support During the Celestial Speed-Up

Perhaps one of the greatest challenges during a time of celestial speed-up is to calmly and gently ride the waves of change. Much happens both within us and external to us during such times. Aldous Huxley articulated a wise way to view rapidly changing times when he wrote, "It is not what happens to us that matters, but what we *do* with what happens to us."

The following four principles can support us during these times of great upheaval at the personal, national, and international level because they provide a perspective of change that is true, reassuring, and strengthening:

Every encounter, every situation, no matter with whom we experience it or what the event, has the potential to show us another way. The Universe generously presents us with multiple and repeated opportunities to learn lessons which guide us to the realization of our true essence. We may have temporarily forgotten qualities about ourselves, either positive or negative. We may need to forgive a grievance we have been unknowingly holding against ourselves or another. Viewed in this way, no person or event can take away our true essence. We are not victims or victimizers; we are students and teachers to each other.

People and events are not as they appear to be. Neither are we upset for the reasons we think. The truth is always beyond the level of the "problem." We need not to deny what is happening, yet see beyond the situation to a greater truth. Being accountable for our projections is the first step to seeing a situation or person differently. Forgiveness is the willingness to search for a truth that lies beyond the situation. Forgiveness is being able to hold ourselves and others in our heart regardless of what has happened.

We are not alone—and our inner strength is found in the moment. The Divine is always with us and we are never separated from our Higher Self. We find and connect with this aspect of the Divine when we are present to it. We disconnect from this strength when we separate ourselves from the moment and move into past or future thoughts. We detach from this inner resilience when we obsess on a negative thought or feeling, as in this way we make real the belief in the separation from our inner divinity and from the divinity of others.

The Universe is constantly giving us feedback, teachings, and support. Synchronicity—the universal principle that links us to others and to outer events at a deep and meaningful level—gives us the gift of vitality, inspiration, and connectedness. It is the Divine spark inherent in our life's purpose—and is the key reminder that, indeed, we are not alone. (For more on synchronicity, see Chapter Two's "Synchronicity ~ Expect a Miracle.")

Riding the Waves of Change

It is our destiny to support one another by doing our part—by **showing another way**—during this time of tremendous spiritual evolution on Planet Earth. We **show another way** when we expect the unexpected, stay connected to our true essence, recognize things are not as they appear, acknowledge synchronicities, have faith that everything is all right, and embrace the celestial speed-up … as we—calmly, gently—ride the waves of change.

> *The only person you're destined to become is the person you decide to be.*
>
> ~ RALPH WALDO EMERSON

To Show Another Way: Applications

1. Journal your responses to two or more of these inquiry questions about the current celestial speed-up:

   ◆ What do I find to be supportive during the present transitional time on our planet?

   ◆ In what ways can I join with others to strengthen both my inner and my outer life?

   ◆ What does it mean that my inner strength is in the present moment, especially when the unexpected happens?

   ◆ Why is it important during a celestial speed-up to **show another way** to be in the world?

2. Support your understanding of this teaching by reviewing the teachings in Chapters One and Two that address the shift from the Piscean to the Aquarian Era.

Radiating Light to All That Is

At times our own light goes out
and is rekindled by a spark from another person.
Each of us has cause to think with deep gratitude
of those who have lighted the flame within us.

~ ALBERT SCHWEITZER

Many years ago I had a friend who was a physician. I noticed a remarkable phenomenon whenever I was in his presence. Whether we were walking in the neighborhood, taking a trip (whether by land, sea, or air), or informally visiting friends or relatives, we repeatedly encountered people in the midst of a life-threatening crisis or accident. These events didn't occur when I was by myself or with other people, and they stopped happening in my life when my friend moved on. What struck me about these synchronistic events was the feeling I had while watching him tend to those who were seriously injured or emotionally traumatized. He seemed to *give himself into* what he was doing with love, care, compassion, and competence. He was present in the moment as he **showed another way,** radiating Self-Light to those he served.

Self-Light

As human beings, we each have the capacity to generate and radiate Light. Spiritual philosopher and self-described "practical mystic" David Spangler refers to the generative source of Light and its spiritual presence within us as "Self-Light." He writes that this Light is naturally within us—it is not Light that we bring down from the higher realms. Although we can also bring Light down from above and extend it into the world, it is essential that we acknowledge the Self-Light we are born with and allow it to radiate forth into the world from within us.

Research shows that the eyes are the most sincere part of our face. When we see a person's eyes glisten, it is highly possible that we are witnessing that person's Self-Light. This may be why the eyes are often referred to as the windows of the soul.

How paltry is our awareness and understanding of the power of our Self-Light! Spangler notes that we too often disown or do not recognize our Self-Light:

> What we forget is that we are that Light…the sun that burns away the fog. The Light is in all of us, but it can be dimmed. If this were not true [if our Light could not be dimmed], we would be living in a very different world, one in which nature is honored and partnered with care and love, one in which the stranger is simply a friend we have yet to meet, one in which each individual represents a potential for discovery and growth, one in which community and collaboration, as well as the honoring of each person's uniqueness, are the hallmarks of life. We want such a world. We pray for such a world … the Light fuels our hope for such a world.

Our Self-Light exists within us as an expression of the will of our Soul—our Higher Self—and can increase or decrease. It increases when we accept the presence and purpose of this Light, when we view Earth as a school in which we learn, heal, and serve, and when we are compassionate, loving, and caring. When our Light is dimmed by doubts, angers, prejudices, hatreds, or apathy, or we turn to outer temptations, distractions, addictions, or self-neglect, ***it is crucial that we ask the Light to illuminate the darkness and show us another way.***

Generating and Radiating Light

We radiate our Self-Light in many ways—in the Light of understanding and wisdom, in the Light of beauty and truth, in the Light of meaning and purpose, in the Light of compassion and love, in the Light of prayer, and in the Light of service to ourselves, others, and Planet Earth. When we infuse our life—its activities, its relationships—with Light, we simultaneously bring heaven and earth into closer proximity. In other words, when we radiate Light, we bring heaven and earth closer together in *every* activity we engage in—walking down the street, driving our car, caring for nature, relating to wildlife and pets, conversing with a stranger, caring for our family, writing letters, speaking on the phone, sharing our feelings, taking a class, working at our job, talking with our boss, interacting with the clerk who checks out our groceries, and so forth. Imagine how uplifting and meaningful our life would be if we radiated Light every day in this way!

The Light of Compassion

Radiating the Light of Compassion—our heart's tender opening to the pain and suffering of others—is critical at this time on Planet Earth. When we hear the call of compassion in action, we recognize **this call begins with ourselves**. We nurture our spiritual growth and cultivate compassion for others when we are first and foremost kind and caring toward ourselves.

Self-inquiry questions help us explore the role of compassion in action in our daily life. We can ask, "What is this for? What is the purpose for my doing this (or not doing this)? What is my intention for this action? My motivation? How can I **show another way** by saying or doing the right thing in the right way at the right time and for the right reason?" Many spiritual teachings suggest that we examine our thoughts and actions with the intent to *do no harm*. This extraordinary principle can be applied in our personal, interpersonal, and work life. We can apply it to all that exists on our planet. In the words of His Holiness the Dalai Lama, "Love and compassion are necessities, not luxuries. Without them, humanity cannot survive. With them, we make a joint effort to solve the problems of the whole of humankind."

The Light of Heaven

An awareness of how to respond purposefully to the ongoing crises of our world emerges when we invite the Light of Heaven to infuse ourselves and others through prayer. Prayer enables us to stand strong when we are buffeted by outer extremes of weather; by cultural, social, and political change; and by inner tensions of fear and distress. Prayer is a powerful response to humanity's cry for help.

Before praying, we pause and connect our heart with the Light of Heaven. The Light of Heaven, also referred to as God's Light, is prayer's sacred power. Prayer manifests as a point of Light shaped like a star. Those who accept a prayer's point of Light within their heart will "wake up" to their spirituality and welcome knowledge, wisdom, conscious knowing, and sacred service into their life.

Years ago, I discovered a Buddhist prayer that radiates Light to others with purity and integrity. The prayer consists of this simple sentence: **"I pray for _____'s highest possible evolution."** The prayer does not focus on what we think the person needs, such as relief from his or her suffering, or a change in the person's behavior, attitude, health, or circumstances. Rather, **the prayer invites the Light to support and guide the person's highest possible evolution at this time in his or her life.**

A New Reality

We stand on the threshold of a new reality that is emerging on our planet. In this new reality, we recognize that all is energy. We welcome Light as the energy of Spirit, the energy of the Soul, the energy of life. We awaken to our spiritual origins. We know that our world is destined to radiate with Light in its many forms—understanding, wisdom, beauty, truth, meaning, purpose, compassion, and love. In this new reality, we literally stand in a waterfall of Light. As we radiate our Self-Light, we rekindle the spark and join with the Light in all we encounter—**showing another way** to ourselves, to others, and to our precious Planet Earth.

If you light a lamp for someone else
It will also brighten your path.

~ BUDDHA

To Show Another Way: Applications

Respond to two or more of the following suggestions:

1. Describe a time when your Light dimmed or went out and was rekindled by a spark from another person. What did you learn from this experience?

2. Describe a time when someone shared that you had rekindled their spark. What specifically happened and what insights did you gain from this experience?

3. Ask yourself: "How might I daily radiate Self-Light as I walk on the sacred path of harmlessness, especially during challenging situations and interactions throughout the day?"

4. Describe an event in which you

   ◆ witnessed someone extending the Light of Compassion to another.

   ◆ extended the Light of Compassion to another.

   ◆ received the Light of Compassion from another.

The Angel in the Marble

I saw the angel in the marble and carved until I set him free.

~ MICHELANGELO

Throughout the writing of *Born to Serve: The Evolution of the Soul through Service,* the first book of my *Soul and Service Trilogy,* I experienced the presence of Michelangelo, the great artist of the Italian Renaissance. Night after night for almost a year, he would appear in my dreams, informing me of the nature of his relationship with the marble he was sculpting. He was teaching me the meaning of **True Service** by providing an energetic experience of his partnership with the marble and the marble's partnership with him. In addition to being a master sculptor and painter, Michelangelo filled his notebooks with writings and poems that would refer to his art as his form of service, indicating that those around him did not see his art in this way. I sensed he wished to make a correction regarding how his art was understood by communicating a teaching to me about sculpting and service. In one of his most moving poems, he discusses being "born to serve"—providing the title for my book. He wanted **to show me** (and the world) **another way** to understand the true meaning of service.

When I wrote *Born to Serve,* I was often either in the consciousness of Michelangelo as sculptor or in the consciousness of the marble being sculpted. In other words, sometimes I was Michelangelo, sometimes I was the marble. I "knew" that a perfected sculpture was a joint goal of both Michelangelo and the marble. Michelangelo and the marble spoke and cooperated with one another until **together they released the statue—the an-**

gel—that revealed the marble's perfected potential. Michelangelo and the marble were one. The sculpture wanted to realize its potential. Michelangelo joined with the marble in purpose by chiseling, burnishing, and polishing the marble until that purpose was fulfilled. Michelangelo's perfected potential as a sculptor was what enabled him to serve the marble by removing what was unnecessary for the statue in its perfection to emerge.

Michelangelo's Metaphor of Service

Metaphors like that of Michelangelo and the marble denote that one kind of object or idea can be used in place of another to suggest a likeness or connection between them. Metaphors reveal something essential to be understood, bringing to light a possible relationship between seemingly diverse forms. For example, Michelangelo's sculpting of the marble is analogous to the server-served partnership. Sometimes, in service, we are the sculptor—the teacher; sometimes, we are the marble—the student. Sometimes we are helping another remove obstacles to his or her soul knowledge, and sometimes another is helping to remove these obstacles from us. Regardless of our role, we serve one another. Our partnership with one another creates a masterpiece of awakening soul knowledge.

I invite you to read the following expression of the Michelangelo metaphor slowly and aloud, deeply imbibing the meaning of the message. (The original Michelangelo metaphor can be found in *Born to Serve*, pages 11-12.)

As certainly as I, Michelangelo, reveal the soul of the marble I sculpt, my soul is revealed through my partnership with the stone; this is how I serve art and, through art, humanity. I reveal my soul through my service. I am always in partnership with that which I serve and am served by, whether people, animals, nature, or task. Serving with the intention of being both the master sculptor and the masterpiece of my life opens the door for the Absolute to create the highest good in any given set of circumstances.

As a sculptor, I see in my mind's eye the figure—the angel—within each massive piece of marble. My heart resonates with the potential sculpture that lives within the stone. The reciprocity between me and the figure within is pure, vibrant, and certain. I cannot force a design on marble that does not agree with its nature. Rather, as I chisel, burnish, and polish its surface, the marble and I speak and cooperate with one another until together we release the statue that reveals both my and the marble's perfected potential. The marble and I are one.

I pound and chisel with force, concentration, and purposefulness until my vision, the soul—the angel—of the marble, emerges from the stone. The marble yields to my blows, not out of sacrifice but out of desire for the figure within to reveal itself. Through this mutual give and take, I remove all obstacles to the marble's complete expression of itself, simultaneously becoming the complete expression of myself in that moment.

The Purpose of True Service

Michelangelo's unique relationship with his art **shows us another way** to understand our soul's relationship to service. The following are principles of life he expressed when engaged in sculpting, his preferred art form:

◆ We are each a sculptor of our life and can use our life experience to remove the superfluous in our inner and outer lives, thereby freeing our soul's knowledge, its already perfected potential.

◆ To recognize and relate to another's fullest potential is to honor that person's soul. Through service, we become equal partners joined in a common purpose rather than being separated individuals doing something to one another. Sometimes we are the sculptor and sometimes the marble; sometimes we are the student, sometimes the teacher. Joined in this way, we release something far greater than is otherwise possible: a holy relationship in which we support the emergence of each other's highest potential into a joint masterpiece. We **show another way.**

◆ The outside forces of painful experiences serve as catalysts for our inner change and transformation. As our personality tendencies and limited perceptions of life experiences fall away, our soul powers are called forth into full expression on the physical plane. In this process, we discover both our human psychology and our

Divine spirituality. The once hidden qualities and features of our soul emerge. With increasing awareness, we **show another way** when we manifest them in the world through service.

◆ The emergence of spiritual knowledge is the destiny of our soul. To release the soul into its full expression requires skills for working with the physical, psychological, and spiritual nature of ourselves and others. This is a lifelong process; it is the reason we are here. In the words of Michelangelo, when our "striving with every nerve" joins with Divine grace, the extraordinary happens. Our will becomes one with Divine Will. We know what to say or do to sculpt our soul's unique masterpiece of service. Only by accepting the rigorous discipline of this partnership can the knowledge of our soul emerge and our fullest potential be attained.

The goal of all work, of all service, is to **show another way** by simply bringing out what is already there—to find and release the angel in the marble in ourselves and others.

Every beauty which is seen here by persons of perception
resembles more than anything else that celestial source
from which we all are come.

~ MICHELANGELO

To Show Another Way: Applications

Reflect on the Michelangelo metaphor and the other information in this teaching before responding to one or both of the following inquiry questions:

1. What did I learn about myself and my relationship to service when I read the passage as if I were Michelangelo?

2. Remember a time in your life in which you recognized that how you were served

allowed an untapped potential to emerge from within you. This memory might be as simple as a comment made by another; perhaps it was an opportunity you were given that awakened a capacity within you—a capacity you had been seeking or maybe did not know you had. Describe your memories, relating them to the teaching of Michelangelo's relationship with the marble he was sculpting.

That Was Then ~ This Is Now

Man was made for joy and woe;
and when this we rightly know,
through the world we safely go.

Joy and woe are woven fine,
a clothing for the soul divine.
Under every grief and pine
runs a joy with silken twine.

~ WILLIAM BLAKE

In my early thirties, I experienced a crisis in my life that stemmed from accumulated regrets and neglect of my physical, emotional, and spiritual wellbeing. In desperation, I decided to share my qualms with a spiritual teacher whose teachings I had grown to trust. I wrote her a letter that described my many regrets and asked for forgiveness. She answered my letter with two sentences that **showed me another way:**

> *"There is nothing to forgive. Use what you have learned*
> *from your life to help others."*

The power of her words dramatically refocused my life. I understood that my teacher's words meant **"that was then—this is now."** "That was then" represented choices I made in reaction to childhood trauma. These choices were not always helpful for me or for others. I acknowledged my emotional pain and subsequently embarked on many years of personal healing combined with an ongoing search for the true meaning of service.

I sensed from my spiritual teacher's message that "this is now" reflected my deep desire to have a heart-centered life and a personal destiny of **True Service.** I recognized that life, with its achievements and challenges, with its joys and sorrows, gifts us with many opportunities to learn, grow, and serve. **We serve when we willingly share, *in some way*, the wisdom we have gleaned from both our uplifting and our hurtful life experiences.** Because our life experiences can teach us what *to* do as well as what *not* to do, each experience or encounter we have has the potential **to show us and others another way.** With this awareness, our life is no longer encumbered by regrets and unfulfilled dreams that impede the spirit of our giving and receiving. Instead, as we saw in the previous teaching ("The Angel in the Marble"), like Michelangelo, we can choose to see the angel within and do the work needed to set ourselves and others free.

Sacred Activism

It is essential that we focus our energies in a meaningful, sacred way if we are to help people grow and evolve psychologically and spiritually during this present perilous and disturbing time in our world. **There is no time to waste.**

Andrew Harvey, founder and director of the Institute for Sacred Activism, writes:

[T]he large-scale practice of Sacred Activism can become an essential force for preserving and healing the planet and its inhabitants … [W]e need to invite concerned people to take up the challenge of our contemporary global crises by becoming inspired, effective, and practical agents of institutional and systemic change. Sacred Activism … is born of a fusion of deep spiritual knowledge, courage, love, and passion, with wise, radical action in the world.

Living and Serving in the Sacred NOW

Three premises support our decision to live and serve in the spirit of the sacred NOW:

◆ **Service pervades all of life**. The spirit of service exists in all activities of life, whether we cook meals, teach school, write books, tend gardens, sweep streets, build buildings, head an organization, or visit someone who is ill. It is present in our varied communications with family, colleagues, friends, and strangers. As we evolve spiritually, service is less about *doing* and more about *being*. More and more, we focus on the integration and quality of our heart and mind while living and working in the outer world.

◆ **The quality of our motivations determines the quality of our service**. We are all servers and we are all being served. Our purest service occurs when we offer others more energy to heal and make helpful choices. To attain this state of **True Service,** we

  ▪ give the right amount of the right thing for the right reason and at the right time,
  ▪ **show another way** to others through the example of our life and interactions,
  ▪ broaden our service to include the wellbeing of Earth and its inhabitants, and
  ▪ extend Light into the world through prayer and meditation.

◆ **We serve when we willingly share, in some way, the wisdom we have gleaned from our life experiences.** A three-stage Life Experience Inventory can help us identify our unique gifts of service in the NOW. The following inventory focuses on using what we have learned from our life to genuinely help others and to participate willingly in sacred activism. Below, I have used examples from my own life to illustrate how the inventory can be used.

LIFE EXPERIENCES INVENTORY

THAT WAS THEN…	THIS IS NOW	
I Life Experience	II Current Status of Heal- ing and Learning	III How Life Experience Is Shared with Others
I know what it feels like to:	*How I feel about it now:*	*How I serve others as a result of this:*
Be in a family where boys are thought to be superior to girls. I felt angry, diminished, and rejected.	I decide to achieve because I want to, not out of spite.	I understand the resentment one feels as a result of being discriminated against.
Have teachers that believe in me.	I feel grateful for these models.	I easily believe in my own students.
Have family secrets.	I see that it keeps family members from being authentic with one another.	I support others speaking secrets without shame or guilt.
Grow up in a farming community with fresh and uncontaminated air and food.	I feel Earth and its inhabitants have been seriously harmed by choices made for materialistic gain without consideration of the greater good.	I support Sacred Activism as a force of compassion-in-action and as a means of creating peace and sustainability.

Showing Another Way

As we heal personally, we have more energy and can become a clearer instrument of healing for others and for the planet. We can choose **to show another way** by

- sharing the lessons we have learned in an appropriate manner and at the right time,
- holding a space for others to be healed of conditions which we have healed or are healing within ourselves,
- broadening our service to include Earth and its inhabitants, and
- participating in some form of Sacred Activism.

Finally, we can remember the wise words of my teacher, which are at the heart of all forms of **showing another way**:

"Use what you have learned from your life to help others."

We have a choice
to give one another
a crown of thorns or
the gift of lilies.

~ A Course in Miracles

To Show Another Way: Applications

Use the blank three-stage Life Experience Inventory on the next page (or draw your own) to record examples from your own life.

LIFE EXPERIENCES INVENTORY

THAT WAS THEN...	THIS IS NOW	
I Life Experience	II Current Status of Healing and Learning	III How Life Experience Is Shared with Others

The Strong Must Be Made Stronger

This is the true joy in life,
the being used for a purpose recognized
by yourself as a mighty one …
the being a force of nature instead
of a feverish, selfish little clod of ailments
and grievances complaining
that the world will not devote itself
to making you happy.

~ George Bernard Shaw

"The strong must be made stronger." Years ago, I had a dream during which these words were repeatedly chanted. At the time, I was well into my service as the head of the spiritual-educational institute I had cofounded years previously. (You can read more about the Institute for the Advancement of Service at the back of this book.) I viewed the chant as a statement of the Institute's mission to support those seeking personal growth and spiritual development. Later, I discovered that the chant had an even higher purpose: to remind us to become stronger as we address our grief and fear concerning this time of crisis on Planet Earth. **We become stronger by** ***showing another way*** **to ourselves and others—maintaining a deep connection to the Sacred Within and taking action in the spirit of True Service.**

Many of us view ourselves as strong, yet we're aware of the presence of niggling concerns that lie just beneath our awareness. We fear we may lack the full inner strength necessary to undergo the multiple threats and uncertainties currently brewing on our planet—global warming, pandemics, wars between nations, financial uncertainty, misused technology, terrorism… the list goes on. Our grief is overwhelming as we learn about the disregard of the health and safety of sentient beings; our despair threatens to defeat us as we witness the brutal treatment and killing of our fellow humans and of the natural world. We wonder if we will be strong *enough* as we weather the acceleration caused by the planet's transition into the fifth dimension. (For a discussion of the planetary transition from the Piscean to the Aquarian Era, see "Humanity's Next Evolutionary Leap" in Chapter Two.) We question whether we will be the ones who can help others during this transition or if we will find ourselves among those needing help.

A Clarion Call

As our world spirals into chaos and confusion, we can choose whether or not to heed the clarion call to be made stronger psychologically and spiritually and to help others do the same. Each of us is being called to become stronger and to engage in **True Service** by making a choice between the old and the new, between what was and what will be. By applying the wisdom of the Universe to help us deepen our collective understanding of what is destined to emerge in the world, we become able to support those who are struggling physically, emotionally, mentally, and spiritually.

The convergence of our inner journey with our outer one leads to the discovery of our soul's unique destiny. Developing inner strength is critical if we wish to fulfill this destiny and save our world from ruin. When we strengthen our own intention, commitment, and practices—when we strengthen our inner state—we become stronger and support the growing stronger of others. In other words, **we show ourselves and others another way** to live on Planet Earth.

Keys to Becoming Stronger

Regardless of how we experience our inner strength, we are wise to take an honest, nonjudgmental look at what we think, feel, and do that weakens our inner strength, and what we think, feel, and do that strengthens it. For example, do we strive to live a life of ease, looking for instant gratification, making excuses, escaping into endless distractions, or engaging in complaining, blaming, and condemning? Or do we strive to practice self-responsibility for our thoughts and reactions, engage in spiritual growth, and tend to our physical, emotional, mental, and spiritual health? Are we committed to becoming stronger and, if so, what supports this happening?

During this transformational time, three practices can help us to evolve if we wish to become stronger and serve others:

- ♦ *Self-Responsibility*—When we are self-responsible, we shift our thoughts, actions, and words to look within rather than without for wholeness.

- ♦ *Aligning with the Sacred*—When we align with what is sacred in us, in others, and in the world in general, we are guided, taught, and protected throughout our life so that we fulfill our life purpose.

- ♦ *Service*—When we are of service, we offer the right thing in the right way at the right time for the right reason and in the right amount.

This teaching's applications offer a series of self-inquiry questions that, if worked with honestly and consistently, can help us grow stronger to support our own wellbeing and that of others at this time of crisis on Planet Earth.

Nothing ever goes away
until it has taught us what we need to know.

~ PEMA CHÖDRÖN

To Show Another Way: Applications

Self-inquiry questions help us discover life patterns that either weaken our inner strength or make us stronger. Select and respond to the following self-inquiry questions that most resonate with you to support your being made stronger.

SELF-RESPONSIBILITY

◆ In what ways am I self-responsible for shifting my thoughts, reactions, and words to look within rather than without for wholeness?

◆ Under what circumstances do I look for instant gratification, excuses, endless distractions, or justification for complaining, blaming, and condemning?

◆ How often do I remember to walk with a light step through life by connecting with nature? How frequently do I lighten things up with fun and laughter when I am with family and friends? How often do I laugh at myself and my imperfections?

◆ With honesty and kindness, how often do I take responsibility for my own choices and allow others to do the same?

◆ In what situations do I tend to forget that patience, gentleness, and unconditional acceptance lessen resistance to change and growth?

ALIGNING WITH THE SACRED

◆ In what ways do I strive to attend to my physical, emotional, mental, and spiritual wellbeing, finding joy in knowing I am supported by both seen and unseen helpers?

◆ How often do I align with my Soul, who guides my life so that I live with integrity, commitment, and gratitude?

◆ Under what circumstances do I put the Divine first in my life, thereby aligning my will with Divine Will and fulfilling my assigned life purpose and mission?

◆ In what ways do I believe I have been given a unique assignment by the Divine and, having accepted this function, live my life with integrity, commitment, and gratitude?

SERVICE

◆ How aware am I that being of True Service is **showing another way** by offering the right thing in the right way at the right time for the right reason and in the right amount?

◆ How often am I aware that, the more conscious I am of the level on which I give and receive, the more helpful my giving and receiving is to myself and others?

◆ In what circumstances do I recognize that Divine Will works through me *as* me when I have no attachment to the form of the task and no expectations of outcome?

Note: These self-inquiry questions are adapted from the Universal Tributes—ten principles that provide a roadmap for becoming self-responsible and attaining self-transformation through service. To deepen your practice of becoming stronger, you are invited to study and practice the Tributes in your daily life.

I first published the Universal Tributes in *Born to Serve* and then again in *The Clarion Call*. The Tributes can also be found on the website of the Institute for the Advancement of Service (www.showanotherway.org).

Awakening to Our Potential

To venture causes anxiety
but not to venture is to lose one's self,
And to venture in the highest
is precisely to be conscious of one's self.

~ SØREN KIERKEGAARD

The chaos currently proliferating on personal, national, and international fronts in our world has transported me back to an experience I had in 1990, when twenty people joined me on my third pilgrimage to Medjugorje, a village in what was then Bosnia-Herzegovina, Yugoslavia. Six teenagers who lived there had been seeing apparitions of the Virgin Mary since 1981. Although my first two visits to Medjugorje were filled with awe and peace, a sense of dread pervaded my third trip.

A Vision in the Sky

On the last day of our visit, our group stood outside the home of one of the visionaries. Someone pointed upwards and said, "Look, it's the Madonna!" In the sky, we saw the Madonna watching two separate images.

In one image, a line of beings moved, ever-changing. At the head of the line was a baby boy; he was soon replaced by the image of a young boy about the age of five. Then, in quick succession, each figure was replaced by an older one: an adolescent, a young man, a middle-aged man, an old man. A skeleton finally replaced the old man and the sequence began all over again. In the adjacent image was a large hole. Through the hole, I could see a man cupping his hands around his mouth like a megaphone and speaking to us. I could see his mouth move but could not hear what he said. Mother Mary stood near the man.

The group watched until night came and the vision vanished. Within weeks, the cruel and bitter civil strife known as the Bosnian War began its six-year span.

Sacred Messages Are at Hand

I realized that what our group and other travelers witnessed in the sky that day was a profound teaching: a teaching that **showed us another way** to view our life on Earth—a way to understand the process of the evolution of the soul. The vision in the sky showed us the endless cycle of humanity reported in spiritual teachings throughout history—the incessant turning of the wheel of karma caused by the belief in our separation from God. Yet the vision showed us that humanity was not left comfortless, for adjacent to this image was the watchful Madonna, an expression of the sacred feminine. Next to her was a representation of the sacred masculine, the man with cupped hands explaining how we could step out of the human cycle of suffering caused by the belief in our estrangement from the Divine—if only we could tune in properly to hear him.

When we fail to communicate with our higher consciousness, we do not hear its words of guidance and direction. We do not learn how to halt the spread of separation made visible in the conflict and warfare within ourselves and between ourselves and others. **The Medjugorje vision suggests that important spiritual messages are always at hand, and that, for whatever reason, we do not take them seriously or follow their counsel.** We have yet to learn how to bring harmony and peace to ourselves and our relationships and to extend the aura of our personal peace into the world.

Three Intentions That Make a Difference

I sense a strong connection between the sacred teachings I saw in the sky that day thirty years ago and how we can make a difference in the world TODAY by **showing another**

way. But where do we start? What is our personal role? How do individuals, families, leaders, groups, businesses, and countries make a difference?

Three intentions can help us discover how to **show another way** to ourselves and others and unveil the potential lying hidden in our intrinsic nature. These intentions remind us to stop ignoring and resisting our capacity for higher consciousness and our role in making a difference. They support us in getting the help we need to identify and address the obstacles that block our inner wisdom and obscure our communication with those unseen helpers seeking to aid us.

Having a safe group or person in our life can be an important support for us as we explore and strengthen the three intentions. A safe person or group might be a spiritual group, a spiritual school (like the Institute for the Advancement of Service—my own safe place), or a spiritual mentor who can listen deeply to us as we explore our life's concerns and advise us from a place of greater awareness. Our time with a safe person or group revitalizes, rebalances, and increases our physical, psychological and spiritual energies so we can return with renewed strength to all aspects of our personal and work lives. We need a safe person or group that provides both practical methods and spiritual gifts.

FIRST INTENTION

The first intention is ***to slow down our life in order to experience spaciousness***. To do this we need to act from awareness rather than automatically reacting with our emotions. Having too much space causes us to lose touch with the qualities of life. Having too little space leaves us dominated by whatever arises, constricting us to such an extent that we try to conquer time by living our life faster and faster. Breathe. Gaze at the magnitude of the sky. With sand underfoot, rest in the expansiveness of the sea.

SECOND INTENTION

The second intention is ***to cultivate the ability to see beyond duality to the bigger picture***. When we see the bigger picture we more easily see how we can **show another way** to ourselves and to others. As if on the wings of an eagle, we rise above the daily fray of "bad news" and strive to reside in a higher vibrational level of consciousness that exists beyond our linear, black-and-white thinking.

We can see that every ongoing conflict has a long history of injustice, typically perpetuated by both sides. Origins of the conflict are commonly buried in the mists of time. The bigger-picture perspective punctures our illusions of what we believe to be true. When we see the bigger picture, we see the greater good of all, where all differences have a win-win resolution. We see events and patterns of events; we see cause and the effect of cause. We shift our awareness from small to large, from constraint to expansion, from limitation to limitless possibilities. We break down outmoded patterns of thinking and being, knowing that a problem is solved at a higher level of consciousness than the level at which it was created.

THIRD INTENTION

The third intention invites us ***to radiate Light and Love to others and to Planet Earth through prayer AND to take some sort of action to bring this about.*** (For an expanded teaching on how to pray for Planet Earth and how to radiate Light to others, see "S.O.S. ~ Pray for Planet Earth" in Chapter One and "Radiating Light to All That Is" in Chapter Five.) When we shine our Light from within out into the world and take action, we make a difference. When we allow that Light to radiate back to us, we can make an even greater difference in the world because we have, as a result, substantially more Light to shine forth in our daily lives—in our every look, our every thought, our every breath.

Awakening to Our Potential

If humanity is to awaken to its potential for higher consciousness and welcome the new phase of life on Earth that is struggling to be born, ***we*** must fully awaken to ***our*** potential. As each individual sleeping soul awakens, we step closer to a global awakening. As a collective, we are poised on the cusp of a gigantic evolutionary leap. No wonder, as individuals and groups, we want to make a difference. In service to humanity and in partnership with our Divine helpers, we have a unique opportunity at this moment in our planet's history to choose to become agents of healing, peace, and harmony—so that we may **show another way** to ourselves and others.

Whatever you can do, or dream you can, begin it.
Boldness has genius, power, and magic in it.
Begin it now.

~ JOHANN WOLFGANG VON GOETHE

To Show Another Way: Applications

Reflect deeply and journal on these questions addressing aspects of making a difference by **showing another way** in today's world:

1. How do I personally relate to the Medjugorje sky vision and its sacred message? Does it change how I view my life? If so, in what way?

2. What do I observe about myself when I view my life through the eyes of the three intentions?

   ◆ To slow down my life in order to experience spaciousness.
   ◆ To cultivate my ability to see beyond duality to the bigger picture so I can more easily see how to **show another way** to myself and others.
   ◆ To radiate Light and Love to others and to Planet Earth through prayer and to take action to bring this about.

3. Do I have a safe person or group in my life where I find practical, psychological, and spiritual teachings and support? If so, how would I describe the role this person or group plays in my life? If not, how might I find such a person or group?

Awakening Leaders and Groups

Beauteous art, brought with us from heaven,
Will conquer nature; so divine a power
Belongs to him who strives with every nerve.
If I was made for art, from childhood given
A prey for burning beauty to devour,
I blame the mistress I was born to serve.

~ MICHELANGELO

D o you see yourself as a leader? If not, think again. **We are all leaders because each of us is the leader of our own life.** It can even be said that each of us leads *two* lives—an inner life and an outer life. We are leaders of our inner life—our feelings, our opinions, our perceptions, our decisions. In our outer life, we lead in a number of different roles. As parents, we lead our families; as presenters or lecturers, we lead our audience. We lead when we care for the elderly or the sick. We lead when we look out for the needs and wellbeing of our neighborhood or when we guide a community project. There is no end to the variety of roles in which we serve as leaders. Of course, there are also leaders of organizations, businesses, committees, and so forth. **As you read the teachings about leadership in this book, I invite you to apply or adapt them to your life, regardless of the kind of leadership roles you play in your public life.** We can benefit from teachings that **show another way** to lead regardless of the form our leadership takes.

We are also each a member of numerous groups. Groups can include nuclear families, extended families, neighbors, communities, towns, cities, or countries. They can be schools and classrooms, businesses, government offices, organizations, departments in the military, or the entire military itself. Groups can be professions, followers of the same religious or spiritual teachings, and activists advocating for the same cause. They can even be drivers on the same road, people walking on the same street or shopping at the same store, or an audience at a public play, concert, or sporting event. The types of groups are endless.

Michelangelo and the Leader-Group Partnership

This teaching shares many similarities with a teaching from Chapter Six—"The Angel in the Marble." In that teaching, I shared how, while writing *Born to Serve: The Evolution of the Soul Through Service*, the first book in my *Soul and Service Trilogy*, Michelangelo, the great painter and sculptor of the Renaissance, appeared regularly in my dreams. In these dreams, he showed me that his relationship with the marble was about being of service. Michelangelo was teaching me the meaning of **True Service** by providing an energetic experience of his partnership with the marble and the marble's partnership with him.

Because leadership is a form of service, the Michelangelo metaphor can be adapted to explain the nature of the leader-group partnership. You will find that, although you have read a version of this teaching in Chapter Six, when the metaphor is used to explain the leader-group relationship, it conveys a unique energy about service for leaders and for group members. I have deliberately used much of the same language to explain both teachings because the energy of the Michelangelo metaphor was "downloaded" from the refined spiritual vibration that pervaded my dreams of Michelangelo. I invite you to allow this teaching to serve as a "deep dive" into your relationship to your leadership and your role as a member of groups. Let the energy of the teaching saturate your consciousness and observe if, over time, your understanding of being a leader and a group member has been elevated or changed in some way for the better.

Creating a Leader-Group Masterpiece

Just as Michelangelo and the marble spoke and cooperated with one another, leaders and groups speak and cooperate with one another until **together they reveal both the sculptor (the leader) and the marble's (the group's) perfected potential.** Michelangelo (the leader) and the marble (the group) are one. The sculpture (the group) wants to realize its potential as does Michelangelo (the leader). Michelangelo (the leader) joins in purpose with the marble (the group) by chiseling, burnishing, and polishing the marble (akin to both the leader and the group members working with their shadow) until that purpose is fulfilled. Michelangelo's perfected potential as a sculptor (a leader) enables him to serve the marble (the group) by removing what is unnecessary for the statue (the group) to emerge in its perfection (by working with its shadow).

Metaphors suggest an implied relationship or a hidden comparison between two apparently unrelated things. The comparison, once revealed, allows us to understand each thing in a dramatically different way. In this case, Michelangelo's sculpting of the marble is analogous to the leader-group partnership. Sometimes, in service, we play the role of the sculptor—the leader—and sometimes we play the role of the marble—the group member. Sometimes we are helping another remove obstacles to his or her soul knowledge, and sometimes the other is helping to remove these obstacles from us. Regardless of our role, we serve one another. Our partnership with one another creates a masterpiece of awakening soul knowledge.

The Michelangelo Metaphor for Leaders and Groups

The Michelangelo metaphor is a helpful model for **showing another way** for leaders and groups to work together. I have adapted the Michelangelo metaphor in the following passage in a new way, where the sculptor—the "I"—refers to you, the reader, in the role of leader. The word "group" has replaced the word "marble."

Read the following slowly and aloud, connecting to the energetic depth of the metaphor's meaning and inviting its message to resonate within your heart and soul.

As certainly as I, the leader, help to reveal the soul of the group, my soul is revealed through my partnership with the group; this is how I serve humanity. I reveal my soul through my leadership as service. I am always in partnership with the group I serve and am served by. Serving with the intention of being both the leader and the masterpiece of my own life opens the door for the Absolute to create the highest good in any given circumstance that occurs in the group.

As leader, I see in my mind's eye the potential within each group member. My heart resonates with the potential that lives within the group. The reciprocity between me and the group is pure, vibrant, and certain.

I cannot force a design on a group that does not agree with its vision. The group and I speak and cooperate with one another until together we release the form that reveals both my and the group's perfected potential, its purpose, vision, and mission. The group and I are one.

I do my part as I pound and chisel with concentration and purposefulness until the shared vision, the "soul" of the group, emerges from within the group. The group and I deliberate and cooperate, not out of sacrifice, but out of desire to reveal our shared destiny. Through this mutual give and take, we remove all obstacles to the complete expression of our potential, becoming the complete expression of ourselves in any given moment.

I am the leader of my life and can use each leadership and group experience to remove the superfluous in my inner and outer life, thereby freeing my soul's knowledge, its already perfected potential. The emergence of spiritual knowledge is the destiny of my soul.

The outside forces of painful experiences serve as catalysts for my inner change and transformation. As my personality tendencies and limited perception of life experiences fall away, my soul powers are called forth into full expression on the physical plane. In this process, I discover both my human psychology and my Divine spirituality. The once hidden qualities and features of my soul emerge, and with increasing consciousness I manifest them in the world through leadership as service.

To recognize and relate to a group's fullest potential is to honor each member's soul. Rather than being separated individuals doing something to one another, through service, the group and I become equal partners joined in a common purpose. Sometimes I am the group member, sometimes the group leader. Joined in this way, we—leader and group—release something far greater than is otherwise possible: a holy relationship in which we support the emergence of each other's highest potential into a joint masterpiece.

Awakening to Our Soul Knowledge

To release the soul of the group to its full expression requires skills for leadership and group life, as well as skills for working with our physical, psychological, and spiritual natures. This is a lifelong process and is the reason we are here on Earth. When our "striving with every nerve" joins with Divine grace, the extraordinary happens. Our will as leader and the will of the group become one with Divine Will. We know what to say and do to help sculpt our unique masterpiece of service. Only by accepting the rigorous discipline of this partnership can the knowledge of our group emerge and our fullest potential be attained.

The goal of all work, of all service, of all leader-group partnerships, is to bring out what is already there, to unveil our souls, and **to show another way** to be a leader and a group member.

The greater danger for most of us
lies not in setting our aim too high and falling short;
but in setting our aim too low
and achieving our mark.

~ MICHELANGELO

To Show Another Way: Applications

1. In silence, imbibe Michelangelo's gift of **showing you another way** to understand service.

2. Reflect and journal on the following inquiry questions:

   ◆ What did I learn about myself **as a leader** (see types of leaders at the beginning of this teaching) when I read the above adaptation of the Michelangelo metaphor?

   ◆ What did I learn about myself **as a group member** (see types of groups at the beginning of this teaching) when I read the above adaptation of the Michelangelo metaphor?

   ◆ How does Michelangelo's view of sculpting marble statues **show me another way** to understand what it *really* means to be a leader or group member?

Living the Destiny of Leadership

A leader is someone you choose to follow
to a place you wouldn't go to by yourself.

~ JOEL BARKER

In Chapter Five, we explored the concept of personal destiny and how it emerges as an expression of **being shown another way** and **showing another way** to others. Recognizing and fulfilling our personal destiny is essential to our happiness and wellbeing. A strong passion, to which we cannot say no, arises from within, driving us forward. It is as though fate itself taps us on the shoulder and assigns us a call to action.

The destiny of leadership shares all the attributes of personal destiny, but has its own unique aspects. When we say yes to leadership, we sense excitement, confidence, determination, and an inner certainty that we can and will complete the task assigned to us, knowing it matches our abilities and talents. Putting in hours of time and shouldering burdens is part of what we are meant to do. Our love and need for self-expression override the drudgery and discipline required to birth a group or to evolve a group that does not work well together into one that does.

As leaders, we discover the destiny of our group or organization in much the same way as we discover our personal destiny. We explore why the group exists and what its role is in relationship to the larger community. The spirit of our personal destiny joins with that of the group we lead.

The Destiny of Leadership

Leaders often do not know how to be effective group members. A competent and confident leader must **first** experience, understand, and honor the role of group member by having learned how to **be** an authentic, competent, and confident group member. When this is not in place, leaders feel separate and isolated from the group and group members feel separate and isolated from the leader. Effective and self-responsible leaders address their obstacles to being effective group members by engaging in personal inner work, removing personality blockages, and working with their shadow tendencies in group settings.

Destined leaders who have healed their conflicted feelings about being a group member emanate an aura of energy and inspiration that attracts others. Robert Goffee and Gareth Jones write in the *Harvard Business Review* that people prefer enthusiastic leaders who create feelings of significance and a sense of community. People feel supported by a leader who appreciates them as valued contributors and makes them feel they are part of an important joint creation. They want a leader to convey excitement and challenge and who makes them feel engaged in the world. A sense of destiny inspires a deep commitment, fueling the energy, enthusiasm, patience, and willingness needed during times of challenge and change. **Destined leaders view their leadership responsibilities as a labor of love.** The leader and group join together to fulfill a specific joint destiny.

As destined leaders, we constantly **show** the group **another way** to be a group and feel safe. Instilled with boldness and courage, we guide our group on a journey to bring its destiny to light. Our intuitive hunches make our task manageable by pointing out the next best step for our group. We understand the meaning of group consciousness and teach this to the group. We persevere through painful setbacks, admit and correct our leadership errors, and celebrate our progress. We honor all aspects of leadership, which include dealing with personnel challenges and even at times emptying trash and straightening closets.

Leadership Destiny Begins in Childhood

The seeds of leadership destiny begin in childhood and unfold thereafter. Our style of leadership in adulthood has its origins in the skills and strength of character we developed when we were children. Even when we deny any interest in leading as a child, the seeds of our leadership destiny are visible in our early years. When I was a young child, I led with stubborn authority. I pushed my leadership out of myself (called "being bossy") to make things happen. I loved to organize the neighborhood children and act out the roles of teacher, restaurant manager, and funeral director. I alarmed my parents when, playing dentist, I would "fill the cavities" in the teeth of my playmates with Concord grape skins from our garden's arbor. As a teenager, I was competitive and driven to lead, to assume responsibilities, to help others, to have a job, to be in charge, and to make decisions. The school principal often asked me to serve as substitute teacher for the lower grades, perhaps setting the stage for my deep interest in teaching. These early traits, improved over many years, provided needed materials to weave the tapestry of my future leadership.

From his earliest memory, **Winston Churchill** believed he was born to a great destiny and intentionally prepared for it by playing with his army of toy soldiers. Churchill credited his sense of destiny with his ability to persist in the face of adversity, a trait developed during long periods of physical and emotional isolation during childhood. His strong sense of destiny led him through a tumultuous political and military career and enabled him to fearlessly espouse his unpopular and sometimes unviable views.

When, in 1911, Churchill was appointed the First Lord of the Admiralty, his daughter, Mary Soames, writes that he "flung himself into this new and coveted job with ardor and confidence. Here was the work for which all his talents fitted him, the task for which he was destined—the defence of Britain." At age sixty-five and anchored in knowledge, foresight, conviction, and oratory skills, Churchill finally became prime minister and led Britain and its allies to victory during the Second World War.

Getting onto the Path of Leadership Destiny

Like Winston Churchill, destined leaders often have the forceful personalities necessary to challenge cultural beliefs and make change happen. **Elisabeth Kubler-Ross**, for example, is known for her straight-talking and unsentimental nature, which she used to transform Western-world attitudes toward death and care of the dying. Even as a child in Switzerland, she challenged dogma, prejudice, and skepticism. She ignored her father's wish that she remain at home and become a secretary for his company; instead, she became a physician. As a young woman working in a hospital, Kubler-Ross fed, washed, and cared for traumatized Jewish refugees who had fled to Switzerland from Nazi-occupied countries. At the urging of a Polish physician, she traveled to war-torn Poland to tend Jewish children in concentration camps. In her autobiography, *The Wheel of Life*, she explains her decision to go to Poland: "My destiny, whatever it turned out to be, was still many miles ahead, somewhere in the desert of human suffering. If I was ever to get there, if I was ever to help, I had to get on the path."

Each subsequent experience of Kubler-Ross' life served her leadership destiny. After World War II, she became a physician and psychiatrist and moved to the United States. She began her pioneering work of educating the public and health professionals about the neglected physical, psychological, and spiritual needs of terminally ill children, AIDS patients, and the elderly. Undeterred by obstacles and disappointments, she never wavered from the path of her destiny, to serve "in the desert of human suffering."

When We Choose against Our Destiny

It is not uncommon that at some point on our leadership journey we make or consider making a choice that goes against the fulfillment of our destiny. We may find ourselves standing at the entrance of a destiny cul-de-sac. We waver between choosing to move into the cul-de-sac or to persist on our path. Standing at this important juncture in our life, we question whether we possess the energy, inner strength, and skills necessary to continue the intense demands of our leadership classroom. We may feel overwhelmed by fear of an unknown future. We may view continuing to be a leader as a burden with too many risks and too little joy. Or, we may still tend to make decisions from the place of our psychological wounds rather than from our intuition, resulting in interpersonal conflicts and errors in judgment.

Choosing to go against our destiny is often accompanied by a profound intuitive sense that we are about to embark upon a wrong path. To make this choice, we must expend great energy to override the intuition with our intellect. Cul-de-sacs can be miles long and have many side roads, and they always lead to a dead end. Inertia sets in and we set up housekeeping. Retracing our steps to return to the main road of our destiny can take years. The longer the side-trip, the more difficult and time-consuming it is to make a correction. **However, cul-de-sacs can be an extraordinary gift if we learn from them and pass that learning on to others.** Also, interventions—called synchronicities—often return us to our destiny's path. ("Synchronicity ~ Expect a Miracle" in Chapter Two explores the power of synchronicities in our life.)

Psychologist Abraham Maslow spoke of the temptation to choose against our destiny as the "Jonah Complex." Jonah was an Israelite prophet who resisted a Divine call to preach repentance to the people of Nineveh, was swallowed and vomited up by a great fish, and eventually carried out his mission. Maslow wrote:

> We all have unused potentialities or not fully developed ones. It is certainly true that many of us evade our constitutionally suggested vocations... So often we run away from the responsibilities dictated (or rather suggested) by nature, by fate, even sometimes by accident, just as Jonah tried in vain to run away from his fate.

The Journey of Our Leadership Destiny

The goal of our leadership journey is to become the leader we are intended to be. Leaders are teachers, designers, and stewards. They are wayshowers. To be an inspired and competent leader, we need multiple skills and many competencies, all of which I identify and describe in two of my previous books, *The Awakened Leader: Leadership as a Classroom of the Soul* and *The Clarion Call: Leadership and Group Life in the Aquarian Era.*

In addition to a range of skills and competencies, because the path of leadership typically includes serious issues within a group or organization, I strongly recommend that a leader have two mentors—a man and a woman. Mentors have experience and skills that can guide and support the leader through difficult situations. I recommend leaders have both a man and a woman mentor for a varied perspective and to represent the masculine and feminine principles in leadership. The incoming structure for leader-ship and group consciousness balances feminine heart qualities of relatedness, nurtur-ing, care, and intuition with the masculine head qualities of rationality, analysis, and problem solving.

As destined leaders, we need plenty of patience as we combine competency, love, and willingness during setbacks and errors in discernment and judgment. As we contin-ually grow in knowledge and application of that knowledge, we serve the highest good of those we lead. As destined leaders, we pursue our vision day after day while attending to both the routine and the unexpected. We ensure we maintain our energies and that the energies of our group are regularly renewed and refreshed. As destined leaders, we are willing to shoulder the burdens of our leadership because we know that **showing another way to lead** is what we are destined to do.

It is a mistake to try to look too far ahead.
The chain of destiny can only be grasped one link at a time.

~ WINSTON CHURCHILL

To Show Another Way: Applications

Reflect and journal on these questions:

1. What does it mean to be "the leader of my life"? How is this made visible in my life?

2. Do I see myself as having a destiny of leadership? If yes, why? If not, why not?

3. If I see myself as a leader, how would I describe my willingness to continually grow and evolve my capacity as a leader and my relationship with those I lead?

4. In what specific ways do I **show another way** to the those I lead?

Discovering the Destiny of Groups

The greatest demand and need for the coming hundred years
are group consciousness, group work, and group cooperation.
Those who cultivate group consciousness will survive
and advance toward a glorious future. Those who try
to base their life on the foundation of past interests,
personal glory, and partisanship will slowly fade away.

~ TORKOM SARAYDARIAN

Throughout my personal and professional life, I have studied, experienced, and written about destiny—not just personal destiny, but also that of leaders, groups, organizations, the country, and the world. In this teaching, I share some of what I have discovered about the destinies of groups and organizations.

In Chapter Five, I define **destiny** as **an unrealized potential within us that persists in its yearning to be fulfilled.** I also note that we have two destinies, personal and spiritual. The same is true for groups. A group by definition is when two or more persons come together for a given purpose.

As we explored in the first teaching of this chapter, every person who lives on the planet ultimately becomes a member of multiple groups. Not only are we members of our immediate and extended families, of our communities, and of the towns, cities, and countries we live in; we are in a group at any time we are doing something similar to, or even in the same place as, one or more other people. Examples of more conspicuous groups would be students in a classroom or workers in an office; people engaged in the same profession, or those who practice the same religion. But as much as a class of students or office of coworkers is each a group, so too are two friends who sit down to play a piano duet together. We don't realize we become part of a group when we get in our car and merge into traffic, when we shop in a store with others, or simply when we walk down the street passing or being passed by people who are also walking on that street. Groups are simply everywhere we look.

Groups, like individuals, use their free will—a gift from the Divine—to determine their purpose, attitudes, structures, and activities, and to choose whether or not to manifest the group's unique destiny. Using their collective free will—the joined wills of group members—they engage in constructive or destructive actions within their own group and in relation to other groups.

Why People Feel Uncomfortable in Groups

If we did not feel at home and safe in our first group—our family of origin—it is likely we will not feel at home or safe in subsequent groups. Being in a group confronts our attachment to our individuality and the belief that we are separate from others. This results in projection and unhealthy boundaries. In Chapter Three, we saw how our individual shadow—the "dark side" of the psyche—is like an iceberg with 90 per cent of its entirety underwater. Our shadow lurks in the unconscious and remains unseen until we are triggered. This is also true for groups: **most energies within a group operate at an unconscious level.** These energies emanate from the unconscious of each individual and combine to form a group shadow. To make a true commitment to a group, as members we must focus on the deep layers of the iceberg and resolve any energetic blockages. **Each group member doing his or her own personal inner work is paramount to group work.**

The deepest layer of any group's unconscious shadow rests in the shadow of the members' first group—their family of origin. Individual members are often unaware that they bring their experiences, unresolved issues, and attitudes about early relationships with parents, siblings, and other relatives into current groups. For example, individuals who had a strong sibling rivalry when growing up might find themselves being fiercely competitive with other members of a current group. Members who have resisted healing their family wounds will resist removing personal blockages that interfere with meeting a group goal. As a group member, I may react negatively to the behavior or appearance of another member because that person reminds me of a family member with whom I experienced conflict. For example, I might project an interpretation onto that group member because he or she reminds me of someone in my family of origin towards whom I still have unfinished business.

When we are triggered by or judge another group member, we might say to ourselves, **"Who does this person remind me of? I'm not seeing this person as someone in his own right but rather as if he is the individual toward whom I still have grievances. In other words, I am projecting my negative feelings onto this person because I have not healed my past relationship."**

When We Are Triggered in a Group

Early school experiences also influence how comfortable we will feel in groups in adulthood. Teachers and classmates play a significant role in determining our feelings as group members because we know we are compared to each another educationally and socially. Our discomfort in groups as a result of early family, school, or other social trauma can result in the separation of a large group into several small groups. Group safety is compromised when its members do not engage in inner work and only function on a mental level. Such tendencies cause group members to accumulate knowledge and philosophize. When we do this as group members, we tend not to know how to cooperate or effectively communicate in the group. We do not solve group problems or make wise decisions in the group with ease or efficiency.

We can also project something *positive* onto another because that person reminds us of someone toward whom we have a high regard or because we deny having that positive quality within us. When this happens, we do not see the person as she is, but rather as someone we imbue with an exceptional or special quality. In both instances, **we *disown our own Light* as we project it onto this "special" person.** Our shadow motivation for this kind of projection can be a hidden intention (hidden to ourselves as well as to the other person) to "make" the person love or esteem us. Projections,

164 ◆ TO SHOW ANOTHER WAY

whether negative or positive, are born in the shadow and therefore are not the authentic actions of our true self.

Learning Healthy Boundaries

Many of us learn unhealthy boundaries from our family of origin. Learning how to have healthy boundaries strongly supports well-functioning group life. **Healthy boundaries increase safety in a group and reduce conflict**. They support the development of a strong sense of self-identity, which enables group members to maintain a neutral space between others and themselves. Boundaries protect our authentic self so we can feel free and safe to be who we are. In *Boundaries and Relationships*, psychologist Charles Whitfield writes,

> [B]oundaries help us … [to] affirm our inner world while granting others the right to have their feelings, thoughts, needs, and viewpoints, which might be different from our own. Through healthy boundaries, we ask to be treated with respect, while extending respect to others.

Establishing guidelines for healthy boundaries is essential for people to feel comfortable and safe in a group. It is the responsibility of group leaders to teach healthy boundaries to group members and to insure members understand, agree to, and practice them as a critical part of the group's structure. In most groups, communication guidelines for appropriate boundaries are not written, reviewed, or accepted by the group. Communication guidelines make the group aware of unconscious tendencies and **show another way** to work with our individual shadow so that we don't project it onto the group. (For an example of communication guidelines, see the Study Guide for Leaders at the back of this book.)

When a group has healthy boundaries, its members are not threatened by thoughts, views, or needs that differ from their own. Group members treat one another with respect and do not have a need to correct or change the point of view of others to agree with what they themselves believe to be true. They are self-responsible for personal reactions and do not project them onto the group. They use inquiry questions to check out their assumptions and understanding of one another's viewpoint. In addition to having communication guidelines that are read and practiced in the group, they establish written guidelines in advance for handling group conflict, assuring that all members understand the group's policies and procedures. Because the cause of a problem often resides below the surface in the group's unconscious, the problem may be different in actuality from what it appears to be. A group with healthy boundaries is willing to resolve conflict and practice the synthesis of a diversity of views.

Recognizing Unhealthy Boundaries

Unhealthy group boundaries typically reflect childhoods that taught members they were incomplete and needed to search outside themselves for what was missing. Common unhealthy boundaries in groups include projection; discounting, critiquing, or negating what another member has shared; gossiping; and making assumptions about a member's verbal communication or behavior. Groups often tolerate inappropriate behavior of members and avoid seeking a solution. Unhealthy boundaries create relationships fraught with expectations and dependencies that result in anger, resentment, and judgments when needs go unmet. Members project onto others what they believe to be missing within themselves, intruding on the boundaries of others by giving away responsibility for their own feelings and emotions. In this way, members abdicate self-responsibility and misuse their personal power.

Group members are often unaware of their personal unhealthy boundary issues. It is essential that group members learn about codependence, identify their symptoms, and strive to heal them. Avenues for healing unhealthy boundaries include codependence support groups, individual therapy, or therapy groups. Unhealthy boundaries include the following symptoms:

◆ Tolerating inappropriate behavior
◆ Failing to set limits by saying no
◆ Failing to see events and people as they are and not as they appear to be
◆ Lacking discernment for who owns a problem
◆ Confusing their needs with the needs of others

- ◆ Imposing their will on others
- ◆ Taking things personally
- ◆ Failing to recognize the complexity of dual relationships

Dual relationships occur when group members have more than one kind of relationship, such as being neighbors, spouses, siblings, friends, therapist and client, or coworkers. They can cause boundaries to be ignored and disrupt group cohesiveness.

Finding Leadership Mentors

It is of utmost importance for group leaders to educate themselves about leading groups and to have a leadership mentor to call upon for guidance and advice regarding leadership and group issues. The mentor needs to be ahead of the leader in understanding group dynamics and group leadership. As discussed in the previous teaching on leadership, to have both a woman and a man mentor to call upon is helpful for their unique vantage points and to reflect, respectively, the feminine and masculine principles in leadership.

Discovering Group Destiny

A group need not be famous or successful in worldly terms to claim a destiny. Destiny is not about competing or comparing ourselves to others. A group may be destined to be a family, a committee, a workplace, a class in school or college, a small business, a department in a large corporation, an academic department of a university, a civic office (such as a fire or police station), and so forth. Alternatively, a group's destiny may be an example of courage, patience, unconditional love, inner strength, or wisdom that emerged during a time of failure, misconduct, loss, or illegal behavior.

Group destiny emerges through synchronicity. The appearance of synchronicity, or the flow of unexpected events, is a signal that a group's destiny is unfolding. Synchronistic events guide the leader and group, alerting them to the next step needed in their destiny journey. Synchronicity events occur at the right time, in the right way, and for the right reason. Many groups feel overwhelmed by problems and demands coming at them at lightning speed. If they wish to notice and benefit from the flow of synchronistic events, groups must slow down. **The more the group slows down and awaits synchronistic events to show the way, the easier it will be for the group to notice when steps in its destiny emerge**. In essence, destiny is always about **showing another way.**

There is one overarching destiny of *all* groups: to discover what it means to be a group and to remember that the planet—our world—is a group that is sacred and must be cared for. As with our individual destiny, a group, large or small, is truly blessed if it can eventually and authentically say, "We are living and fulfilling our highest potential. We have said *yes* to our destiny." Such a group has said *yes* **to showing another way** to live and be on Planet Earth.

The Evolution of a Group Destiny

Groups typically experience challenges in attracting the right environment to live out their destiny. A group may have an outline of the story of its destiny, but there are different ways this destiny can be lived. For example, because a group is not isolated, its destiny story can be shaped by the choices of others, such as group members' families, the group's larger community, and local, national, and international events, including the results of elections and the choices of civic and world leaders, governments, countries, and so on. In addition, individual group members, using their free will, make choices that can enhance, shift, or impede a group's destiny journey.

I have observed that groups (as is the case with individuals as well) tend to expect their destiny to be quickly and easily revealed and even fulfilled. They therefore do not take time to educate themselves about how to work together towards fulfilling their destiny. Destiny emerges step by step over time. For example, the organization I cofounded—the Institute for the Advancement for Service—has changed its name four times, with each name change reflecting a significant shift in the Institute's purpose, vision, and mission. Our destiny has only just emerged—in our fortieth year.

Destiny does not happen instantly. A wise motto for a group to remember is: **It takes time to save time—it takes time for a group to be born well and to stay well.** When we take time to be born well and stay well, we save time because less time and effort are needed to solve problems and conflicts. Unresolved problems become embedded and resistant to change. Said in another way, we save time if we listen to the whispers before the whispers become screams.

We are all citizens of Earth and thus are blessed with a precious life. I can think of no topic as important in today's world as that of joining together to fulfill the destiny of a group or organization that **shows another way** to serve and be in the world. Such a destiny is a clarion call from the heart: it must be heeded if we are to truly live—as individuals and groups—completely and well.

> *One of the most important things that we've learned from research*
> *is that the actualization of our potential*
> *is heavily influenced by the groups we are a part of.*

~ KEN WILBER

To Show Another Way: Applications

1. Select a group of which you are presently a member and journal about what makes you comfortable or uncomfortable in the group. Relate this awareness to how you felt as a member of your first group—your family of origin.

2. Respond to the following questions:

   ◆ If I feel uncomfortable in this group, why might that be so?

   ◆ What unhealed feelings might I be projecting onto members of this group?

   ◆ In what way can I withdraw this projection and engage in inner work that can heal my unfinished business with the person this individual reminds me of?

   ◆ How willing and open is the group to having communication guidelines?

   ◆ How willing and open is the group to learning about healthy boundaries and why healthy boundaries are essential in a group?

Living America's Destiny

America will never be destroyed from the outside.
If we falter and lose our freedoms,
it will be because we destroyed ourselves.

~ ABRAHAM LINCOLN

When I was on the young side of life, I wanted to be a poet and a writer. As time passed, I did become a writer, largely because acquiring left-brain skills were essential if I were to obtain a PhD and teach at a university. My poet self never fully emerged beyond the occasional poetic phrasing in some of my academic and personal writing. That is, it didn't manifest until I was introduced to "medicine poetry."

Medicine Poetry

Stephen Levine, in his book *Becoming Kuan Yin: The Evolution of Compassion*, writes that the Chinese goddess of compassion, Kuan Yin, urges her students to write medicine poetry, telling them, "The right word at the right time is strong medicine." She explains that medicine poetry is intuitive and comes from the heart, not the head: "How quiet one must be—a single thought can muffle it." Medicine poetry heals us, whether we write it or read it.

Kuan Yin's teachings about medicine poetry **showed me another way** to awaken my poet self. I mustered the courage and self-confidence to put pen to paper and began writing poems. To write medicine poetry, one must abandon all thoughts and merge with feelings, not knowing in advance what the poem will say or how it will evolve. The intent is to allow the poem to flow from the heart, expressing authentic feelings, whether of pain or glory. Once the poem is completed, the poet experiences the peacefulness and balm of the "medicine." The genuine truth of one's feelings releases the pain. One's truth has been spoken; one's truth has been heard.

One of the first poems I wrote was about Abraham Lincoln. In it, I expressed the intense pain I felt for our country—the pain of self-forgetting, the pain of polarization, the pain of focusing on the self at the expense of the greater good of humanity and the planet.

America's Pain—America's Choice

I wrote that poem about Lincoln and about my feelings. Later, another poem emerged written from the perspective of Lincoln himself, the great wayshower, responding to our nation's collective pain. Although already significant at the time I wrote the first poem, our national grief had continued to increase dramatically. In the poem, Lincoln identifies the core dilemma our country now faces and conveys **the SAME message—showing another way for our country to heal—that he proposed during the Civil War over 150 years ago.** He answers our nation's call for help with a call of his own, showing us we have a choice—a challenging choice, yet a healing one. As citizens of this conflicted country, it is a choice we must make if we are to move through and beyond our current state of chaos and strife.

ABRAHAM LINCOLN'S CLARION CALL

I sit in my marble chair
Living inward— gazing outward
To all who come to visit me:
I see your magnificent souls

I hear your appreciation
I know your pain

Remembering my time in history
I remain with you in spirit
Witnessing history repeat itself
The greater truth
The Civil War never ended
The cause unhealed
Unity unattained
The true cause
Unaddressed

Now crises
Of epidemic proportions
Blanket our country
Few imagined
The manifold events
That now shatter
Our reality

Even so
Consciously forewarned
And prepared or not
No one is exempt from
Life-altering truths
Our country now faces

Together
We entered into the darkness
Of bewildering inner
And outer chaos

Of psyches
Homes
Lands
Beliefs
How the world functions
Ways we operate within it
We have dimmed
Into a barren blend
Of mist and smoke

Much of what once was
Cannot be reconstructed
Cannot be revised
Yet tucked among
The ashes of the past
Are durable remnants
And cherished seeds
Still vibrating with life

I promise you:
A door of sacred fortune
WILL open before you
We WILL cross a threshold
Together

What our ears once silenced
We will soon hear
The irrepressible
Clarion call of life
A call sounded
At the beginning of time
When we forgot

Who we were
Why we had come
Hearing the clarion blast
We awaken
To our injured world

Together
Believing
We disconnected
From the Sacred Source
From one another
Now we know
Our connection
Always remained
That it was
Our awareness of connection
That called to be returned

I invite you
To move into inner silence
Write medicine poetry
Acknowledge your personal pain
Focus on what really matters
Smooth the eagle's feathers
Celebrate the learned lessons
Of equality
Of greater good
Of unity within diversity
God doesn't care
If we make mistakes
God only cares
If we learn from them

I, Abraham Lincoln,
Remind you
Of an unwavering Truth
I upheld
For our country's wholeness
Proposed during the Civil War:
We may ACT separated
And divided
But we ARE not
We remain
ONE UNIFIED COUNTRY
Destined to answer
A clarion call
Of life and action

Called by our Sacred Source
To attain our True Destiny
Live with unconditional
Love and compassion
As
A global family
In a world
Of One

To Show Another Way: Applications

Respond to one or both of the following suggestions:

1. Place your awareness in your heart. Write a medicine poem that expresses your truth about healing our country.

Remember, writing medicine poetry requires that we allow the words to flow, abandoning all thoughts and merging with feelings, not knowing in advance what the poem will say or how it will evolve. In other words, we allow our inner poet to **show us another way** to express our authentic feelings. When thoughts distract us or words cease, we return to the silence of our heart's awareness. Once the poem is written, we breathe in the "medicine" of calm and peace.

2. Select an issue or topic in your life that you would like to heal using medicine poetry. Write the name of your topic at the top of a blank sheet of paper or on a blank page in your journal. Keep your pen and paper or journal nearby. Meditate for several minutes.

   Place your awareness in your heart. When thoughts distract you, return to the silence of your heart's awareness. Allow the words to flow. If the words cease, return to the silence within.

Falling in Love with Our Will

Never doubt that a small group of thoughtful,
committed citizens can change the world;
indeed, it's the only way that it ever has.

~ Margaret Mead

The teachings in this chapter introduce one of the most powerful spiritual gifts we have been given by the Divine… our **WILL**. This boon is likely the most underappreciated of our multiple spiritual attributes. Understanding and en-livening our will is an essential aspect of our life on Earth. The following teachings about the will are a tiny sip (though, for those new to the complexities of the will, they may feel like a huge gulp) of a topic the importance of which is fundamental not only for our own soul development, but for the soul development of our family, our coworkers, our fellow citizens, and Planet Earth. The intent of this chapter's teachings is to **show another way** to understand our will and use it wisely.

Bridging Spirit and Matter

My deep interest in discovering a model of the psyche that supports an understanding of just *how* we **show another way** to ourselves and others led me to the work of Roberto Assagioli, an Italian psychiatrist who developed a model of the psyche—the soul—which he referred to as "psychosynthesis." The goal of Assagioli's model is to guide us to create a personality that fully expresses our spirituality, bridging spirit and matter. He describes the human psyche as an integration of physiology, psychology, and spirituality and refers to this process as "self-realization"—a term that implies we have the potential **to show another way** to ourselves and others. Psychosynthesis includes an in-depth model of the will, including the roles of our *Transpersonal Will* (the element of our will that is Divine) and our *witness* (the element that observes without judgment), as well as the aspects, qualities, and stages of the will. This chapter and its four teachings introduce the key elements of Assagioli's model.

A Psychospiritual Path

Many of us view our will as stubborn, uncooperative, the cause of our failures, and the perpetuator of our unhappiness. **Happiness, believe it or not, is the result of the RIGHT use of our will.** Our will actually wants us to be happy and lighten up!

The will embodies and expresses all psychological and spiritual qualities, aspects, and development. When viewing the will in this way, it becomes apparent that the right use of the will is a psycho-spiritual path within all spiritual paths. It is likely that you are reading this teaching in this book at this time in your life because you have responded to your soul's call to bring your will out of hiding and into its full glory.

The right use of our will helps us find our right place in life—that is to say, our will helps us discover our destiny. Have you noticed how happy you are when you find your right place? When you know what you are meant to do and be in your life? You have your will to thank for that.

The Encompassing Role of the Will

Have you ever wondered how your will spends its time or what its job description is? The will lives with its partner, the witness, in the center of our personal soul (located in the heart) and in our Transpersonal Soul (our Higher Self—located above the head). The Transpersonal Will and the personal will are in partnership—they do not exist exclusive of one another, and are connected by a line of Light or energy. As for its job description—the will selects, integrates, harmonizes, and either directs or inhibits our emotions, thoughts, ideas, reactions, responses, imagination, intuition, desires, senses, images, movements, and actions. Our will is active and extremely busy. It plays an encompassing role as the source of every action and inaction in our life—physically, emotionally, mentally, and spiritually.

Parenting and the Will

As a young child, I had an abundance of energy. My parents described me as being strong-willed, determined, and having a mind of my own… meaning that I often went against their wishes and therefore got into trouble. Many years later, my father told me that he and my mother felt they didn't raise me because I raised myself! Most of us were blessed with strong will energy as children. This is true even if we don't remember it or if others did not tell us this about ourselves. What happened to this blessing? What happened to the strong will energy we had as a child?

Our will energy is like the wind. Where did our will energy blow to? Was it channeled and nurtured, or distorted and denied? Who or what stopped the flow of this energy? To feel safe, did *we* stop the flow? Where did the fire in our belly go? The great American mystic Edgar Cayce writes that children with strong will energy are extremely difficult to raise. Without wise, capable parenting, strong-willed children risk traveling a treacherous and unfulfilling path in life.

Indeed, will and parenting are the two most important influences in our human lives, and yet most adults know very little with respect to either. How do parents deal with a strong-willed child? How does a strong-willed child deal with parents who don't know what to do with him or her? When I was a child, I actually thought children were born wild. I believed they had to be tamed and molded into human beings. The method needed? You might be familiar with "the NO approach": "You can't do this, you can't say that… you can't, you can't, you can't." For the child, this soon becomes, "I won't, I won't, I won't," and "You can't make me!" We become angry and defiant whenever our will is imposed upon. At any age, our will can have a tantrum.

Survival and Wounding of the Will

We pay an enormous psychological and spiritual price for poor parenting of our will. Very early in life, we start to deny our true feelings and force ourselves to conform—or rebel, or "numb out"—in order to survive. There's so much over which a young child has no control, including how it is born, the makeup of the family it was born into, and the helpful and harmful events or accidents that happen in its early life. It is our will that keeps us alive in early childhood and ensures that we survive physically and emotionally. All of this is complicated by the fact that, according to the natural development of our psyche, we first *experience* the emotional energy of the will (using our *heart*—the feminine principle) and then *explain* our feelings (using our *head*—the masculine principle). The head does not always interpret the emotional energy correctly, and it often rationalizes. Soon, we don't know WHAT we feel—and thus begins our denial, the pattern of lying to ourselves about how we feel because we don't actually *know* how we feel. In the process, our will is being wounded.

It's important to note that we can use the negative experiences and wounding of our will to **show us another way** to live and serve. Negative experiences can act as models for how NOT to act, inviting us to do the opposite as we raise our own children—or even as we "re-parent" our own will, treating it with gentleness and compassion. Negative experiences are as fruitful for **showing us another way** as positive experiences when we recognize how much we can learn from them, how they serve us, and how, as "anti-models," they teach us how NOT to serve.

The Neurology of the Will

Denials of being imposed upon begin when we are in the womb. The circumstances of our nine months in gestation and the quality of our birth matter. Our misuse of will begins with how our lower brain centers respond to this earliest experience of life. To address this, we need to know how our will has been "wired." We need to understand our neurology, which explains how the lower brain centers influence the will's job description.

When we deny our experience and feelings beginning in early childhood, our will protects itself by hiding in our unconscious. When this occurs, a portion of our will energy is not available to our conscious self. We become lethargic, sluggish, dispirited, passive, depressed, and unmotivated. We use distractions to move away from our feelings, especially painful ones, and become "busy-busy," addicted, or collectors of material things. We become unaware of our true feelings and who we really are. This is the result of the wounding of our will.

As we grow, we begin to force or control our will, wounding it further. We decide that the will is not helping us "find our bliss," so we take matters into our own hands and put our will under total control. We make the will our enemy because it won't do what we want it to. We feel a victim of our will. We may even feel our will will go out of control. We force our will to cooperate… but does it? No! Our will howls with pain and humiliation as it digs in its heels in an attempt to resist being imposed upon. Rather than becoming "The Little Engine That Could," we become the little engine that *can't* and *won't*.

Collectively, we have not developed healthy wills. Our wills are desperately out of control, resisting and rebelling against this violent treatment as they try to survive. At the present time, virtually all human souls on Planet Earth are living with a damaged will, leading to ineffective decision-making regarding the greater good of ourselves, others, and the planet.

An Invitation

You may be thinking that what you are learning about the will is depressing, discouraging, and irreversible. It's true that most of us have been in denial that our will has been severely damaged—and the will *will* continue to "act out" as a way to survive *until* we welcome its need for understanding and healing.

Let me **show you another way** to think of your will. I encourage you to state the following aloud:

Will, if I gently take your hand, educate myself about your functions and extraordinary capacity, and walk with you to freedom, you will feel alive and honored and can trust me. I will then have the treasured will I was meant to have as a spiritual being in a human body.

Walking with Our Will

You are invited to experience a sacred respect and love for your will. Embrace it, honor it, and begin to heal it. **Our will is at the center of our life. Joined with our witness self, our will is the center of our soul, which connects us to our Divine Will.**

When we walk with our will, we experience freedom and happiness rather than inertia. We become playful, have lots of elbow room, and enter into the swing of things. Instead of walking through molasses, we skip through daisy fields. When we walk with our will, we become the person we were meant to be. When we walk with our will, we walk with the Divine.

Where there's a will, there's a way.

~ PROVERB

To Show Another Way: Applications

Guided Visualization ~ A Walk and Talk with My Will

Directions: Sit comfortably in a quiet place where you will not be disturbed. Practice the guided visualization silently in your mind until you are instructed to speak aloud to your will.

Take the hand of your will and invite it to go for a walk with you in nature. Note the age of your will and how it is dressed.

Talk with your will as if it is someone you love and honor but have misunderstood and therefore harmed. Express your regrets for blaming it for your failures and problems in life. Then, share how you are going **to show another way** of relating to your will. Express how you plan to be kind, patient, respectful, and open to learning who and what your will truly is—its nature, qualities, functions, talents, and gifts.

Say the following *aloud* to your will:

◆ Will, I accept who I am, what I am, and where I am, and welcome your gifts into my life. I know we can both heal as I welcome changing my relationship with you.

◆ Will, I will give you space so you can breathe. To do that, I will stop making a big deal about how unhappy I am when you don't do the things I demand of you. I will soften around that attitude and change it to patience and appreciation for your gifts.

◆ Will, I will be honest with myself by not denying my emotions about how you have been damaged by others and how I continue to hurt you.

◆ Will, I want to develop a partnership with both aspects of you—the personal will and the spiritual will. I know I can be in alignment with both of these parts of you and view you in terms of "both-and" rather than "either-or."

◆ Will, I promise to notice when I blame you for my choices and instead I will ask myself these questions:

   ▪ How do I feel when I don't want to _____?
   ▪ In what way is my personal will out of alignment and partnership with my spiritual will?
   ▪ How can I **show myself another way**—the way of a healthy, happy, helpful will?

Where There's a Will...

Not applying what we know dissipates our energy and undermines our will.

~ Edgar Cayce

lthough many of us adhere to the proverb, "where there's a will, there's a way," we tend to interpret it as giving us permission to use the forceful quality of the will that demands things of us. For example, this "pushy" aspect of the will might demand we immediately solve a problem—without reflection, without educating ourselves on what we might need to know to find a solution, without "sleeping on it," or without seeking guidance from a trusted friend or mentor. Demanding the will perform leads us down a path of control, and control leads us up a mountain of resistance. We go against the will as if it were an enemy.

Commitment to a Spiritual Intention

Recently I asked a colleague, who often speaks of her resistance and indecision, how she uses her will. To my surprise, she responded by saying she uses her will by being obstinate, stubborn, intractable, reluctant, grudging, oppositional, indecisive, and indifferent. She then added, "I want to want to **want** to use my will to change and grow but I'm stuck. I have a to-do list that spans into eternity and I have yet to make any of it happen."

Clearly, our will does not thrive when squeezed into a box. Rather, it flourishes in the spaciousness of the deep and profound desire of our heart and when it is allowed "to do its job" of **showing another way** to be in the world. **Capacities of the will evolve naturally when we commit to a spiritual intention that we want to manifest in our life**. Once our intention is in place, the hard work of self-effort begins. It is our responsibility to place ourselves in settings that serve as a spacious container for our will to thrive and thus for our spiritual intention to manifest. Likewise, it is our job to surround ourselves with inspiring and supportive people. We need many skills and competencies to successfully fulfill our intention **to show another way** to be in the world.

An Example from My Life

Many people have asked me how I became a founding leader of the Institute for the Advancement of Service, an educational and nonsectarian spiritual organization that serves as a wayshower for those who wish to heal and serve humanity during these challenging times. They wanted to know what I did to "make it happen."

The Institute is the ultimate manifestation of a deep, unshakeable spiritual commitment I made as a young child when I "knew" I was not to waste my life. Rather, I was "here"—on Earth, in a physical incarnation—to help people. This commitment first came into being in my work with children and adults with communication and neurological disorders and then in the cofounding of a holistic and multidisciplinary university training program that prepared specialists in this area. However, for years I knew my inner life was in shambles and in need of healing. At age forty, I chose to make a commitment to inner peace. I did not make a to-do list that would lead to the creation of an Institute, nor did I visualize the Institute as a fully formed organization. Rather, my psyche—my soul—held fast to my spiritual goal of inner peace. That's all I wanted. I decided to surround myself with people striving to do the same. I read many spiritual and self-help books, attended multiple inner work and spiritual workshops and classes, developed a spiritual practice, connected with nature and animals, and found a spiritual teacher.

Soon after I made my commitment to inner peace, a synchronistic event occurred. I was offered an opportunity to cofound and lead an educational and spiritual service organization—the organization that would become the Institute of the Advancement of Service. For the past 40 years, I have had the opportunity daily to practice inner peace and to help others do the same. My intent as the Institute's leader is **to show another way** to others—a way to attain inner peace through psychological and spiritual support and by being of service to others.

Creating a Nurturing Environment

When we establish a spiritual intention for our life and truly mean it, we benefit from placing ourselves in settings and with people that nurture our intention. When it is nourished, our will naturally develops in all of its aspects—strength, skill, goodness, and connection to the Divine. Why is this so? Our psyche is very suggestible and is neurologically rewired by what we are exposed to in our external physical, emotional, mental, and spiritual environments. If we wish to have a strong and healthy will, we need to allow a nurturing environment to manifest. In a nurturing environment, our will gradually becomes healthier **all by itself**. In such a setting, our will awakens and moves toward health, wholeness, and integration with other functions of our psyche.

When Our Will Is Undeveloped

Have you noticed that almost no one knows very much at all about the nature of his or her will? This lack of knowledge has resulted in a distortion of individual will and responsibility. Without a healthy will, we are not equipped to solve the crises we currently face in so many aspects of our world: ecological, economic, biological, psychological, and physical. Damaged and undeveloped wills are visible behind the upheavals of the transitional age in which we are now living.

Four Aspects of Our Will

We continue our pursuit of knowledge about the will with the introduction of its four aspects. (As discussed in the first teaching of this chapter, this model of the will was developed by Italian psychologist Roberto Assagioli.)

1. **Strong will** is the energy of the will. The will needs energy to move, to take action.

2. **Skillful will** is the ability to develop a strategy for every activity, thought, emotion, action, or movement. Skillful will is needed to **attain desired results with the least amount of energy expended** and is not necessarily the most direct and obvious route to success. For our skillful will to function effectively, we need to know ourselves—our functions, desires, drives, habit patterns, and so forth. Strong will provides the energy needed to use the skillful will.

3. **Good will** is essential if we want our strong and skillful will to be governed by ethical considerations. To be fulfilling, the will must be good and not cause harm to ourselves or others.

4. **Transpersonal Will** is beyond the personal and resides in the spiritual domain. We seek to have our personal will aligned with our Transpersonal Will so that we live a purposeful life, expressing the qualities emanating from the Divine.

The aspects of our will help us understand the meaning of our life. When we see meaning in our life, we gain a surprising degree of inner strength. The purpose of life is to use our will to find ways to express the qualities emanating from Transpersonal Will—the aspect in us that directs us to act for the highest good.

Right Use of Our Will

Deep within our hearts, we desire to serve others by **showing another way**. We do this by engaging the right use of our will to transcend our personality limitations, joining with our Transpersonal Will to experience the union of will and love. Does this seem like a lofty goal—perhaps out of your reach? Let me remind you that capacities of the will evolve naturally when we commit to a spiritual intention that we want to manifest in our life. In other words, where there's a will, there's a way.

Discovering your own will is a revelation
that can radically expand your self-awareness
and your potential for inner expansion and outer action.

~ ROBERTO ASSAGIOLI

To Show Another Way: Applications

In Chapter Four, we explored this application from the slightly different perspective of "The Jewel Within." Here, the Jewel is represented by the Transpersonal Self, which is also known as the Higher Self, the Soul, and the Solar Angel, as well as the Jewel Within. This application invites you to align with "Transpersonal Will," an expression of the Transpersonal Self. Transpersonal Will is the aspect of the will that allows us to transcend personality limitations through union with something greater and higher—the union of will and love. Alignment with our Transpersonal Will allows us to live a purposeful life, expressing the qualities emanating from the Divine.

Transpersonal Will Alignment

Purpose: To align daily with the Transpersonal Will, which is an expression of the Transpersonal Self. Through the personal will, the Transpersonal Will calls forth those abilities and skills needed to express Itself more fully in the world.

When to Align: Aligning with our Transpersonal Will can be done at any time. Doing so is especially helpful at the beginning of the day or before any activity in which we wish to have support and guidance. Conversing with our Transpersonal Will is helpful when we have a problem about which we seek insight and resolution.

Directions: The soul is located in the heart and has two parts—the witness and the will. The witness is the part of our soul that observes ourselves without judgment. The will is the directing agent that actively selects and initiates action in the external world. Our Transpersonal Will is located about eight inches above the head.

Sit in a comfortable position when doing the alignment and in a quiet place where you will not be interrupted. ***Pause at least 10 seconds between each step.***

1. Take three deep breaths to calm your physical body. (pause)

2. Take three deep breaths to calm your emotional body. (pause)

3. Take three deep breaths to calm your mental body. (pause)

4. Focus your awareness in your heart, the home of self (soul) and personal will.

5. Visualize a line of energy extending from your heart down to the heart of the Mother of the Earth.

6. Visualize a line of energy from your heart to your Transpersonal Will, located eight inches above your head.

7. Visualize the energy extending from your Transpersonal Will to Divine Source.

8. In silence, hold this alignment from the heart of the Mother of the Earth to Divine Source. See the Will energy of Source moving down the alignment to the heart of the Mother of the Earth and then back again to Source, creating a circuit (circular movement) of energy carrying Divine Will to all levels of manifestation. Sit in silence and meditate (20 minutes is recommended).

Embracing the Nature of Our Will

Spirit and Will are partners in the Body
and must find their balance in the Heart...
help with the understanding of this process is necessary.

~ CEANNE DEROHAN

If we wish to live with purpose and integrity on Planet Earth and serve ourselves and others by **showing another way,** it is essential that we understand the nature of our will. How harmoniously the will functions determines the quality of our life—physically, emotionally, mentally, and spiritually. Having neglected its care, we must embrace our will and take it to our heart with enthusiasm, affection, and gratitude—especially at this critical time in the history of our world.

Unfortunately, we were not taught about the nature of our will by our parents, nor by our primary schools, high schools, or colleges. Consequently, the lack of knowledge and compassion for our will—as well as for the will of others—has existed since the beginning of our life. Out of ignorance, not only has our personal will been harmed, we have harmed the will of others as well.

Self: Witness and Will

As in the other teachings of this chapter, in this teaching we use Roberto Assagioli's psychosynthesis model of the human psyche to further explore our understanding of the will.

The **self** consists of two parts: our **witness** and our **will.** The **self** is also known as the psyche or soul and is located in the heart. Its two parts, **witness** and **will,** form a unity of feminine and masculine principles: love (feminine) and will (masculine); observation (feminine) and action (masculine).

The **witness,** the *passive part* of the self, is a spectator—a pure, objective, loving observer of what is happening within and without. The witness watches the flow of events without judgment.

The **will,** the *active part* of the self, is the aspect of the self that is the will-er—the directing agent that actively intervenes to orchestrate the various functions and energies of our personality. The will makes choices and instigates action or inaction in the external world. The will regulates, integrates, harmonizes, and directs psychological and physical functions.

The Self and "I"

The **self** (lower case initial *s*) is connected to the **Self** (upper case initial *S*), which is an extension of Divine Source. The self is an integrating center which *is* the essential individual—the self is ME and YOU, with our underlying roles, behaviors, feelings, thoughts, and their manifestations in action.

The **self** and **"I"** are considered synonymous in psychosynthesis. However, the "I" is a movable point of identification that can become entangled in aspects of the personality, such as the mind or the body. For example, when I identify with my body ("I am sick," "I am fat," etc.), I am not identified with my **self.** The self remains constant at center. The experience of self occurs when the "I" identifies with the self. Conversely, this explains what we are experiencing when we say, "I am not myself."

The **self** is the center of pure awareness (witness) and intentionality (will). It is from this center that we make the choices that determine our life's direction, style, and form. The self is without qualities; it is pure awareness, without content. **The will's energy of intention and choice find their source in the self.**

Self-Personality Fusion

The Self, a luminous source, manifests through the personal self and the many functions of the personality. The Self is consciousness acting and creating through the will, whether at the Transpersonal level or the personality level, in the world. It is important to develop and train the will to bring the personality functions into effective relationship with one another. As personality functions are balanced and harmonized, they can be used to express superconscious qualities and carry out purposes of the Self.

Summarizing the Nature of Our Will

◆ The **self** is also known as the psyche or soul and is located in the heart.

◆ The **self** consists of two parts: our **witness** and our **will.**

◆ The **witness** is the *passive part* of the self and observes what is happening in us and outside of us without judgment.

◆ The **will** is the *active part* of the self that does the willing, making choices and instigating action or inaction in the external world.

◆ When I identify with my body ("I am sick," "I am fat"), I am not identified with my **self.** The self remains constant at center.

◆ The **will**'s energy of intention and choice finds its source in the **self.**

◆ The **self** is connected to the **Self,** which is an extension of Divine Source.

◆ The **Self** manifests through the personal **self** and the many functions of the personality.

◆ By training the **will** to bring the personality functions into effective relationship with one another, the personality becomes fused with and can carry out the purposes of the **Self.**

The More We Love Our Will...

You are beginning to see the complexities of the self and of the nature of the will. In this chapter's first teaching, you were invited to fall in love with your will. Are you ready now to embrace its nature? Your commitment to learning about the will (an act of will in itself) is the first step in this love affair. The more you know and love your will, the more you'll be able to work with, walk with, and embrace this profound gift you were given at birth to help you live your life and carry out its destiny. I invite you to choose NOW—through an act of your beloved will—**to show another way** to serve our struggling planet and its fellow inhabitants by embracing the nature of your will.

> *Strength does not come from physical capacity.*
> *It comes from an indomitable will.*
>
> ~ MAHATMA GANDHI

To Show Another Way: Applications

Practice the Dis-identification—Self-Identification exercise below **daily.**

◆ Note any changes in your ease in making commitments and choices and in instigating action or non-action in the external world.

◆ Consider how this practice is **showing you another way** to be in the world.

Dis-identification—Self-Identification Practice

Purpose: We are dominated by, or attached to, everything with which we become identified. When we are identified with something, we cannot direct and use our will well. When we dis-identify and engage our **witness** (our observer), we can use our **will** to wisely direct and utilize everything from which we dis-identify. We learn discrimination, detachment, and discernment.

Our **witness** observes our actions, thoughts, and behavior without judgment or interpretation. Our **will** strengthens our capacity to discern the truth of our life experiences. From this place, we accurately determine how best **to show another way.**

Note: You can also create your own dis-identification exercise that addresses your unique needs at this time in your life.

Directions: Sit in a comfortable and relaxed position. Slowly take a few deep breaths. Then make the following **dis-identification** affirmations, slowly and thoughtfully.

♦   I *have* a body but I *am not* my body. My body may find itself in different conditions of health or sickness, it may be rested or tired, but that has nothing to do with my **self,** my real "I." I value my body as a precious instrument of experience and of action in the outer world, but *it is only an instrument.* I treat it well, I seek to keep it in good health, but it is *not* my **self.**

    I *have* a body, but I *am not* my body.
    I am more than my body.
    I am the constant and unchanging Self.
    I am the Self.

♦   I *have* emotions, but I *am not* my emotions. My emotions are diverse, changing, sometimes contradictory. They may swing from love to hatred, from calm to anger, from joy to sorrow, and yet my essence—my true nature—does not change. "I" remain. Though a wave of anger may temporarily submerge me, I know that it will pass in time; therefore, I *am not* this anger. Since I can observe and understand my emotions, and then gradually learn to direct, utilize, and integrate them harmoniously, it is clear that they are not my **self.**

    I *have* emotions, but I *am not* my emotions.
    I am more than my emotions.
    I am the constant and unchanging Self.
    I am the Self.

◆ I *have* thoughts but I *am not* my thoughts. My thoughts are a valuable tool of discovery and expression, but they *are not* the essence of my being. They are constantly changing as they embrace new ideas, knowledge, and experience. Often, they refuse to obey me! Therefore, they cannot be my **self**. My thoughts are *an organ of knowledge* in regard to the outer and inner worlds, but they are **not** my **self**.

I *have* thoughts but I *am not* my thoughts.
I am more than my thoughts.
I am the constant and unchanging Self.
I am the Self.

◆ After the dis-identification of my **self**, of the "I" from the contents of consciousness such as sensations, emotions, and thoughts, *I recognize and affirm that I am a center of pure self-awareness.* I am *a center of will,* capable of observing, directing, and using all my psychological processes and my physical body.

I **am** a center of pure self-awareness.
I **am** a center of will, capable of mastering and directing all of my energies:
    physical, emotional, mental, and spiritual.
I **am** the constant and unchanging Self.
I **am** the Self.

Sit in silence, experiencing the truth and depth of your awareness.

Short Version

I have a body, but I am not my body.
I am the one who is aware.

I have emotions, but I am not my emotions.
I am the one who is aware.

I have thoughts, but I am not my thoughts.
I am the one who is aware.

I am the center of pure self-awareness.
I am the center of will.
I am the one who is aware.

Happiness Is... a Healed Will in Action

*It is always true that love and will become
more difficult in a transitional age;
and ours is an era of radical transition.*

~ ROLLO MAY

Did you know that happiness is the result of the right use of our will? Right action of a healed will enables us to develop meaningful relationships, make right decisions in our choice of work in the world, be responsible for caring for our physical, emotional, mental, and spiritual wellbeing, and be a compassionate, caring person in our chosen service in the world.

The first three teachings of this chapter explore how important it is to learn about the human will and to develop and use our will with competence, wisdom, and compassion—in other words, to use our will as it was meant to be used. This final teaching about the will addresses how to heal our will and use our healed will in our actions. Ultimately, working with the will is a spiritual path. A healed, developed will is essential if we wish **to show another way** to live and be in this world—appropriately and with integrity.

Healing Our Will

Have you noticed you're happy when your will is happy? Have you perceived how distraught you feel when you discover your will is not happy? Have you observed how distressing it is to know that the wills of most people on our planet are wounded and out of control? The present troubled state of our beloved Planet Earth is a manifestation of a collective misuse of the will. To correct this, we must heal our personal will and use our healthy will to **show another way** to take action and contribute to healing the planet.

What are some ways we can begin to heal our will self-responsibly and with integrity?

- ◆ By unconditionally accepting ourselves—accept "who I am, what I am, and where I am." This acceptance is the first step in healing our will.

- ◆ By giving space to our will. How desperately our will needs space to breathe! We give space to our will when we don't make a big deal about how unhappy we are with it for not doing our bidding. Soften around it. Be honest with yourself— don't deny any emotions and don't act them out if they're hurtful.

- ◆ By developing a partnership of our healthy personal will with our Transpersonal (spiritual) Will— do not view these as either-or but both-and. Learn to be in alignment with both.

- ◆ By asking questions when we observe that we are doing what we don't want to do and are blaming our will for it. Questions could include: What's not right here? How do I feel when I don't want to _____? Am I out of alignment with my spiritual life purpose? Is my personal will out of alignment and thus out of part-nership with my Transpersonal Will?

- ◆ To be happy requires that we use our will in a way that allows us to thrive in the spaciousness of the deep and profound desires of our heart. When we do so, not only are we healing our own will, we are participating in the healing of the col-lective will of our world. According to a spiritual principle of group energy, when one is healed, ALL are healed.

Seven Qualities of the Will

In this teaching, we continue to explore the will through the psychosynthesis model of Roberto Assagioli, which includes seven *qualities* of the will. **The qualities are modes of expression of the will in action.** Qualities can be evoked as needed in the proper way and in the right amount. The healed will knows how to achieve a balance among all the qualities. We can call on any of the seven qualities of the will at any time for any reason throughout our daily activities and when we wish **to show ourselves and others another way.** All qualities of the will are effortless to activate when we are aligned with our Transpersonal Will.

The qualities are sometimes related here to the four *aspects* of the will as discussed in the second teaching of this chapter, "Where There's a Will…" The four aspects of the will are the *strong will*, the *skillful will*, the *good will*, and the *Transpersonal Will.*

The seven qualities of the will are as follows:

1. **Energy:** dynamic power; intensity; a naturally outstanding characteristic of the **strong will;** needs to be associated with other qualities and balanced as can be misused in domineering, oppressive, forbidding way; we may need the quality of energy to overcome opposing forces, as in sports

2. **Mastery:** control; discipline; regulates expression; guided, constructive use of biological and psychological energies (not repression); used to learn necessary skills and techniques

3. **Concentration:** one-pointedness; attention; focus; sustained effort; we can't have a *strong will* without this; can compensate for a weak *strong will*, like a lens concentrating the sun's rays; can be inner- or outer-directed (performs tasks, such as meditation and contemplation); occurs when one is absorbed; at first may require an act of will and then can persist without effort or tension

4. **Determination:** decisiveness; resoluteness; promptness; deliberation but without too much lingering; not to decide is also a decision and may not be a good one

5. **Persistence:** endurance; patience; steadfastness of purpose needed even more

than energy, like dripping water wearing away stone; tenacity; endurance; not giving up; willingness to accept unavoidable suffering without self-pity

6. **Initiative:** courage; daring; risk-taking that has purpose and value; recognizes there is no complete security in our life— craving for security at any cost is self-defeating

7. **Organization:** integration; analysis plus synthesis; enables will to fulfill its specific function; operates through inner synergy plus outer activities

Six Stages of the Will—The Act of Willing

We are not taught how to use our will. We are unaware of the act of will which tells us how to consciously use our will to identify and direct the steps needed to complete a task. Identifying and directing the steps needed to complete a task are known as the *stages of the will.*

According to Assagioli, we need to master all the stages of the act of will. Think of the six stages (the act of willing) as links in a chain. A chain is only as strong as its weakest link. Therefore, success in performing an act of will, such as that needed **to show another way**, depends on effectively completing each stage. We need to identify those stages where we may have difficulties—the weak links in our chain. Also, depending on the action or task, certain stages may be more significant and require more attention than others.

1. **Purpose/aim/goal:** The purpose or goal must have meaning and value as well as be manageable so we are motivated to take action toward achieving it.

2. **Deliberation:** We deliberate and determine which goal is preferable to initiate at this point in time. We may have to use restraint to put other goals aside for now.

3. **Choice and Decision:** We state our decision to work toward achieving a certain goal and set aside others.

4. **Affirmation:** We confirm our choice and decision by affirmation, stating positively what our decision is. It is important to imbue the affirmation with clarity,

certainty, and enthusiasm, as these energies provide the "juice" needed to achieve the goal.

5. **Planning and Programming:** We create the details of the plan. To accomplish our goal, we need to consider the various means that are available to us, the timing, existing circumstances, resources, the need to include others, and so forth.

6. **Direction of Execution:** We use our will to make skillful use of our personality, using energies such as thinking, imagination, perceptions, intuition, feelings, and impulses, as well as our physical means of action. The will is like the director of a theater production, not one of the actors.

It is common for people to have difficulty carrying out one or more of the stages of the will. Some deliberate and deliberate and cannot make a decision. Some may be able to make a decision but have difficulty implementing it. Some may jump to action without careful consideration or without weighing the consequences of all their actions. Even though we use each stage in varying degrees depending on the situation, we need to be familiar with all of the stages and develop them so that they are available to us when we need them.

The Healed and Happy Will

Each of us has a will. We use our will in everything we do, even something as simple as getting up in the morning. Assagioli's model of the will is a structural framework to help us look at our will, explore it in a meaningful way, and develop it. Studying its parts—its aspects, qualities, and stages—strengthens our understanding of the will and, in doing so, strengthens the will itself.

Consider which of these elements of the will you've used in studying this chapter about the will. If you look closely and apply the teachings, you can see which elements of your will are thriving and which need healing. Check in with yourself: how happy is your will right now? Chances are, just reading this chapter will have tickled your will and started you on the journey to being the proud companion of a healed and happy will.

Our greatest weakness lies in giving up.
The most certain way to succeed is always
to try just one more time.

~ THOMAS EDISON

To Show Another Way: Applications

1. Contemplate this question: "Am I ready and willing at this time in my life to be **self-responsible** by making a commitment to have a healed and happy will?"

   If the answer is yes, select one or more of the following suggestions to begin and/or continue your healing process.

   ◆ Refer to Teaching Two of this chapter concerning the **aspects of your will**—strong, skillful, good, and Transpersonal. Acknowledge which aspect(s) is your strongest and which one(s) needs developing. Identify ways you might strengthen the development of your weaker aspect(s).

   ◆ Refer to Teaching Three and the explanation of the **relationship between your witness and will.** How would you describe the quality of the relationship between these two parts of your self? How might you strengthen this relationship?

   ◆ Refer to Teaching Four and the section titled *"Seven Qualities of the Will."* Select one or two qualities that you feel need development. In what ways might you strengthen these qualities?

   ◆ Refer to Teaching Four and the section *"Six Stages of the Will*—The Act of Willing." Apply these stages to a current action or task in your life, following the stages in the order they are given.

2. If you wish to explore ways to deepen the healing of your will, I invite you to explore the following references:

◆ Roberto Assagioli's *The Act of Will* (Amherst, MA: Synthesis Center Press, 2010) and www.aap-psychosynthesis.org

◆ Molly Young Brown's *Unfolding Self: The Practice of Psychosynthesis* (New York: Helios, 2004)

◆ Piero Ferrucci's *What We May Be* (Los Angeles: Tarcher, 1982)

Wherever You Go, Go with Your Heart

The warmth of the sun and the warmth of the heart are our life-givers.

~ AUTHOR UNKNOWN

Perhaps the rarest treasure we can embody or witness in another is a compassionate, joyful, and patient heart. Such a heart can pour out blessings, offering the gift of Love and Light to individuals, countries, nations, nature—indeed, to all living creatures and all aspects of our world. A healing, transforming, uplifting heart offers the most magnificent gift we can find within ourselves or discover in another—the opportunity **to show another way.**

In universal spiritual and metaphysical[*] teachings, the heart is described as the core of our being—our essence and True Self or Soul. These teachings, known as the Ancient or Ageless Wisdom, predict that gifts of the heart will eventually emerge in people across the planet and permeate our world. These gifts of the heart will lead humanity into a golden age. When this happens, the enlightened heart will guide all that the mind does, charging it with the vision of the future. The awakening of the heart has already begun;

---

[*] Metaphysics is the study of "first causes." The prefix "meta-" means beyond, higher, after, or transcending. Physics deals with the "physical" world; *meta*physics refers to what goes beyond the delimitations of time and space and is concerned with a higher order of laws—the laws of the Universe or God's laws.

it is this awakening that will ultimately save Planet Earth from ongoing harm and from being destroyed.

Spiritual Laws of the Heart

For the Ancients, the heart was the Holiest Temple in which dwelled the Most High. In the presence of the Most High, the heart unfolds and radiates the fragrance of the Divine. This fragrance, a kind of sacred energy, brings a flood of Light, Love, and Divine Power to our solar system and to Planet Earth. The human heart is the assimilator and communicator of these sacred energies as their Light, Love, and Power inundate the Earth. Only the heart—only the core of our being—can serve as the "translator" of these high vibration energies into the practical, day-to-day realities of our world on Earth.

These metaphysical teachings describe the human heart as a golden, twelve-petaled lotus located behind the physical heart and about four to six inches away from the body. Twelve flames radiate from the center of the heart, forming an electromagnetic energy field. At the center of this field is a blue-orange flame that originates from the Self, a Spark of God. Human hearts can be in various stages of development: their lotus may be only a small bud, have just a few petals open, or be fully developed.

To understand the heart as it is described in this teaching, we look to a higher order of spiritual laws. These laws are explored at length in *The Flame of the Heart* by Torkom Saraydarian. At this level, our heart is capable of doing the following:

◆ healing,
◆ offering serenity and peace,
◆ feeling deep compassion,
◆ extending joy and sacred service,
◆ offering courage, daring, striving, and patience,
◆ increasing love, unification, and inclusiveness,
◆ establishing synthesis, bringing together all the heart's aspects,
◆ evoking beauty,
◆ understanding timelessness, knowledge, and intuition,
◆ becoming creative and receiving visionary inspirations,

◆ transmuting energy from negative to positive, and

◆ recording heartfelt experiences.

When we place our awareness in our heart and use our heart's intelligence, we can share the fruits of our healing by giving away what we have learned in service to others.

A Heart-Centered Prayer for Our Times

The Great Invocation is a prayer that was designed to support humanity as it enters the Aquarian Era. (For a discussion of the transition from the Piscean to the Aquarian Era which our planet is currently undergoing, see Chapter Two's "Humanity's Next Evolutionary Leap.") It was given to spiritual writer and teacher Alice Bailey in 1945 and has been translated into over seventy-five languages and dialects. **The Great Invocation is used by millions of people worldwide of all religious faiths and spiritual traditions.** It is a heart-centered prayer to help manifest the full expression of the Divine Plan on Earth. As such, its intent is **to show another way**.

The Great Invocation voices the basic needs of humanity—the need for Light and Love, for an understanding of Divine Will, and for the ending of evil or separatism. It refers to humanity's sacred responsibility to spread Light and Love to manifest Divine Will on Earth.

Praying the Great Invocation gives people everywhere a means of contacting and circulating powerful spiritual energies that contribute to the transformation of humanity and our world. This prayer gives voice to our heart's role in meeting the needs of humanity at this time on Planet Earth.

The Great Invocation

From the point of Light within the Mind of God
Let Light stream forth into human minds.
Let Light descend on Earth.

From the point of Love within the Heart of God

Let Love stream forth into human hearts.
May the Coming One return to Earth.

From the center where the Will of God is known
Let purpose guide all little human wills—
The purpose which the Masters know and serve.

From the center which we call the human race
Let the Plan of Love and Light work out
And may it seal the door where Evil dwells.

Let Light and Love and Power restore the Plan on Earth.

The Great Invocation Explored

In the **first stanza,** the prayer gives voice to one of the great needs of humanity—to bring Light into the world for the purpose of raising the consciousness of the planet. Light is cast into dark places of human activity revealing what needs to be exposed and healed. When minds are illuminated, we see things as they are and take the needed steps to create right relations with others, an urgent necessity.

In the **second stanza**, Love is an energy which must reach the hearts of people everywhere so that loving understanding—love plus intelligence—permeates all that we do. This will lead to a flowering of Christ Consciousness in the world—to concord, peace, plenty, and unity. This flowering will mobilize a tremendous reaction against hate and separatism. People all over the world will form groups to promote good will and the creation of right human relations. These groups will be an influential force in the world.

In the **third stanza**, we pray that all people will be aligned with Divine Will, even though we cannot fully grasp the purpose of God. Divine Will remains a great mystery, but we know that it has to do with goodwill, raising consciousness, and establishing right relations between all sentient beings. This includes our relationship with nature.

In the **fourth stanza,** having invoked the power of Light, Love, and Will in the first three stanzas, we ask that these powers be anchored in humanity so that we can express them through our thoughts and actions as compassion, wisdom, harmony, grace, and oneness. To "seal the door where evil dwells" is symbolic: there is no particular place where evil dwells. This phrase expresses the idea of disabling evil purposes and rendering them powerless. The door is kept open by humanity through greed, selfishness, hatred, prejudice, separateness, love of power, cruelty, materialism, and so forth. As the qualities of Light, Love, and Will become dominant, the door where evil dwells will slowly close through the sheer weight of public opinion and right human desire.

Healing the Heart

Because the Great Invocation came directly from Source with the express intention to help humanity establish the Divine Plan on Earth, its vibration is very high and its reach infinite. It is a prayer for both our darkest moments and our brightest days. Reciting it can calm animals and ease the dying. As you speak it aloud or say it silently within, allow this supreme gift from the Masters to permeate your heart. Allow the prayer to **show you another way** to live and be as it heals, transforms, and uplifts your heart—so you may **show another way** for others to do the same.

Wherever you go, go with your heart.

~ Confucius

To Show Another Way: Applications

Recite the Great Invocation aloud as part of your morning and/or evening practice. If you are experiencing a major challenge or crisis in your life, **repeat the prayer many times in one sitting.** Doing so comforts both you and any others who are part of the situation, whether they are physically present or not.

The Lion and the Unicorn

You are free to choose,
but you are not free
from the consequence
of your choice.

~ A UNIVERSAL PARADOX

A paradox is a statement that appears self-contradictory or opposed to common sense, yet under examination can prove true. Paradoxes are dualistic by definition, yet their two opposing aspects come together to produce a single larger truth. Similarly, the human psyche is dual by nature—think of the popular representations of the angel on one shoulder who bids us do the right thing and the devil on the other who urges us to do whatever we feel like doing, regardless of the consequences. We've been taught to believe these two aspects of ourselves are at war with each other and "never the twain shall meet." But if we honor the psyche's opposing aspects, they unite in partnership and form a paradox—a single larger truth that helps define our capacity as human beings.

The lion and the unicorn are an unlikely couple that have represented the United Kingdom since 1603, when King James VI of Scotland became King James I of England—unifying the Scottish and English kingdoms. The union of lion and unicorn into one combined symbol—the union of two separate realms—provides a fitting symbol for the opposing aspects of psyche, whose masculine (lion) and feminine (unicorn) principles appear clearly divided or separate from each other. Yet if we honor and acknowledge both aspects within us, they can ultimately be joined to form a united, authentic self.

The Dual Nature of the Human Psyche

The nature of the human psyche is one of duality—of opposites and polarity. From birth, our mind is conditioned to think this and not that, to avoid that and grasp this, to believe this to be right and true and that to be wrong and false. Depending on what we deemed essential for physical and psychological survival as children, as adults we form unbending opinions, assumptions, and beliefs, holding rigidly to right-wrong thinking and seeing ourselves, others, and the world in absolute terms.

By middle age, many of us tire of this seesaw of oppositional thinking and it slowly dawns on us, if we are alert, that the middle ground is the best. Jungian analyst Robert Johnson writes that, "To our surprise, that middle ground is not the gray compromise that we feared but the place of ecstasy and joy… that middle place is the product of honoring both extremes." He notes that, in Ancient China, this was called the Tao, where the middle way was "not a compromise but a **creative synthesis.**" Johnson uses the teeter totter metaphor to help us understand this concept from a Western perspective:

> [S]tanding in the middle of the teeter totter, [we stand] with one foot planted on either side so we can balance easily. This honors the duality but keeps both elements within reach. Each tempers the other and no serious split occurs. This is not a gray compromise but a strong and balanced life."

This, in other words, is paradox.

The two complementary energies of the feminine and the masculine **exist within every human psyche regardless of gender.** Naturally, women are more in touch with the feminine principle and men with the masculine. We diminish the value of both when we embrace one without honoring the other. The goal is to have the masculine and feminine energies work in partnership and move into wholeness, a creative synthesis of opposites. **The goal of the human psyche is to have the lion and the unicorn—the contending solar-lunar, masculine-feminine forces within us—learn to work together as a team.**

The Paradox of Feminine and Masculine Union

This union of feminine and masculine principles represents a challenging paradox. Masculinity has relevance only in contrast to femininity. Femininity has relevance only in contrast to masculinity. The feminine principle is that part of our psyche that expresses relatedness, softness, tenderness, nurturing, and synthesis. The feminine principle knows when to listen, when to wait, when to keep still, when to choose, and when to act. The masculine principle is that part of our psyche that is rational, sequential, impersonal, productive, action-oriented, political, scientific, and verbal. We devalue this paradox when we embrace only one aspect (masculinity **or** femininity) without acknowledging and paying tribute to the other. Both aspects must be equally honored. Degrading paradox into contradiction can lead to personal suffering.

    The feminine principle and the masculine principle exist in each person, regardless of gender. What differs is that women more often have an easier access to the feminine principle and men have easier access to the masculine. Learning about these principles will **show another way** to all genders as they remember their wholeness—their integrated selves.

    Jungian analyst and author Jean Shinoda Bolen uses the metaphor of a committee as a way to remember and acknowledge all parts of ourselves. She refers to the committee in each of us as unconscious patterns of God and Goddess archetypes or subpersonalities. In any given circumstance, the goal is to call forth the appropriate committee members—Gods (aspects of the masculine principle) or Goddesses (aspects of the feminine principle). Machaelle Small Wright, cofounder of Perelandra, a nature research center where she develops flower essences and other energy medicine in collaboration with nature, states that, whether man or woman, the goal of our human development is to have our inner masculine and feminine principles **working in partnership.**

Creative Synthesis

When our inner masculine and feminine principles are in partnership, we move into a creative synthesis of opposites. We have access to a deeper source of wisdom, authenticity, and spirituality. The inner masculine and feminine partnership energizes us and gives us a sense of meaning and self-acceptance.

When we accept opposing elements, we prepare the way to embracing paradox. This gives us the inner presence and self-confidence to remain unbiased, clear, and down-to-earth. With one foot on either side of the teeter totter, we unify action and reflection, process and productivity, the predictable and the spontaneous, the "devil" and the "angel"—uniting the lion and the unicorn. In this process, our psyche becomes integrated, allowing us consciously to call forth the qualities and gifts of masculine *and* feminine principles to guide us in making choices that **show another way** to serve the highest good of humanity and Planet Earth.

> *I have found the paradox that if you love until it hurts,*
> *there can be no more hurt, only more love.*
>
> ~ Mother Teresa

To Show Another Way: Applications

Step One: Inventory

This teaching explores how the feminine and the masculine principles are complementary presences within the human psyche. That is, **these energies exist in each person regardless of gender**. As you read through the lists of lion and unicorn qualities, place a plus sign (+) by those you feel you fully embody and a minus sign (-) by those you feel are not present or are underdeveloped in you. You may wish to place both a plus and minus sign (+-) next to those you feel are partially developed.

LION—represents the solar, masculine principle

◆ Productive, product-oriented, action-oriented
◆ Verbal
◆ Orderly
◆ Discriminating and discerning
◆ Mental—mind-oriented to life
◆ Predictable
◆ Analyzes problems before taking action by questioning how something works, how well it works, and what it's used for
◆ Protector, defender
◆ Prefers communication that is linear, analytical, rational, and impersonal

UNICORN—represents the lunar, feminine principle

◆ Emphasizes relatedness, collaboration
◆ Marked by softness, tenderness
◆ Process-oriented
◆ Aware of feelings (heart) and connection with the body
◆ Knows when to listen, when to wait, when to keep still, what to choose, and when to act
◆ Loving container for suffering and conflict
◆ Accepts life as it is without judgment
◆ Translates the theoretical by appraising the theory with the heart and selects a heart-directed action; intuitive; synthesis thinker
◆ Preferred communication modes are stories, humor, art—modes that reflect spontaneity, receptivity, reflection

Step Two: The Nature of Your Psyche

Based on your personal inventory of lion and unicorn qualities, describe what seems to be the nature of your psyche. To assist you in doing this, complete the following three sentence several times:

- ◆ I am a person who is _____.
- ◆ I am a person who isn't (or doesn't) _____.
- ◆ I am a person who is _____ about _____ but not about _____.

For example, you might write "I am a person who is very orderly," or "I am a person who isn't very orderly," or "I am a person who is orderly about my financial records but not about papers on my desk."

Step Three: Showing Another Way

Describe how knowing that the masculine and feminine principles are both present within you supports how you **show another way** to yourself and to others.

What Hurts and What Helps the Heart: Part I

In prayer it is better to have a heart without words
than words without a heart.

~ MAHATMA GANDHI

In the coming years, people all over the world will discover the critical importance of the heart. The foretold balance of the heart and the mind will lead humanity to a new level of understanding and awareness. The flame of the heart will enlighten our thoughts and guide our minds. Humanity's commitment to a true heart-mind connection is destined to create a new vision for our planet and **show another way** to live and be in our world. **To have a true heart-mind connection, we need a pure heart.**

This two-part teaching is based on the writings of Torkom Saraydarian, an internationally recognized scholar and author of comparative religions and philosophy whose work centers on a universal approach to spirituality. For a deeper study of Saraydarian's work, I invite you to seek out and explore the TSG Foundation (www.tsgfoundation. org), publisher of Saraydarian's 170 books, which have been translated into multiple languages.

What is a Pure Heart?

Our heart is the central organ in our body—physically, psychologically, and spiritually. As such, it continuously receives energy from and distributes energy to each system in our body. The responsibility of our physical heart is to distribute blood (energy) throughout our system. Our emotional heart distributes feelings, sensations, and moods throughout our body. Our spiritual heart connects us to our Divinity, including our Higher Self (our Soul), the Angels, and the Great Ones (the Masters).

If our heart is pure, our mind will make the right decision. If impure, the heart can interfere, distort, and override the mind's reasoning and logic. At the same time, higher aspects of the heart cannot be developed without the striving of the mind. Wrong decisions are therefore the result of an imbalance between heart and mind.

What Hurts Our Heart and Damages Its Energy Network

When our heart is harmed or damaged physically, psychologically, or spiritually, our ability to live a meaningful life and have healthy relationships is disrupted.

The energy network of our heart can be hurt or damaged in the following ways:

◆ The heart is highly sensitive and easily influenced by sound. It stands to reason, then, that it is *noise pollution* that most harms the heart. Noise pollution pervades our planet. Research has shown there is now no place on Earth that is uncontaminated by noise. External noise comes from traffic, machines, airplanes, industry, and sirens. Noise pollution in the home environment emanates from refrigerators, air conditioners, heaters, loud music, and lawn equipment from our yards, among other things.

◆ *Other environmental factors* also damage the heart, including electrical currents, insecticides and chemical products, air pollution, fluorescent light bulbs, radioactive elements, electronic devices, and toxic heavy metals in batteries.

◆ *Negative thoughts and emotions* pollute, contaminate, and poison the heart, blocking it from receiving light and intuition. Invisible to the naked eye, the heart's energy network is damaged by such low-vibration energies. The list of negative emotions and thoughts that damage the heart is long: fear, anger, hatred, jealousy, greed, slander, conflict, and self-interest. Accumulated poison from negative thoughts spreads into the heart and body and results in a life devoid of happiness and joy. Ugly thoughts disintegrate our body's aura and its magnetism. Past pains and sufferings, when we have not forgiven their source, echo continuously within our heart and can destroy blood and nervous systems.

What Helps the Heart and Heals Its Energy Network

Our heart's energy network is pervasive in our body, involving the physical, psychological, and spiritual aspects of our heart and the effect of these aspects on our body's various systems. We must identify healing approaches to repair the damage this network has suffered from its inner and outer environments and **show another way** to ourselves and others that will keep our heart safe from harm. In addition to protecting our own heart and the hearts of fellow humans, we must safeguard the hearts of our pets, of animals in the wild, and, indeed, the hearts of all living beings, large and small.

The following practices can support healing the energy network of our heart:

- ◆ choosing to live our life with an intention to purify our heart by overcoming selfishness, clearing vanities, checking motives, developing a spirit of worship, having aspirations, being devoted to a cause, dedicating ourselves to higher ideals, renouncing the ego, not obsessing, not controlling the lives of others, not speaking evil, seeing beauty in everyone, and obeying the heart,
- ◆ practicing forgiveness (for a specific forgiveness practice in this book, see Chapter Three's "The Gift of Lilies"),
- ◆ allowing our heart to receive appreciation, honor, love, and respect,
- ◆ facing our challenges with inner strength, enthusiasm, peace, clarity, creativity, and beauty,
- ◆ striving to have a meaningful life and healthy relationships, and

◆ cultivating virtues of the heart: group consciousness, humility, service, patience, tolerance, compassion, and gratitude.

Transcending the Impossible

As the heart heals, it goes through the process of purification. When a pure heart partners with a developed mind, the heart absorbs the mind and acts like a diamond with three facets—pure reason, pure love, and pure will. With our thoughts under the control of the heart, our mind turns into its servant. Fueled with the energy of a pure heart, our thoughts can move mountains. As we transcend the impossible, we **show ourselves and others another way** to live the vision of a healed, harmonious, and flourishing Planet Earth.

You can change your life by changing your heart.

~ MAX LUCADO

To Show Another Way: Applications

To support the healing and expansion of your heart's energy network, write an intention for two or more of the following heart virtues:

1. **Group Love or Group Consciousness** is when we begin to live for the benefit of others. We never think, speak, or act in a way that hinders the progress, success, or development of group members. Group love holds the members together in cooperation.

   My intention to show another way **to express group love and group consciousness to a current group in which I am a member is to:**

2. **Humility** is the awareness of our exact place on the ladder of perfection. We need to know consciously where we stand on the ladder. When we look up, we

see millions of people ahead of us. When we look back, we see millions of people behind us. We feel responsible for those behind us and feel admiration for those out ahead.

My intention to show another way **from the place where I stand on the ladder of perfection is to:**

3. **Service** is used to uplift, to heal, to lead, and to direct us toward a higher understanding of those in need. Service is the radiation of the Light of the soul, which purifies, gives joy, enlightens, and creates striving. Striving is an inner effort to make our life better and more useful.

   My intention to show another way **when being of service is to:**

4. **Patience** is the ability to observe the situation or condition in the light of endlessness, knowing that things follow the laws of nature and that we cannot make a tree grow in one day.

   My intention to show another way **of being patient is to:**

5. **Tolerance** is the ability to understand others and give them a chance to grow. People sometimes think that we must tolerate another person's ugliness. This is not tolerance. Tolerance is not passivity but rather a double-edged sword. One edge is love, respect, and understanding; the other is balance, sternness, and fortitude. If we misunderstand tolerance, we turn into a football being kicked around on a field of self-seeking people.

   My intention to show another way **of being tolerant is to:**

6. **Compassion** is the ability to see all conflicting forces and the reasons for their conflict. It is the ability to see the *contribution* of conflicting forces. Compassion is understanding and love that is inclusive.

   My intention to show another way **to be more compassionate is to:**

7. **Gratitude** is the ability to accept the beauty and glory of existence and to appreciate the gifts of life given to us—the air, the sky, the ocean, and the beauty of other people, of animals, and of our own bodies and consciousness. It is the appreciation of the various kinds of help we receive on all levels from the Universe. Gratitude is appreciation for the forces which work for us, which protect us, and which give us the opportunity to transcend our level of being.

   My intention to show another way **of practicing gratitude is to:**

What Hurts and What Helps the Heart: Part II

The best and most beautiful things in the world
cannot be seen or even touched.
They must be felt with the heart.

~ HELEN KELLER

I n Part I of this teaching, we explored Saraydarian's view of what hurts and what heals the heart's energy network. He also explores what helps or harms our heart by viewing it through the lens of the psyche's masculine and feminine principles. In this context, there are three general kinds of people:

◆ those who focus on developing their mind (masculine principle) and ignore their heart (feminine principle),

◆ those who focus on developing their heart (feminine principle) and ignore their mind (masculine principle), and

◆ those who focus on developing their heart and mind simultaneously (partnering masculine and feminine principles).

The ambitious nature of our country's culture and its demanding work-ethic values hurt the heart beginning early in life by perpetuating an imbalance of mind (the masculine)

and heart (the feminine). We can transcend this imbalance by simultaneously developing both mind *and* heart, the masculine and feminine principles.

When We Develop Our Mind and Ignore Our Heart

American culture highly values the work ethic. A work-ethic culture is one that favors productivity and assumes that all problems can be solved through hard work and action in the world. Desiring to make the world "work," those who overvalue the work ethic prepare themselves to help this process through education, training, and experience that emphasizes the power of the mind rather than the power of the heart.

Although work-ethic values can begin in the home, they are firmly established by the educational system. At every level of our schooling, from kindergarten to postgraduate higher education, we have a bias towards educating the mind and intellect at the expense of teaching us what it means to have a pure heart and a true partnership of heart and mind. This has created mental giants and a culture lacking in pure hearts. Sadly, without a true connection to our heart, we may experience a mental breakdown, take drugs or seek other ways to "numb out," or engage in other destructive activities that impact the general public, harm ourselves and others, and even destroy life on Planet Earth.

Our thinking mind can bring us success, prosperity, and victory—defined as a good job or report card, a generous paycheck, or accolades from our school or employer. We develop our minds through academic studies and college educations, then go on to develop them as scientists, physicians, lawyers, business leaders, politicians, educators, philosophers, communicators, theologians, financiers, and so forth. In the process of achieving success using the mind-centered orientation typical of our present academic and corporate culture, we develop separatism within ourselves. We build a wall in our minds—the lower side of our nature is deprived of our higher, Divine nature. Without the information from this higher, heart-centered aspect of ourselves, we can become destructive and try to hurt the interests of other people. This is the cause of revolutions, conflicts, and wars.

Desiring to be a valuable person in today's world, we develop an ego. We think degrees, knowledge, position, possessions, and hard work make us valuable. We manipulate and exploit others and develop an urge to dominate, rule, and force our will. The "heart-less" mind gives us a sense of power and the urge to control the lives of others, bringing them under our will—a trait found both in politics and world religions. If not balanced by a combination of reason and compassion, power is self-destructive. Our desire to possess without limit, whether objects, property, or people, can lead to materialism and criminality.

My Personal Story

I was born in a small midwestern town into a family that prized a strong work ethic. My father and mother were devoted to having the smartest, most self-responsible, and best-behaved kids in town. As a scientist, my father was mainly head-centered and placed an exceptional value on intelligence and productivity. Although my mother was heart-centered and artistically talented, she bore the pain of a troubled childhood and a life of thwarted dreams.

Witnessing my mother's intense pain from not living her dreams, I became determined that I would learn from her mistake and live my own dream of helping others. To achieve this goal, I needed to do well in school and then in college. The conflict between my mind and heart emerged with intensity when I attended college and then went on to get my master's and doctorate degrees. I soon discovered that doing well at two elite universities meant I had to put my heart aside and focus solely on stretching my mind. The stress of needing to do this, year after year, was severe. When it was time to research and write my doctoral dissertation, I fell apart. My heart was so traumatized, I didn't think I could survive emotionally. My doctoral advisor told me I needed to put my emotions aside and focus on the mental task of the dissertation. But my mind and emotions were now oceans apart. My physical heart literally ached.

Two close friends came to my rescue and day after day, for months, walked me through the process of writing and editing my dissertation. When I finally defended my dissertation, I was amazed that I passed and was actually awarded the PhD. The crippling writer's block that began with the writing of my dissertation continued to afflict me for several more years.

Then, Providence—the protective care of God—moved into my life. I was given a rare opportunity—that of designing a graduate program to train clinicians in diagnosing and teaching children and adults with brain damage and neurological disorders. I joined two colleagues to develop a two-year training program that was both heart-centered and mind-centered. As chair of the department, I asked the graduate student clinicians to meet with me at the end of each semester to set physical, emotional, mental, and spiritual goals for the subsequent term. A mind-heart approach to education and training continues today to pervade my role as head of the Institute for the Advancement of Service.

When We Develop Our Heart and Ignore Our Mind

Our culture values "nice" people who give to others and sacrifice their own desires, health, and wellbeing. When we say yes to every request, we become all-giving, developing our heart and ignoring our mind. We lose our identity and self-esteem. It is not possible to reach out authentically to others and serve them unless we have a sense of our own individuality. Giving is dangerous if we encourage weakness in others, make others dependent on us, or develop pride in giving and sacrificing. It is also dangerous for our physical health, as giving while refusing to receive depletes our energy.

Love is not an emotion but a light kindled by the mind. It is not an act of controlling others or surrendering ourselves to them. Love is an energy that must be applied intelligently. We develop our questioning mind with our heart, not agreeing with everything. We engage the mind by examining and analyzing a situation before our heart chooses an action.

If we develop our heart and ignore our mind, we can be taken advantage of or exploited by those who do the opposite—develop their minds but not their hearts. We must be mindful of legislators and leaders without heart, as they can dominate large groups of people. Those with greater intellectual capacity and knowledge can tyrannize those who have less or no intellectual power.

Our mind's knowledge about science and technology is far ahead of our heart's knowledge of its capacity. As a result, masses of people, even in a democracy, are unknowing victims of the decisions made by intellectuals with no heart. Only a minority of people in any given country have developed both heart and mind. Such people cannot be deceived. If their voices are heard and given credence, humanity will be able to transcend its challenges. It is also vital to recognize that, if we develop the heart only, we can become a visionary, but our vision will be floating aimlessly in the air like a balloon. To actualize our vision, we must call upon the gifts of the mind.

When We Develop Both Our Mind and Heart

The heart is idealistic and the mind is practical. When we develop both, we bring higher values into manifestation:

- The heart is intuitive and the mind is intelligent; when we develop both, we can introduce spiritual values to others in effective ways.

- The heart uses synthesis and the mind uses analysis; when we develop both, we see the bigger picture as well as its parts.

- The heart is sensitive and the mind is creative; when we develop both, our impressions can be manifested in various ways through creativity. We need not engage in traditionally creative pursuits (i.e., writing, painting, dance) to manifest our creativity; we can engage in our work, our relationships, and our day-to-day lives in newly creative ways.

- The heart has feelings and the mind explains them; when we develop both, we can follow our feelings, as well as discover and explain their source.

- The heart is all-giving and the mind is discriminative; when we develop both we take the right actions with what we give—we give the right amount at the right time of the right thing in the right way.

- The heart works for freedom and the mind sees limitations; when we develop both, we sense the right direction and follow it.

- The heart searches for beauty and the mind seeks knowledge; when we develop both, we evoke Divine Will to support us in using knowledge to help and not harm.

- The heart sees the needs of humanity and the mind takes action; when we develop both, we have the courage to take *right* action.

Universities of the Mind and the Heart

Higher aspects of heart cannot be developed without the striving of the mind. When heart and mind join together, we experience the beauty of life. We experience goodness and love as we travel with the Divine day after day, hour by hour, moment by moment. An inspiring tenet of metaphysical teachings posits that someday we will have universities that study and develop not only the mind, but the partnership of mind *and* heart.

May your mind whirl joyful cartwheels of creativity.
May your heart sing sweet lullabies of timelessness.
May your essence be the nectar of the open blossom of your joy.
May your spirit soar throughout the vast cathedral of your being.

~ Jonathan Lockwood Huie

To Show Another Way: Applications

Select the suggestions below that serve the needs of your heart and mind at this time in your life.

1. Explore these questions: After reading and reflecting on this two-part teaching, how would I describe my mind-heart development? Do I sense a need to develop my heart? My mind? My heart and mind together?

2. Review the following suggestions and put a check mark by those that will support the next step in your mind-heart development:

Ways to develop my heart:

◆ Bring beauty and joy into my life in some way
◆ Express respect, love, and gratitude to a person or group
◆ Deepen and expand my love by feeling the suffering of others and Planet Earth

- Pray for individuals, groups, and Planet Earth
- Meditate daily, focusing my awareness in my heart
- Engage in service to animals
- Maintain loving support for family, friends, and coworkers
- Protect my heart from negative energy

Ways to develop my mind:

- Read and study a new subject or learn a new language
- Participate in a group that explores a certain school of thought
- Share and discuss ideas about developing my mind with a trusted friend
- Find a mentor to help me organize projects in my personal and/or work life

Ways to develop my heart and mind together:

- Study what it means to approach life with both heart and mind
- Engage in creative arts, such as painting, composing music, or sculpting
- Learn sacred dance
- Engage in activities and projects that require use of both mind and heart
- Explore what it means *practically* that higher aspects of the heart cannot be developed without the striving of the mind
- Approach my work in the world by focusing on both my heart and mind
- Learn how to be a student, leader, and group member who uses both mind and heart
- Parent my children by teaching them to use qualities of both heart and mind

Service as the Means to Happiness

I slept and dreamt that life was Joy,
I awoke and saw that life was Service,
I acted and behold, Service was Joy.

~RABINDRANATH TAGORE

Despite the learning, accomplishments, and skills we've gathered throughout our lifetime, we continue to feel discouraged, overwhelmed, and joyless. We wonder what's missing. Why don't we feel enthusiastic and inspired about our life and our place in the world? Where is the inner joy we seek? How can we be happy when our world is falling apart and our planet is collapsing? There is one answer to all of these questions: we must **be mindful when we have the opportunity to show another way.** It is our sacred responsibility to reach beyond our self-absorption and in some way help another person, animal, group, or our planet. When we take up this sacred responsibility to serve, we create an opportunity for joy in our life and happiness in our world.

Inner Joy

According to psychiatrist and spiritual teacher David Hawkins, a widely known authority within the fields of consciousness research and spirituality, "another way" to live and serve that we can show to ourselves and others involves inner joy. Inner joy emerges naturally and miraculously as we begin to transcend our love for particular individuals only and shift more and more into an unconditional love for the benefit of all humanity. In this process, joy becomes a constant presence in all activities and arises in each moment from within rather than from an outside source. When we experience the energy of joy, life is effortless and the world is rife with synchronicities. Joy is what happens when our personal will merges with Divine Will, the powerful energy source of joy. When this merging happens, we are able to serve others by **showing another way.**

Hawkins writes that the capacity for joy evolves out of our capacity for "enormous patience and the persistence of a positive attitude in the face of prolonged adversity," and that the primary characteristic of this state is compassion: "People who have attained this level have a notable effect on others," he writes. "They're capable of a prolonged, open visual gaze, which induces a state of love and peace."

Joy eludes us when we hold fearful, judgmental, and limiting beliefs and behaviors, and when we are self-absorbed, materialistic, and have expectations of outcome. These beliefs and behaviors reduce the vibration of our energy because they separate us from the source of joy. We experience an energy drain, a lack of concentration, an inability to apply what we know, and a growing disinterest in reaching out to help others.

If we do not experience joy in our life, we cannot experience joy in our service. If, as the poet Tagore writes, life is service and service is joy, when we give our life completely to joy, we give it to service. When we can give our life completely to service, we are filled with joy. Viewed in this way, service is self-transformational and can be practiced in every action of our life. The transformational nature of service opens the way for us to practice *selfless service.*

Selfless Service

In Eastern traditions, service is known by the concept of *seva* or selfless service. *Seva* is a state of high consciousness and is a combination of self-effort and Divine Grace. Virtually all spiritual paths acknowledge the concept of this highest level of giving in the service of mystics and saints. Even though such service may seem unreachable to those of us less advanced on our spiritual journey, our desire and subsequent *intention to practice selfless service* sets in motion the alchemical shift in our inner state which allows us to taste this experience ourselves.

In *Born to Serve*, I wrote that selfless service arises from union with the Absolute:

> [T]he server is totally open to the Divine view of serving the world. Every action is a prayer, a service to the True Self within oneself and others, and an acknowledgement of love for humanity. In this way, service is the altar of devotion.

The benefits of selfless service are often unexpected and difficult to put into words. Selfless service is not tinged with inertia, boredom, or negative emotions of selfishness, pride, or judgment. Every tiny act of service, whether smiling at a stranger, caring for a pet, peeling potatoes, or cleaning the house, is offered for the sake of service *because we want to*—and not for any purpose other than joy. Offered in this way, service purifies the heart and the mind. As the heart and mind are cleansed through selfless service, our service becomes a joyful spiritual journey. In essence, practicing selfless service is **showing another way** to live and be in the world.

There is no experience of service that does not present us with the opportunity to bring us joy, inner peace, and a deep sense of wellbeing. As a spiritual teacher once said to me, "Thank you for your recognition of service as the means to happiness." And so it is.

The great sea has set me in motion,
Set me adrift,
Moving me like a weed in a river.
The sky and the strong wind
Have moved the spirit inside me
Till I am carried away
Trembling with joy.

~ UVANUK, A NETSILIK INUIT WOMAN WHO, IN A SINGLE MOMENT OF MYSTICAL UNION, RECEIVED THIS SONG. WHEN SHE SANG IT, SHE WAS ABLE TO HEAL OTHERS.

To Show Another Way: Applications

Take an inventory of the presence or absence of joy in your life by responding to the following inquiry questions:

1. Do I feel something vitally important is missing in my life? If so, what do I think is missing?

2. Do I feel enthusiastic and inspired about my place in the world? If so, in what ways? If not, what do I sense is absent in my life?

3. Where might I find the inner joy that I seek?

4. Have I ever practiced selfless service—giving free from personal desires or hidden motives (remembering that service could be our work, our relationship with our spouse or children, caring for a pet, any menial task, or, indeed, any act at all)? What were the circumstances in which I was able to do this?

5. What can I be and do that would bring me joy in the midst of the chaos of our present world?

The Tao of Receiving

To give and to receive are one in truth.
I will receive what I am giving now.

~ A COURSE IN MIRACLES

D id you know that our ability to receive directly affects our ability to care for ourselves on every level—physically, emotionally, mentally, and spiritually? We live in a culture in which we value giving over receiving, as if they are not two sides of the same coin, and may never have considered that receiving is critical to our health and happiness. **We become integrated physically, emotionally, mentally, and spiritually if what we receive nurtures us and permeates our entire being.** In the process of receiving, we become healed—we experience our wholeness.

If we discover we are not open to being nurtured, we can ask ourselves: What personal issues are interfering with my accepting nurturing? Why do I resist being nurtured and thus neglect my self-care? To ask these questions is the first step to opening ourselves to being nurtured. Exploring the answers to these questions begins the process that will **show us another way** to view the cause of our self-neglect.

Unconscious or subconscious ways we relate to receiving that may lead to self-neglect:

◆ Resistance to receiving
◆ Disowning our Light when we reject a compliment or quiet the person who praises us

- ◆ Beliefs that tell us we should not receive and, if we do, we should feel guilty
- ◆ Lack of knowledge about why receiving is essential to our total wellbeing
- ◆ Childhood wounds that tell us it is not safe to receive
- ◆ Feeling unworthy to receive all that is good

Receiving on All Levels of the Self

Physically, our body receives the food we give it. How well our body functions will depend on the quality and nourishment of the food it receives. When the body receives what it needs, it responds by giving back to us by serving our life. Saint Francis of Assisi reminds us of how often we fail to thank our body for all it does for us. When he was seriously ill, he wrote that he regretted he had neglected his "Brother Body" and had not thanked it for its service to him.

Emotionally, we respond with inner strength and depth when we receive healthy and constructive emotional experiences. We can turn all emotional experiences into healthy and constructive ones when we explore what these experiences are teaching us. In this way, we can use negative as well as positive experiences **to show us another way.** We are nurtured as we personally acknowledge our gifts and steps in growth. We are not psychologically nourished when we absorb negative and destructive emotions or discount our self-worth and self-confidence. Our lack of emotional health affects our wellbeing and impacts that of others.

Mentally, we receive by gathering knowledge and deepening our understanding of life and the world around us. What would we have to give if we had not received knowledge and wisdom from others and from our schooling and life experiences? Even if our experiences were negative and hurtful at the time of their occurrence, they offer us the gifts of knowledge and awareness if we allow them **to show us another way**—the *opposite* way—to live and to serve.

Spiritually, we receive impressions from the Divine of our potential for compassion, wisdom, intuition, and understanding. We learn to live from right action, giving the right amount in the right way for the right reason and at the right time. We care for our spiritual vessel through prayer, meditation, contemplation, and serving others. When we neglect our spiritual needs, we fail to fully benefit from the gifts of the soul.

Giving and Receiving Are the Same

Contrary to what many believe, service cannot be defined solely as giving. Lao Tzu's *Tao Te Ching*, one of China's best-loved books of ancient spiritual wisdom, states that we live in conscious harmony with the natural law of service through receiving. This law states that **what we give to others, we first give to ourselves—we first** *receive*. In other words, we *cannot* give what we have not previously received. Another way to think of this is that we cannot give from an empty vessel. The vessel must first be filled or there is nothing to give from it. Because self-care fills our vessel, **caring for ourselves is the first priority to giving.**

To maintain and strengthen what we have, the law of receiving requires us to give what we have within ourselves. To give without expectation of reward, we must first unconditionally receive, accept, and integrate all that is given to us. **Our ability to receive eventually dies when we are not open to receiving.** The inability to fully receive arises from the ego's need to defend itself against love. In this painful paradox, we become narcissistic, focusing unceasingly on our lack and on our desperate need to have our vessel filled from someone or something outside ourselves.

Giving and receiving create a feedback loop that can be conscious or unconscious. We are typically unaware of the nature of the energy we are giving or the nature of the energy we are receiving. That is, we tend not to be conscious of receiving energy—positive or negative. If we are receiving negative energy from someone and do not recognize it, we will feel depleted of energy once we are out of that person's presence. We know this occurs if we always feel exhausted after being with a certain person. If we receive positive, uplifting energy from someone and are not conscious of it, we might notice or say that we always feel better after talking or being with that person.

This also works in the other direction: if I send positive energy to someone, or they say they always feel better after talking with me, this is evidence that I have that energy within myself or I would not have been able to give it to the other. Because giving and receiving is a loop of dynamic energy, we will receive in return the positive energy we give. This is true whether we send positive or negative energy.

Aligning with Our Higher Self (Our Soul)

As a vessel, we are full when we allow the Life Force to flow continuously through us. Our energy will not be impacted by another, regardless of the quality of that person's energy, when we remain aligned with our true source of positive energy, our Higher Self (our Soul), which is in alignment with the energy of Divine Source. When we strengthen our alignment with our Higher Self, we open to the *Tao* (the Divine Way) of receiving and allow ourselves **to be shown another way** to heal and be whole. From this place of wholeness, we can live in conscious harmony with the natural law of service—and **show others another way** to do the same.

> *Just as you cannot receive without giving,*
> *so neither can you give without receiving.*
>
> ~ PEACE PILGRIM

To Show Another Way: Applications

"The Tao of Receiving" shows us ways to sustain our energy when interacting with others. This application invites you to explore the following inquiry question:

How do the following practices **show me another way** to care for my physical, emotional, mental, and spiritual energies?

◆ Practicing compassion for myself
◆ Practicing compassion for others
◆ Determining whether I am in my right place (see the Chapter Four teaching, "Am I in My Right Place?" for help understanding this practice)
◆ Investigating ways to be creative
◆ Having no expectations of outcome

The Dimensions of Service

*Giving is what opens your eyes—
the inner eye, the eye of wisdom.
Learning to give and having the willingness
and good karma to receive—
that is the greatest gift of seva.*

~ Swami Chidvilasananda

Have you ever considered that at the heart of all acts of service is *love,* plain and simple? Whether we move to a war-torn country to assist the wounded, or help a stranger reach something on the top shelf in the grocery store, each gesture of assistance or support, large or small, is based in *love* for the fellow beings who share this planet with us, or even for the planet itself. One common thread that weaves itself throughout the teachings of all world religions is that—once we remove the obstacles of unawareness, lack of understanding, and resistance that obscure it—**we each have an inner call to live a life of *love through service.***

Each of us views the concept of service through different lenses depending on our culture, societal values, religious background, and the form of the service itself. Five of the world's major religions—Buddhism, Christianity, Hinduism, Islam, and Judaism—identify **four primary dimensions of service: duty, charity, purification, and devotion.** Regardless of our present religious or spiritual orientation, these four dimensions have much to teach us about service—and about love. If we wish to serve more consciously and move closer to union with the Divine, we can be supported by exploring, developing, and integrating the qualities of these dimensions within ourselves.

We serve others at more and more sublime levels as we love and serve the Divine. Each dimension **shows us another way** to serve others. No matter what the outer form of our spiritual path, we move from unenlightened to enlightened, from being caught in the world's illusion to being spiritually liberated, and from chaotic, antisocial behavior to **True Service** and mystic union with All That Is.

Service as Duty

Through the dimension of service as duty, we set aside our personal and individual interests for a greater good. Through duty, we show honor and respect to some authority beyond ourselves. Duty demands discipline—the ability to develop a self-controlled pattern of behavior. We practice duty by giving, doing good works, having a spiritual practice, and using it as a container for all activities in our life.

Duty is commonly associated with rigidity, constraints on individual freedom, and even punishment. Around the world, there are religious and politically based sects that make adherence to duty and rules the principal responsibility of members. Many who experience the negative attitudes and punitive approaches of these groups resist the concept of duty and of service as duty. Yet duty can be the basis for heroic acts, push us to take risks, and bring out the best in us.

Through duty we simply do what needs to be done. Teaching children, caring for the unfortunate, and respecting elders all involve the self-discipline and individual responsibility characteristic of duty. In fact, virtually all forms of employment, even at the most high-ranking and lucrative levels, require a commitment to duty—respecting authority, engaging our self-discipline, and adhering to the greater good. In its highest form, duty is the moment when our will meets God's Will. We act in total consciousness and without analysis, judgment, or expectation of reward.

Service as Charity

Synonymous with altruism, compassion, and unconditional love, charity is the kind of love that exhibits unselfish concern for and total acceptance of another.

True charity always helps the person who gives it as much as it helps the person who receives it. To establish this reciprocal relationship, we must master four skills of giving:

◆ **giving the right amount** by being sensitive to what the recipient is able to receive,

◆ **giving the right thing** by expanding people's choices rather than making the choices for them,

◆ **giving for the right reason** by giving without expectations of response or reward, and

◆ **giving at the right time** by trusting our intuition and knowing that it comes from our True Self.

By modeling adept giving and receiving, givers also make it possible for those who receive their service to master the skills of giving and receiving for themselves.

Service as Purification

Through the conscious practice of service as duty and charity, we increasingly let go of personal desires and stay focused on the desires of the soul. Service then becomes not only the extension or result of our spiritual development, but the means for the soul's purification and evolution. By using service as a mirror, it is possible to identify and then remove the obstacles we place in the way of recognizing our true identity and that of others. That is, as we are purified, so is the quality of our service; as our service is purified, so are we.

Service as Devotion

We do not have to wait until we become mystics to practice service as devotion. In fact, **service as love in action** can be practiced at any time in any situation. We can practice service as devotion by putting whatever interaction or activity we are engaged in on an altar of devotion. When we do this, we drop our fears of inadequacy and release our judgments about ourselves and those we are serving. Instead, we focus on qualities of understanding, patience, and compassion.

A Critical Choice

Whether service is practiced as duty, charity, purification, or devotion, the call to service expresses the desire to love through action. As we explore the dimensions of service, we discover service *is* life, rather than something we *do* in life; we discover that everything we do is service.

The pervasiveness of service requires that we work diligently to chisel away all that stands between us and our soul's full expression. This involves a willingness to examine the shadow aspects of ourselves—aspects from which we spend much of our lives hiding. Working with our shadow exposes our natural state of grace.

In the Michelangelo painting on the ceiling of the Sistine Chapel illustrating the biblical creation story, in the moment before he is born into the world, Adam lifts his finger to touch God. Without lifting his finger—without making this *choice*—not only would his birth not have taken place, but the human race would not exist because Adam would not be there to beget it.

Michelangelo's version of the Old Testament creation story represents a critical moment of choice—and can serve as a metaphor for the choice we have to engage with our shadow. Will we lift a finger to touch God and be born to our True Self? Will we choose to come out of hiding and work with our shadow—to remove the obstacles of unawareness, lack of understanding, and resistance that obscure our inner call to service? To work with our shadow is itself an act of True Service—an act of Divine Love—toward our self. Without making this choice, we cannot truly serve others because we cannot serve from our authentic self. **It is when we choose to "take birth" as an integrated self that we choose *to live a life of love through service*.**

Lord, free me of myself so I can please you!

~ MICHELANGELO

To Show Another Way: Applications

You are invited to respond to one or more of the inquiry questions regarding the four dimensions of service in your own life:

Service as Duty

◆ What experiences as a child and/or adult have most influenced the view I hold today about service as duty?

◆ What aspects of my current life do I view as my duty? What is my attitude/philosophy about these responsibilities? Do I view these aspects of my life as *spiritual* duty? If so, why? If not, why not?

Service as Charity

◆ What is an example from my life when I was given the right amount of the right thing for the right reason at the right time? What was the impact of that experience on my life? Did the experience shift how I view helping others or how I view being helped? If so, in what way?

Service as Purification

◆ What is an example from my life in which the person(s), animal(s), group, or situation I served mirrored something back to me that showed me my motivation was not pure? As a result of this feedback, what inner work did I do? Did this experience shift my motivation for service?

An example: You meet someone with a life-threatening illness and ask her how she is doing. As she starts to tell you, you interrupt her and talk about what happened to your relative who has the same illness. Later you notice the person with the illness avoids you. From this feedback, you are informed that you need to purify your motivations and learn certain communication skills. The situation has shown you that you have inner work to do to chisel away the obstacles that exist between you and your soul's full expression.

Service as Devotion

◆ What is an interaction or activity of service I wish to place on the altar of devotion? After doing this, what shifts in my feelings and attitudes do I observe?

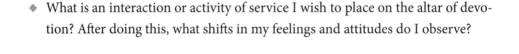

Robin Williams' Gift of Service

Isn't it funny how I can bring great happiness
to all these people but not to myself?

~ ROBIN WILLIAMS

Sometimes an event has such inherent power that it dramatically impacts people worldwide. The August 10, 2014 suicide of comedian Robin Williams was such an event. Unsettled by his death, people felt driven to share their grief and their good memories of this master of comedic talent. News of his death was the focus of conversations throughout the world—conversations that were personal, deep, and life-changing. Why was this so?

The teaching I published about Robin's passing remains the most widely read of any on my blog. I realized the reason we were so impacted by Robin's emotional and spiritual pain is because **his pain was akin to our own and his death personally served us in some way.** Most of us have experienced depression and despair at some point in our life; perhaps we are experiencing this pain now, as we watch our planet collapsing and our "civilized" world breaking down. Through his tragic death, Robin Williams became a mirror: when we looked at him, we saw that he was us, you and me, and was giving us an opportunity to choose a different path. In his mirror, *we recognized ourselves.*

Robin's death felt personal, as though we were participating in a drama just like our own. Our inner self emerged from the depths of our unconscious and seemed to say,

"Pay attention to your reaction to this event… it represents a vital teaching for you. If you imbibe this teaching, its truth has the power to heal you. This event can **show you another way**."

Separation from Our True Self

I decided to examine my response to Robin's death by acknowledging I felt his death was not by suicide, but by *despair*. What seemed key to me was the depth and intensity of his longstanding depression and anguish. For days after his death, I had images of my former, desperate self—feelings that had begun in my early life and extended well into my forties. I had been depressed for years, but not until the depression became despair did I realize I was in trouble.

Depression and despair are points on a continuum. Depression begins to develop when, over time, we fail to notice how we really feel, emotionally and spiritually. We separate our psyche into two selves, the personality self and the spiritual self. The face we want to present to the world (our personality) becomes our truth rather than the face of our True Self (our inner spiritual reality). This split produces anxiety and self-hatred because the energy of our psyche is *pulled apart*. When our energy is used in this way, we descend into depression because we no longer know who we are, where our safety lies, what meaning there is in our life, or where we stand in the world.

As we become increasingly separated from our True Self, we spiral into despair, a state of utter meaninglessness and dejection. Despair is inert energy that resides at the very bottom of our belief in separation from what is real—our True Self. The pain of this belief is unbearable. We become so separated from the awareness of our True Self that we believe there is nowhere to go but *out—out* of this life, either by numbing ourselves with addictions or ending our life by suicide.

Finding Meaning and Purpose

How do we start climbing out of the abyss of despair? Hands reach out to help us, but we often decline them or don't even notice their presence. We are the ones who must "wake up" and choose to begin the long climb out of the depths of despair. There is only one way to begin this climb: admit the truth of our condition and then, with humility, pray and ask for help from the Divine and from all of the Angels and High Beings who are, in reality, just waiting for us to ask them to help us. It doesn't matter if we believe this is so—it only matters that we are humble enough to ask for help.

Once we are sincere about asking for help and are willing to accept it, *help will come*. We will be **shown another way**. *How* it will come is inevitably a surprise. Synchronicity—unusual or mysterious "coincidences" that appear random but are genuinely meaningful—is the method extended to us by the Divine and our Helpers. We MUST look for synchronicities, as they WILL come. It could be something someone says to us or a book someone hands us that shifts our perspective. We might have a dream that leaves us feeling lighter.

A despair-reversing synchronicity can take virtually any form. It can be the action of a loving pet or a deep sense of peacefulness we unexpectedly experience from walking in a silent wood or witnessing a new dawn. It could be the impulse to call a hotline. Perhaps someone describes a healing method that has helped her and we recognize it might also help us. As we begin to climb out of despair, we'll have an urge to use what we've learned to help others. We'll begin to refocus our life. Finally, we'll find meaning and purpose for being on Planet Earth.

Healing Our Lives

At the time in my life when I was in the depths of despair and drowning in self-hatred, I noticed a colleague I knew seemed much happier than she had been in recent weeks. I asked her why. She said she had taken an *est* training (the self-realization workshop developed by Werner Erhard) and also learned to meditate. I had no idea what *est* was about but I respected her opinion and enrolled in it myself. For most of the training, I was extremely miserable, mired in my wretchedness. Then, a woman in the group stood up and told her story… and it was *my* story she was telling! Listening to her talk about her life, I suddenly saw my own situation clearly and knew what I needed to do. I understood in that moment that ***I had a choice to change how and with whom I lived my life***. I was not the victim of my circumstances—in fact, I had helped create them. Knowing this to be true, I could create something different in my life by accepting responsibility for my past choices and making choices going forward that were healthier and wiser. I recall in that moment literally dancing with joy, chanting over and over: "I have a choice! I have a choice!"

Later, this same colleague said to me, "Someday you'll look back on this time in your life and see all that you've learned. Then, you'll naturally want to give away what you learned by taking the hand of others in pain. You can do this because you've been there and know it's possible to make a different choice and heal your life."

Choosing the Inner Way

Robin reminded us that we have a choice. By his actions, he taught us not to give up in despair and neglect our souls, but to search for and **show ourselves another way** to look at our pain and discouragement—an inner way, a soul-oriented way. We won't find inner peace if we reside only in our personality and its attainments in the world. Inner peace is found within us as a spiritual quest, as our soul's journey. Why are we on Earth? We are here to heal our emotional traumas and learn how to create a meaningful, soul-focused life that helps others do the same.

What is the gift of service that Robin extends to us? *It is not what we do in the world that matters but the love and spirit we experience within that nourishes our soul and allows us to fulfill our life's purpose on Earth.* Our life has meaning when our personality becomes infused with our soul's essence. This wholeness, this integration, is where our true happiness resides. We are not strengthened by how much money we make, how hard we work, how many relationships we have, or how often we make people laugh. *It is the energy we receive by connecting to our soul that sustains us.* In the intensity of silence that is the soul's domain, we experience the depth of our strength.

> *You will have bad times,*
> *but they will always wake you up*
> *to the stuff you weren't paying attention to.*
>
> ~ ROBIN WILLIAMS

To Show Another Way: Applications

Sit in silence and reflect on your personal reaction to the news of Robin Williams' death. Then, respond to these inquiry questions:

1. What did Robin's life and death teach me about how to climb out of the abyss of despair?

2. After contemplating this teaching, what changes in my life am I now considering?

3. How will I use what I've learned from Robin Williams **to show others another way**? How will I use what I've learned from my own life challenges to help others?

Service as an Altar of Devotion

To serve is beautiful, but only if it is done
with joy and a whole heart and a free mind.

~ Pearl S. Buck

Throughout this book, I have emphasized it is our experiences that provide the learnings we need to develop as souls and truly serve ourselves and others. We learn from both our positive and negative experiences to understand how **to show ourselves and others another way** to live and be in the world.

If we learn from our experiences, it stands to reason that our experiences serve as our teachers. Yet our greatest life teacher of all is service itself. Service provides us with an opportunity to monitor our inner state when we shift our mind from an outer focus to inner contemplation. Our inner contemplation, in turn, allows us to investigate our motives for serving. When, as helpers, we explore our motives for serving, service becomes our most powerful spiritual teacher of all.

Service as an Inner Spiritual Process

In the ancient, sacred language of Sanskrit, the word for practicing selfless service is *seva*. Virtually all spiritual paths acknowledge that mystics and saints offer *seva* as the highest level of service. Even though such service may seem unreachable to those of us less spiritually attuned, our desire and subsequent intention to practice selfless service sets in motion a shift in our inner state, resulting in our tasting *seva's* nectar. *Seva* is a state of high consciousness and is achieved through a combination of self-effort and Divine Grace.

Seva is giving that is free from personal desires or hidden motives. When we practice *seva*, we experience the profound truth that giving and receiving are the same. In *seva*, the purity of our service washes away resentment, anger, feelings of superiority or inferiority, and the sense of being separate from others and from the Divine. We subsequently touch feelings of joy and a profound lightness of being.

When we decide to practice *seva,* we recognize that our *seva* could be our work, our relationship with our spouse or children, any menial task, or, indeed, any act at all. Practicing *seva* necessitates that we take responsibility for our inner state when helping others. Those we serve reflect back to us the nature and quality of our inner state, aspects of our unfinished business, and reminders of the reality of Divine Love. This mutuality of giving and receiving is essential for our emotional and spiritual wellbeing.

Dissolving the False Needs of the Ego

A common mental model of *seva* is that, by surrendering to the Divine, we must sacrifice our individuality and/or our own needs. This assumption fails to recognize that surrendering to the Divine allows us to be suffused with Divine energy—the Life Force— which dissolves self-preoccupation and the false needs of the ego, allowing the True Self to emerge.

False needs of the ego to be aware of include

- ◆ the need to be recognized for our service,
- ◆ the need to "get the task done" above all else,
- ◆ not recognizing that it is not the form of the task, but the state we are in when we do it that really matters, and
- ◆ feeling pride or specialness for what we may see as our advanced state of spiritual evolution.

Practicing Seva

When we practice *seva*, we strive to achieve a state of true purity of motive. Divine Grace hears our call and brings up our unhealed emotions and thoughts in order to purify them in the high spiritual frequency of this commitment. We notice our inner state and continue to surrender our thoughts and feelings—"good" and "bad"—to the sacred commitment we have made to **True Service.** We release our attachment to outcome and receive the gifts of *seva,* devoting our life **to showing another way** as we allow ourselves to receive the Divine Grace that flows back to us through this practice.

We do not have to wait until we become a mystic to practice service as devotion. In fact, service as love in action can be practiced at any time in any situation. We can practice service as devotion by putting whatever interaction or activity we are involved in on an **altar of devotion**. When I wrote *The Soul and Service Trilogy*, my editor joined me in placing each of the three books on an altar of devotion as they were being written and edited. I imaged this altar in my mind's eye. I did not focus on those aspects of my personality that might interfere with the ease of my writing or my fears about receiving corrections from my editor. In other words, I did not focus on my insecurities, judgments, or self-limitations. Rather, I was devoted to welcoming any help and feedback that would ensure that each book's highest potential was realized.

The Altar of Devotion

It is only when we are able to truly practice *seva* that service becomes an altar of devotion. We feel the first inkling of the oneness of *doing* and *being*, of acting *in* the world while not being *of* it, of loving others without conditions and of the bliss of love for the Absolute. To serve others, we listen to our Inner Voice (the voice of our Soul), see the inner strength and rich resources in others, and have no expectations of outcome.

As we begin to practice service as an altar of devotion, we increasingly take responsibility for our perceptions and choices, **showing ourselves another way** to be in the world, holding the reality of the presence of Divine Love within ourselves and in our interactions with others. As we help others with the desire and intention to practice service as *seva*, we become increasingly capable of responding to them with understanding and compassion. In doing so, **we show them another way** to serve—and to be served by those *they* serve. In this process, the circle of giving and receiving is complete. At the same time, a NEW circle begins, as those we serve go on to serve others in their turn.

Thus it is that service becomes our greatest teacher of all.

Seva is work performed without attachment;
duty fulfilled without any desire for personal gain;
service offered without any motive,
without any of the objectives that
cramp one's actions or contract the heart.

~ Swami Chidvilasananda

To Show Another Way: Applications

Contemplate these questions:

1. As I review my life, under what circumstances have I served others by **showing another way**?

2. What are my obstacles to service?

3. What are my goals regarding **showing another way** as a way of life? (Include both motivations and desired actions.)

4. How do I intend to practice service as an altar of devotion? What are some examples?

The Evolution of the Soul Through Service: Part I

Do your little bit of good where you are;
it's those little bits of good put together
that overwhelm the world.

~ Desmond Tutu

Saint Teresa of Ávila, the sixteenth century Spanish mystic, envisioned the soul as an "interior castle" into which the soul spends its life going deeper and deeper into a sacred awareness of the Self. This castle is made up of seven "mansions" or "dwelling places," each representing a progressive stage of faith. Teresa wrote her book for those leading a monastic life—for the sisters of the Carmelite order, which she founded. In my book, *Born to Serve: The Evolution of the Soul Through Service,* I expand upon Teresa's seven stages of faith as **evolutionary stages of soul development.** These stages provide a blueprint for those of us in the world seeking a way to serve without expectation or agenda, from a place of freedom and joy.

The Seven Stages of Soul Development

The seven stages of the evolution of the soul describe the developmental nature of our unfolding identity as individuals. As we gain life experiences and actualize our potential, we evolve into an authentic self that reflects our wholeness. **In this process, we show ourselves and others another way,** becoming the best we are capable of being.

The seven evolutionary stages of service are developmental, interrelational, and multidimensional. Our inner state evolves from the initial stage of having little or no conscious motivation to serve, to the final stage of *being* selfless service. Stages one through four focus on *dependence*—seeking our value from something or someone outside ourselves; stages five and six focus on *interdependence*—where we seek our value from within through the care of the self and the practice of service in the world.

A Brief Overview of the Stages

Stage One ~ *Awakening to Serve*	The primary focus is on caring for one's own physical and material needs. Those in Stage One have little or no motivation to help others as their focus is on their own needs.
Stage Two ~ Work Ethic	Outer-focused, those in this stage are doers who work to meet their physical and material needs and to bring order out of chaos. They help others as a natural extension of their work ethic.
Stages Three and Four ~ *Missionary Attitude* and *Wounded Healer*	Both stages serve with an unconscious motive of helping someone or something outside themselves at the expense of their own physical and emotional needs. Those in Stage Three focus on activism as a right-wrong way to "save" the world; those in Stage Four focus on sacrificing their own needs by meeting the physical and emotional needs of others.

~ Transition from outer-focused to inner-focused ~

Stage Five ~ Healing the Healer	Inwardly focused, those in Stage Five are self-responsible, doing inner work and acknowledging the need to balance care of self with care of others.
Stage Six ~ Selfless Action	Those in this stage have no attachment to the form and outcome of their service. They are often referred to as mystics.
Stage Seven ~ Beyond the Physical	Souls continue to serve after death.

Progression and Regression

The stages reflect a deepening relationship with the Divine and how that deepening affects our motivation to serve others. Rather than a straight line or ascending ladder, the soul's development progresses in a spiral—gradually going deeper and further into the interior. At the same time, we can, in the span of a moment, drop back to a lower stage from wherever we are, which often happens under stress. Usually, such regression gives us an opportunity to reassess and recommit to **showing ourselves and others another way.** Sometimes, we regress and choose to continue an old pattern.

It is not possible to skip stages of development without negative consequences. Just as, to dance freely, we must first master walking, rhythm, and a myriad of discrete movement and listening skills, the soul's evolution through service requires us to acquire and integrate specific abilities at beginning, intermediate, and advanced levels. How the soul expresses itself is unique for each individual.

The Nature of the Stages of the Soul's Evolution

Each stage has certain characteristics: a state of the self, a worldview, a relationship with God, shadow issues, a mode of service, a major obstacle or fear, a specific learning that is a gift to us, a primary gift we offer to the world, and a period of transition into the next stage. Each stage has a range of possibilities for its expression.

One developmental stage is not better than another. Rather, we bring what we have learned from one stage into the next (for example, our skills and wisdom). Because the stages are developmental (we move through them as we move from infancy through adulthood), it is not possible to skip a stage, although we sometimes attempt to bypass a stage out of personal woundedness.

Although there is an ideal time at which we pass through each stage of service, delays occur for one reason or another. People differ in how long they stay in a stage, but we are primarily in one stage at a time. We can stay in one stage for our entire life, or we can move through some or all of the stages. We may stay at different lengths of time in any given stage depending on life circumstances, woundedness, our soul age, or the choice not to move forward in our psycho-spiritual growth.

We may regress or drop back to an earlier stage under stress and may briefly experience a future stage as a glimpse of our potential.

Stages are not related to the form of service we are doing in the world but to the motivation for doing that service. Our level of consciousness determines the essence of our service. For example, it is possible to be an activist from the third (Missionary) stage and view the world as black and white, or we can serve as an activist from the fifth stage (Healing the Healer) and view our service as sacred activism.

A Roadmap into the Castle

As Saint Teresa well understood, the soul has many "dwelling places"—stages—and each offers us important gifts, including knowledge about the very deepest aspects of ourselves. Part II of this teaching takes us further into each of the stages, providing a more detailed roadmap for our journey into the castle—and into the sacred depths of our soul.

The important thing is not to think much,
but to love much; and so,
do that which best stirs you to love.

~ SAINT TERESA OF ÁVILA

To Show Another Way: Applications

This exercise invites you to identify the many ways you have served others throughout your life. You are invited to list the ways you have helped others, beginning in childhood and extending to your present age. This inventory will reveal the variety of ways service has existed in your life thus far.

Use a broad definition of service. For example, between the ages of five and twelve, you might recall helping your mother prepare a meal or running an errand for your father. Between the ages of thirteen and eighteen, you may remember mowing your neighbor's lawn, tutoring a fellow student on his homework, or supporting a friend who was upset about something. Record several examples of the ways you have helped others when in the following age groups:

- ◆ Ages 5 to 12
- ◆ Ages 13 to 18
- ◆ Ages 19 to 30
- ◆ Ages 31 to 50
- ◆ Ages 51 to 64
- ◆ Age 65 to present

The Evolution of the Soul Through Service: Part II

The meaning of life is to find your gift.
The purpose of life is to give it away.

~ AUTHOR UNKNOWN

P art I of this teaching provided an introduction and overview of the soul's seven evolutionary stages of service, the nature of their progression (and periodic regression) through Saint Teresa's "interior castle," and the stages' relationship to one another. In Part II, we explore the stages in greater depth and how they apply specifically to individuals, leaders, organizations, and groups.

A comprehensive study of the stages can be found in the three books of my *Soul and Service Trilogy*. Each book explores the unique ways that the stages of soul development—also known as the stages of *service*—can be applied specifically to individuals (in *Born to Serve: The Evolution of the Soul Through Service*), to leaders (in *The Awakened Leader: Leadership as a Classroom of the Soul*), and to groups and organizations (in *The Clarion Call: Leadership and Group Life in the Aquarian Era*).

Stage One: Awakening to Serve

As *individuals* in this stage, we move from being "asleep" in regard to self and serving others, to a beginning awareness that life is more than just meeting our own needs. We have little interest in helping others and are self-preoccupied with the intensity of our own pain. Consequently, we view life as a series of duties and obligations necessary for our physical and emotional survival. In this stage, we tend to express our lack of identity and personal power through passive-aggressiveness, right-wrong thinking, and an extreme desire to control. Our overdependence on opinions and directions from others reflects an inability to connect with our own inner resources. In Stage One, our self-preoccupation impedes our ability to have healthy relationships.

As *leaders* in this stage, we find the leadership role a challenging and emotionally painful one—and subsequently do our best to avoid serving as leaders. Should we find ourselves in this stage as leaders, we compensate for our lack of inner strength and sense of self through rigid control of our outer world; we can become coercive and demand immediate compliance. When awakening to serve as leaders, we may be indecisive and passive-aggressive, tending to make decisions that please others. We find it difficult to articulate our ideas and often fail to bring these ideas into reality.

Groups and organizations in this stage often flounder, as members have undeveloped leadership and organizational skills and cannot grasp group needs. As individuals in this stage, we may find ourselves attracted to organizations with clear structure and expectations. Because, as Stage One individuals, we look to others for our identity, we are susceptible to groups that promise protection and right-wrong beliefs and behaviors.

Stage Two: The Work Ethic

Individuals in this stage believe that to live is to be productive, to make things happen, to transform chaos into order, and to fulfill one's duty by earning a living. In Stage Two, we view the outer world of work as the means to our physical and emotional survival. Lacking self-responsibility for our thoughts, we fear and thus ignore our inner life—the consequence of which can result in denial, lack of self-care, and acting-out behavior, including addictions and misuse of power and money.

Leaders in this stage are driven to be productive and make things happen. Our leadership style in Stage Two is typically coercive (demanding immediate compliance) and pacesetting (expecting excellence and self-direction and setting high standards for excellence). When our motivation for effective change includes openness and willingness, as Work Ethic leaders we may refocus our leadership style to be authoritative (mobilizing people toward a vision).

Groups and organizations in this stage focus on materiality and productivity. Although community-minded, Stage Two groups do not see the impact of their work on humanity as a whole (such groups, for example, would not acknowledge the consequence of technology or business on the planet's ecology). Second stage organizations are addicted to productivity and competition at the expense of the personal wellbeing of their members. Such groups can deny individuality and adopt a collective persona. As members of Stage Two groups, lacking personal power (a sense of inner worth), we may act out our need for power or value by violating ethical principles, dominating others, telling white lies, and hungering for physical or material pleasures (sex, power, and money). It is common for these groups to project blame and engage in addictive behaviors.

Stage Three: The Missionary Attitude

Not finding personal fulfillment by laboring in the world, *individuals* in this stage seek self-identity by engaging in a social cause, in institutions, or in organized religion. In this stage, we can do much social good, although it is with the intent of having definitive answers to a broken social or spiritual world. As Stage Three individuals, our strong adherence to an absolute right way can trigger the desire to annihilate the wrong way(s). We compensate for inner feelings of powerlessness by projecting outer power—that is, our psyche attempts to rebalance its energies through an opposite action. We develop a strong personal persona at the expense of exploring and developing our inner (psychological and spiritual) life. As such, we become vulnerable to acting out what we "forbid" in ourselves and others. Our projections onto others reflect our rigidly held right-wrong thinking.

Leaders in Stage Three prefer coercive (demanding immediate compliance) and pacesetting styles, expecting excellence and self-direction and setting high standards for excellence. These styles provide Stage Three leaders with the energy (power) to initiate and sustain social causes.

Groups and organizations in this stage include religious groups, activist groups, and self-help, spiritual, and new-age organizations claiming that, "if only others used our way, the world would be saved." Through right-wrong thinking and behavior, in third-stage organizations we project our individual and group shadow onto those who oppose our group's view. As members of such groups or organizations, we are vulnerable to acting out the group's shadow in the forbidden areas of sex, power, and money. As members of Stage Three groups, we often punish or condemn those who act out traits we have forbidden in ourselves.

Stage Four: The Wounded Healer

Individuals in this stage use relationships as the final place to seek self-validation in the outer world. In Stage Four, we hope to be made whole and complete through our relationships with others. Though generous and skillful in what we do, we serve others as a means of getting our emotional needs met. We hope not to rescue but to *be* rescued. Such ideas and behavior lead to unhealthy boundaries and codependency. In this stage, we have not integrated knowledge with practice and expect others to do what we have not done ourselves. Boundary and codependency issues arise for us when we need others to meet our emotional needs. In this stage, we tend not to seek help and instead approach feelings of inadequacy by seeking answers in yet another training, book, or system of knowledge.

Leaders in this stage seek harmony, empathy, and communication in relationships. As Stage Four leaders, the leadership styles we prefer are affiliative (creating harmony and building emotional bonds) and democratic (building consensus through participation). When transitioning to the Healing the Healer stage (Stage Five), as leaders we begin to sense an early ease with mobilizing groups toward a vision and preparing them for the future.

Groups and organizations in this stage expect their members to serve (to do, to perform) at the expense of inner work. Many helping professions and self-help, human-resource, religious, spiritual, and new-age groups are in this stage. Unhealthy boundaries and codependency issues abound within Stage Four organizations. As members of these groups, we project blame onto others (including those we serve) when we don't get our emotional needs met, and this leaves us feeling betrayed and abandoned. Stage Four organizations defend against receiving help—"You people need help but we don't." We think our organization and its members can bypass inner work and self-care on behalf of caring for the needs of others. As members of these groups, we have a high incidence of mental and physical burnout.

Stage Five: Healing the Healer

When we move into this stage as *individuals,* we are self-responsible for our inner state and our outer actions and make a commitment to our psychological and spiritual well-being. We view what happens to us and others as opportunities to learn and to grow. In this stage, we view serving others as being solely about the inner state of the server. At the later phases of this stage, we see our personal healing and growth and our service as one and the same. Our vulnerabilities in this stage include pride and the projection of weakness onto others, which make us feel "special," and a tendency to be impatient for the rewards of our hard work.

As *leaders* in Stage Five, we tend to be anchored in the authoritative style (mobilizing people toward a vision) and the coaching style (developing people for the future). Our flexibility is unique—when appropriate, we can also call upon styles we used in earlier stages. Motivated to master self-awareness, self-management, social awareness, and social skills, we are oriented to teamwork and collaboration.

Groups and organizations in this stage encourage their members to do boundary and shadow work and to integrate their inner work with service (action). As members, we are encouraged by our groups to apply what we know in our work and personal lives. Some spiritual and helping professional organizations are able to work very successfully with this stage. As members of these organizations, we are susceptible to spiritual pride, believing our group has special powers, qualities, and talents to give to others that others don't have. We can project weakness onto others and not see their inner strength. Our major challenge in Stage Five groups is to give up attachment to outcome. We can deny what remains unhealed in our individual and group shadow and become impatient for rewards of our endurance and arduous efforts.

Stage Six: Selfless Action

In the Selfless Action stage of soul development, we move, as *individuals,* into full awareness that a force greater than us is the doer. While participating in the world, we become a spontaneous radiation of the Self, living and serving with equal vision and non-attachment to the fruits of our actions. At this stage, we are vulnerable to the shadow of any personal quality we have not sufficiently developed and mastered in the earlier stages.

As *leaders* in this stage, we can effectively engage in any leadership style that is required and have developed self-awareness, self-management, social awareness, and social skills.

Groups and organizations in this stage are rare in today's world. Such organizations would not speak of their inner state as being one of selfless action, as their humility is pure. The dangers for groups at this stage include relaxing their vigilance and neglecting their inner work and spiritual disciplines. They may succumb to shadow issues of sex, power, and money if they have not fully experienced and integrated all the lessons of the previous stages. Group members in Stage Six may deny weakness and be prideful of attainments.

Stage Seven: Beyond the Physical

The evolution of service continues after death. After the transition, individuals and groups may choose to become unseen helpers of those on the physical plane. Unseen helpers have different missions and are at various stages of awareness.

A Roadmap to Soul-Inspired Service

The seven stages of soul development can serve as a roadmap for each of us—as individuals, leaders, and groups—as we pursue a new way to learn, heal, and serve at this time of crisis on Planet Earth. Within every soul stage, we benefit from being supported around our concerns and vulnerabilities while capitalizing on our strengths and capabilities. Within each stage, as we follow the spiral of growth deep within ourselves, **we show ourselves another way** to be and serve in the world.

Progress through the seven stages of soul development—the seven mansions of Saint Teresa's interior castle—takes us deep within our authentic self by way of our soul's journey. The deeper we penetrate the castle, the deeper our relationship with the Divine. The deeper our relationship with the Divine, the deeper our commitment **to showing another way**—through the growth and self-actualization of our soul, through our development as spiritual beings, and, ultimately, through our soul-inspired service.

> *One act of humility is worth more*
> *than all the knowledge of the world.*
>
> ~ Saint Teresa of Ávila

To Show Another Way: Applications

Reflect on two or more of the following suggestions:

1. Select and write about the **one** stage you feel matches you at this time, including how you **show another way** to others in this stage. Remember you **cannot** be in more than one stage at a time. Write about your observations and feelings if you sense you are in transition from one stage to another.

2. If you are a leader, identify the stage you are in. Note your observations about being in this stage and how you **show others another way** as a leader. Write about your observations and feelings if you sense you are in transition from one stage to another.

3. Members of a group, company, or organization of which you are a part **can be in a different stage than you personally are in**. Consider one of the primary groups you are a part of (for example, your workplace, or your family). Note whether you and the group are in different stages and how this difference impacts your participation in and attitude toward the group. Note whether this awareness brings you understanding and compassion. How do you **show others in your group, family, company, or organization another way?**

4. Describe what you've learned about your life and what changes you'd like to make now that you know about the stages of service. Include how you would increase the times you **show others another way.**

Flying on the Inside~
The Power and Safety of Love

*It isn't outcomes that matter. It's people,
our relationships, that give meaning to our struggles.
If we free ourselves from hope and fear, from having
to succeed, we discover that it becomes easier to love.
We realize that we truly are in this together,
and that's all that matters.*

~ Margaret Wheatley

The great naturalist John Muir, living and writing at the turn of the twentieth century, was an early advocate for the preservation of the wilderness. Considered a patron saint of environmentalists, his writings have inspired millions. Muir studied and explored nature by living in it for extended periods of time. Among his most famous writings is the story of Stickeen, the pet dog who accompanied Muir on many of his outdoor adventures. The dog had an enduring and joyous relationship with Muir and liked to join him even in the middle of storms and in treacherous country. This particular story occurred on a trek across glaciers in Alaska.

The Answer to Life's Challenges

Muir discovered as night was falling that he and Stickeen faced an enormous crevasse that was passable only by a precarious, ice-sliver ledge. Muir realized that there was no alternative but to cross the deep and broad chasm by walking the narrow, ice-covered ledge.

Muir knew there was no way he could safely carry the dog across with him. With great remorse, he left the dog behind. Stickeen watched intently as Muir walked the ledge to safety. Muir looked back at the sad and lonely dog who loved him so much. At first the dog paced back and forth as he deliberated whether to walk across the ledge, facing the hope of walking safely across and the fear that he would not be able to do so.

It seemed an impossibility to Muir that the dog could make it. After much thinking and pacing, Stickeen finally decided to walk across the ledge—willing to risk his life in order to be with his beloved friend.

The dog made his way slowly across the dangerously narrow ledge. Safe at last on the other side, Stickeen instantly became wild with joy. Muir captured Stickeen's remarkable behavior at this moment in the following description:

> [Stickeen] ran and cried and barked and rolled about fairly hysterical in the sudden revulsion from the depth of despair to triumphant joy. I tried to catch him and pet him and tell him how good and brave he was, but he would not be caught. He ran round and round, swirling like autumn leaves in an eddy, lay down and rolled head over heels.

Stickeen Shows Us Another Way

Muir notes that, prior to walking across the icy ledge, Stickeen had been a rather troubled animal, distant and aloof toward human beings. After he successfully crossed the ledge, Stickeen was a delight to all he met. He had transformed into a loving and devoted dog who joyfully interacted with others. Muir wrote that Stickeen had "enlarged my life, for through him as through a window, I have ever since been looking with deeper sympathy into all my fellow mortals."

Wherever Muir went, people begged to hear the inspirational story of Stickeen, a story that reminded them of how profound and exhilarating it is to face our fears by engaging in the power and safety of love. Over time, Stickeen's story has **shown many people another way** to face their fears.

Stickeen's Gift of Service

To successfully cross the treacherous ice-sliver ledge, Stickeen needed to "fly on the inside." We, too, can cross over from fear to love when we find the inner strength and commitment to fly, to move rapidly across the many ice-sliver ledges in our life. Just as Muir could not make the choice for the dog, others cannot make this choice for us. We cherish Stickeen for showing us the loving and healing outcome of a courageous choice. His gift of service **shows us another way.**

Love was the ultimate reason Stickeen made the decision to cross—the love that he and Muir had for one another and the love the dog had for the gift of his precious life. On a spiritual level, Stickeen chose not to be separated from the Love of God that emanated through his precious friend, John Muir. Muir himself was clearly flying on the inside when he, too, crossed the icy ledge in spirit with Stickeen.

Humanity can learn from Stickeen as we face the challenge of crossing the ice-sliver ledges of the many life-threatening crises currently confronting our beloved planet. Stickeen **shows us another way** to view and experience our current critical predicament, a way that allows LOVE—for ourselves, all of humanity, and nature—to carry us from our present harmful way of living on Planet Earth to a loving, kind, and spiritual one.

Flying on the Inside

When Stickeen made his decision, acted upon it, and then triumphantly reached the other side, he felt the elation that comes when we choose *courage* (the root of which, *cor,* is the Latin word for *heart*) over fear. The personality change that came over Stickeen after his crossing suggests that, when he made the courageous choice to cross, a deep spiritual healing took place for him—as it can for us.

When we successfully cross our personal—and global—ice-sliver ledges, like

Stickeen, we are transformed from a fearful being into one who lives a life filled with love. Stickeen teaches us that we can turn our fears of human and planetary devastation founded in the current state of our collapsing world into vital actions that bring about, not only our own personal healing, but the healing and restoration of our cherished planet. Like Stickeen, each of us can find the inner strength and commitment to walk across the ice-sliver ledge—arriving safely on the other side and flying on the inside.

In every walk with nature one receives far more than he seeks.

~ JOHN MUIR

To Show Another Way: Applications

Contemplate or explore in your journal the following questions:

1. In what way is Stickeen a teacher of **showing another way** for me?

2. What is the gift I received from John Muir's reaction to Stickeen's successful crossing of the ice-sliver ledge?

3. How does learning about Stickeen's gift of service shift how I view the current upheaval of our world and the critical state of our planet?

Consciously practice using Stickeen's gift this week with family members, friends, colleagues, people you pass on the street, fellow drivers, store clerks, your helping professionals, and so forth. Ask yourself: What did I discover as a result of this practice?

Becoming the Master Gardener of Our Soul

*A man sooner or later discovers
that he is the master gardener of his soul,
the director of his life.*

~ JAMES ALLEN

We live in a world that constantly asks us to adapt to simultaneous technological, financial, political, and international crises; a world that demands we recalibrate our lives around mental and physical health challenges, relationship disturbances, family unrest, violent acts, humanitarian upheavals, and ongoing natural disasters. To survive the onslaught of such circumstances, we have two choices: pretend the situation doesn't exist by blaming others and burying our head in the sand, or face the situation and **show another way** by becoming *the master gardeners of our soul.*

James Allen, a British writer known for his inspirational books and poetry, writes:

[A] man has to learn that he cannot command things, but he can command himself, that he cannot coerce the will of others, but that he can mold and master his own will, and things serve him who serves truth, people seek guidance of him who is master of himself.

According to Allen, who coined the phrase "the master gardener of the soul," we become the director of our life by molding and mastering our will.

Becoming a Change Agent

As master gardeners of our soul, we become "change agents" on behalf of ourselves, humanity, and the planet. A change agent influences positive and constructive change directly or indirectly in how things are done and how ideas are viewed. As change agents, we are not only self-responsible for our worldview and our actions, but we also serve as teachers and guides who encourage others to be self-responsible. In other words, as change agents, we serve to **show another way.**

As master gardeners of our soul, we develop our talents and abilities. We have a passion to learn and teach others. We pass on what we have learned from our own personal struggles. We are enthusiastic and willing to learn. We have a love of all living things. We are nurturers and gentle in our manner. We accept responsibility to care for nature. We are patient and choose not to expect instant gratification. We have a forgiving nature and a sense of humor. In any given circumstance, we become, as Gandhi urged us to, the change we wish to see in the world. We are self-responsible for every decision we make and every action we take. We **show another way.**

Becoming Self-Responsible

Self-responsibility is fundamental to becoming the master gardener of our soul. It is the state of being answerable or accountable for what we think, say, and do. It requires developing *ourselves* rather than blaming others for situations and circumstances. It means *living* our values and purpose—with honor. Each of us carries the responsibility for the consequences of our choices and decisions.

Being self-responsible **shows us and others another way** according to the following tenets:

- ◆ Whenever we make a choice about anything, we are immediately responsible for that choice and for its positive or negative consequences.

◆ Self-responsibility begins within us and is expressed when we take ownership of our choices, thoughts, and reactions.

◆ Being self-responsible means we acknowledge the choices we've made that have contributed to creating what harms the world we live in as well as what helps it.

◆ When we are self-responsible, we are aware that we use our free will to make choices.

◆ Self-responsibility is the gift of being able *consciously* to make choices or to avoid making choices that benefit or harm humanity.

◆ When we are self-responsible, we understand that others are not responsible for our problems or the solutions to our problems.

◆ When we are self-responsible, we do not waste precious years believing there will be more time tomorrow than there is today.

◆ When we are self-responsible, we understand that, when things are working, we are responsible—and when they are broken and need fixing or healing, we are also responsible.

◆ When we are self-responsible, we follow the principles and laws specific to Planet Earth that result in our leading a responsible life—where we care for our personal property, pay our bills, and have a job with income that meets our needs.

◆ When we are self-responsible, we choose actions that reduce reactions, positively influencing the future of our life and of our world.

◆ When we are self-responsible, we do not deny problems or avoid responsibility for finding positive and constructive ways to solve them.

When we are self-responsible, we understand that, although we cannot control all circumstances in life, we can learn from them. We can choose to live a life of integrity, satisfaction, and fulfillment by using every circumstance to make us stronger, wiser, more knowledgeable, more skillful, and more loving.

The following anonymous "poem" succinctly summarizes the essence of self-responsibility and how to **show another way**:

I can do things on my own.
When I turn it on, I turn it off.
When I unlock something, I lock it up.
When I drop something, I pick it up.
When I open something, I close it.
When I make a mess, I clean it up.
When I find something, I return it.
When I borrow something, I give it back.
When I take something out, I put it back.
When I am assigned a task, I complete it.
When I earn money, I spend it wisely.
When I give my word, I keep it.
I choose to be self-responsible.

The Garden of Wellbeing

When we choose to practice self-responsibility, we **show another way** to ourselves and others, becoming change agents, as well as teachers and guides who encourage others to do the same. As proponents of self-responsibility in our own life, we clear the weeds of distraction and lethargy, allowing the seeds of our being to grow and thrive—which in turn allows us to show others how to do the same. When we hold fast to the garden path of self-responsibility, we are well on our way to becoming the master gardeners of our soul.

Everything you do is based on the choices you make.
It's not your parents, your past relationships, your job,
the economy, the weather, an argument
or your age that is to blame.
You and only you are responsible

for every decision and choice you make.
Period.

~ WAYNE DYER

To Show Another Way: Applications

Through the eyes of self-responsibility, reflect on the choices you have made in your life that have **shown you another way**. Ask yourself these questions:

1. In general, how have I viewed self-responsibility during the major challenging events of my life? In what ways have I been aware of being self-responsible for my thoughts and actions during these times? What were the consequences of these choices? What have I learned from these experiences?

2. Am I motivated to become the master gardener of my soul? If I *am* motivated to do so, what do I see as my next step? If I'm not motivated, why am I not?

3. What one or two choices have I made in my life that **showed another way** by impacting the quality of my life and/or the quality of the lives of others?

4. As I refer to the above poem that begins, " I can do things on my own…. ," what is my personal response (true or false) to each line? For example, do I pick something up when I drop it? Or, when I am assigned to a task, do I complete it?

Becoming a Master Gardener of Groups

Gardens are not made by singing, "Oh, how beautiful,"
and sitting in the shade.

~ RUDYARD KIPLING

In the previous teaching, we explored the spiritual imperative of personal self-responsibility. What about self-responsibility in groups? A group is defined as two or more people who have come together for a given purpose—family, friends, coworkers, classmates, committees, and so forth. Do groups have a collective responsibility? What is the responsibility of a group when all is going well? What can happen in a group when it experiences a disruption? Can responsibility be shared in a group?

The self-responsibility of members of a group is similar to the self-responsibility of individuals. Every person is responsible for his or her group experience. The ability of a group to share responsibility depends on the personal development of each group member and the willingness of each member to be self-responsible for learning how to be a member of a group. ***How we function in groups relates to the unfinished business with our first group—our family.*** If we have healed our first group relationships, we will feel more at ease and more open to learning how to be in subsequent groups. (For an extended exploration of how our family experiences influence our experience of groups, see Chapter Seven's "Discovering the Destiny of Groups.")

Becoming Group Master-Gardeners

Our awareness and evolving understanding of group consciousness has been seeded by energies and ideas of the Aquarian Era. Whereas the Piscean Era focused on the authority invested in the leader, the Aquarian Era shifts its focus to the group, embracing the authority of individual members' *inner knowing* through group cooperation and discovery. Inner knowing occurs when we receive the soul's input and insight. The Aquarian Era asks both leaders and groups to shift the style, purpose, and form of their leadership and group life. (To read more about our planet's momentous transition from the Piscean to the Aquarian Era, see "Humanity's Next Evolutionary Leap" in Chapter Two.)

Aquarian group life serves as a classroom of the soul. In this classroom, we learn how to be in a group as an expression of higher consciousness rather than individual personality. It is only when groups decide to engage wholeheartedly in the evolutionary process that they enroll in the unique curriculum of the soul classroom of group life. *Group soul lessons* provide a practical means to bring Aquarian group life into reality. Aquarian groups have the singular potential to become group master-gardeners.

The Soul Lessons of Groups

The group master-gardener course of study consists of five soul lessons, all of which **show another way** to be a responsible member of a group. The first four lessons are *shared vision, greater good, right relations,* and *service.* Once a group has mastered these four lessons, it can attain the ultimate soul lesson—*to stand strong in group consciousness.* Each soul lesson has challenges and integrates experience with knowledge unique to each stage of soul development. Practicing co-responsibility will shift existing groups and bring new groups into reality.

Shared Vision

The soul lesson of shared vision serves as the underpinning that supports all other soul lessons of group life. A group successfully creates and manifests a shared vision when it learns: (1) how to translate personal vision into shared vision; (2) how to develop, ground, and sustain a shared vision; and (3) how to evolve a shared holographic philosophical framework.

Greater Good

To understand and apply the concept of a group's greater good is a complex and profound group soul lesson. For a group to learn this soul lesson depends on its emotional, mental, and spiritual maturity; on the development of its members' intuition and will; and on the practice of synthesis within the group.

Greater good is an ideal of the group mind. Greater good means more good for the entire group, including each individual in the group. The greater good for the group *is* the greater good of the individual, and vice versa. Greater good as applied to groups has *cooperation* at its heart—*living* goodwill and *being* the will to good. Greater good is the embodiment of sisterhood and brotherhood.

Right Relations

The right relations group soul lesson determines the physical, emotional, and spiritual health of the group. Right relations foster cooperation and group consciousness among group members. The right relations soul lesson for groups includes three values: healthy boundaries, friendship, and integrity. All three values are spiritual principles that hold the intention to see the soul in others and create partnership and group consciousness among group members.

Service

The group soul lesson of service is unique in that it integrates the previous soul lessons of *shared vision, greater good,* and *right relations.* This integration occurs when groups learn to see the bigger picture or destiny of their group and practice **True Service,** viewing their service as a classroom for spiritual development and group transformation.

To Stand Strong in Group Consciousness

To attain the Aquarian values of partnership, cooperation, and standing strong in group consciousness, groups must first master the four group soul lessons of *shared vision, greater good, right relations,* and *service.* When the first four soul lessons have been assimilated, the group is open to and can embrace the fusion of the group personality with the Group Soul. A significantly increased and vitalized energy now begins to move through the group as the Group Soul's energies flow unimpeded through the group instrument, bringing greater service into its sphere of influence.

Groups of the Future

The time has come to welcome and support groups as they bring their next evolutionary step into reality. To do this, as leaders and group members we are called to discover the potential of "groups of the future." There can be no delay, as the future has arrived. We must remember that we are, in fact, *one* group… the group of humankind. Regardless of what challenges lie ahead, it is time to stand strong in the Light and claim our True Voice. It is time, as group master-gardeners, **to show our group and other groups another way** to tend our plots (to be in groups) so they may sprout, grow, and blossom into the splendid and bountiful gardens they are destined to be.

> *A society grows great*
> *when old men plant trees*
> *whose shade they know*
> *they shall never sit in.*
>
> ~ GREEK PROVERB

To Show Another Way: Applications

Select a current group in which you participate as a member or a leader. Contemplate or respond in your journal to the following questions regarding this group:

1. What is the group's purpose?

2. In what ways is the group practicing or not practicing co-responsibility for attaining its purpose?

3. Identify the primary soul lesson your group is currently working on. How might the group leader and members be co-responsible for learning about and practicing this soul lesson in your group meetings? (Include yourself as leader or group member.)

Becoming a Master Gardener of Nature

Nature is probably our greatest healing resource.
From the plants, we gain medicines and beauty.
From the trees, we get fruit and strength.
The stones gift us with color, light, and electrical
frequencies of health. And the animals
guide, teach, and protect us.
We are blessed by Nature. It touches each of us
in personal and special ways.

~ TED ANDREWS

Not until I moved to Alaska in the 1960s and participated in a research project sponsored by the Arctic Health Research Center did I fully appreciate the spiritual power of nature. As the research team audiologist, I flew by bush plane or traveled by dog sled to various villages across Alaska, testing the hearing of three-to-five-year-old Inuit children. Hearing loss is a major health issue for Alaskan natives from an early age due to chronic middle-ear disease. This disease often results in a severe infection requiring major surgery and causing deafness. The center's research concerns included issues of medical treatment for the disease and the age of its onset.

One of my flights by bush plane flew to the village of Eek, whose river flowed into the Bering Sea. The instant I saw the Bering Sea, I became overwhelmed by its radiant beauty. My awareness suddenly expanded as an intense, peace-filled energy entered every cell of my body. Only later, upon reflection, did I realize I had tapped into the energy of Providence, the protective care of God and spiritual power of nature, the purpose of which is to sustain and guide our destiny.

I traveled to many other villages and survived a number of accidents that took place during the bush plane landings and takeoffs. My awareness of Providence and initiation into the spiritual power of nature stayed with me the entire time. Providence continues **to show me another way**—by sustaining, inspiring, and guiding me to be a master gardener of nature during this time of crisis on our beloved planet—and to encourage others to do the same.

Healing from Nature-Deficit Disorder

The first step in becoming a master gardener of nature is **to show another way** to humanity. As a group, we have failed to fully recognize and appreciate the physical, psychological, and spiritual gifts that nature generously and unselfishly offers us. Richard Louv, author of *Last Child in the Woods: Saving Our Children from Nature-Deficit Disorder*, asserts that both adults and children are not receiving nature's gifts and are becoming alienated from nature because they spend less time outdoors. This has resulted in a wide range of behavioral problems he calls "nature-deficit disorder."

Louv reports on the results of ten research studies that document how we can benefit from increased contact with nature. In countless ways, nature **shows us another way** to learn, heal, and serve at this time of crisis on Planet Earth. Louv shows how nature improves our memory, helps us recuperate, and brings our senses alive. He notes that we are hardwired not only to need exposure to the natural world, but to *love* our contact with nature. We suffer pain when the place where we reside is not connected in some way to nature.

We become master gardeners of nature when we bring nature into our life more fully, slowing down our pace, monitoring our busyness, and increasing our sense of peacefulness. Louv offers many ways to do this in his book and other writings (see bibliography for references), as do various sources regarding work-life balance, detoxing from technology overload, and general health and wellness.

Helping Wildlife

The second step in becoming a master gardener of nature is to own our responsibility for the care and wellbeing of wildlife. The wildlife in our urban and suburban environments is barely surviving. Any action we can take, no matter how small, can help restore the world to its natural balance. Consider some of the following ideas to support the wildlife in your immediate environment:

- ◆ Engage in Sacred Activism, a transforming force of compassion in action that calls on courage, wisdom, love, and passion. The focus of Sacred Activism is to become a force for preserving and healing Planet Earth and its inhabitants. Seek out the work of Andrew Harvey, founder and director of the Institute for Sacred Activism, for practical guidance on how to become a Sacred Activist.

- ◆ Connect with the Perelandra Center for Nature Research, an organization that works with the intelligence inherent in nature and teaches methods to care for our health, our gardens, our home and work environments, and our planet. In addition to its unique processes for working with nature intelligence and energy medicine, Perelandra provides excellent resources on practical ways to live sustainably in our own homes and communities.

- ◆ Do some internet research on simple ways you can support wildlife in your own backyard. Some ideas include minimizing landscaping to preserve animal habitats, refusing to use pesticides, keeping cats indoors to prevent them from killing birds, and finding an alternative to bug zappers and tiki torches, which attract and kill far more bugs than are in your immediate vicinity and which would otherwise serve as food sources for other wildlife.

Loving Planet Earth

The third step in becoming a master gardener of nature is **to show another way** by actively joining with others in specific ways to heal our planet. This includes praying for the health and wellbeing of nature and radiating Love and Light to all who call Planet Earth their Home. (For specific instructions on how to radiate Love and Light to the Earth, see Chapter One's teaching "S.O.S. ~ Pray for Planet Earth.") Sufi teacher Llewellyn Vaughan-Lee writes in his book *Including the Earth in our Prayers*:

> It is our love for the Earth that will heal what we have desecrated, that will guide us throughout this wasteland, helping our dying Earth to regenerate, and help[ing] us to bring light back into our darkening world. Love links us all together in the most mysterious ways, and love can guide our hearts and hands.

The fourth step in becoming a master gardener of nature is to acknowledge how nature continuously and in multiple ways **shows us another way** to live on Planet Earth. To love Earth is to rekindle our wonder of its animals and plants, its trees and insects. Nature speaks to us every day in the sound of wind in the trees, the loving gaze of a pet, the slow rising of a harvest moon. If we develop a higher perception of Earth's reality and welcome its knowledge, we will recognize that nature is an integral part of a joyous human life.

The books of gifted teacher Ted Andrews—*Animal Speak: The Spiritual and Magical Powers of Creatures Great and Small* and *Nature-Speak: Signs, Omens and Messages in Nature*—deepen our love of nature's magical ways. He writes:

> When we choose to walk the path of Nature, we open ourselves to initiation. Initiation has taken on many meanings in recent years, but simply put, it is a beginning. It is a beginning of new perceptions. It leads to an awakening of deeper levels of consciousness.

Andrews **shows us another way** to understand and be with the natural world that invites us to become more peaceful and loving. Receiving his teachings into our life for study and contemplation is another way to express our love for Planet Earth and support our becoming master gardeners of nature.

Restoring the Garden of Our Planet

We can learn from nature. We can speak to nature and nature can speak to us. We can invite nature to become our teacher and our companion. We can walk together with nature, and we can heal together. As master gardeners of nature, we can steward with love and honor the magnificent garden that is our planet—and help restore our world to the paradise it was always meant to be.

> *The glory of gardening:*
> *hands in the dirt, head in the sun,*
> *heart with nature. To nurture a garden*
> *is to feed not just the body,*
> *but the soul.*
>
> ~ ALFRED AUSTIN

To Show Another Way: Applications

1. Nature needs our prayers and Light as much as it needs us to clean up its rivers and recycle our trash. Choose one of the following teachings to review and practice anew its applications that **show another way** to live and serve on Planet Earth:

   ◆ Chapter One's "S.O.S. ~ Pray for Planet Earth"
   ◆ Chapter Five's "Radiating Light to All That Is"
   ◆ The last teaching of this chapter: "Becoming a Master Gardener of the World"

2. Consider the ideas discussed in this teaching for bringing nature more fully into

your life. Choose one or two ideas that particularly appeal to you. How might you make time daily or weekly to bring these ideas into being?

Becoming a Master Gardener of the World

Walk as if you are kissing the Earth with your feet.

Every step we make should be peace.
Each step we make should be joy.
Each step we make should be happiness.
If we are determined, we can do it.
We don't need the future.
We can smile and relax.
Everything we want is right here in the present moment.

Walk as if you are kissing the Earth with your feet.

~ Thich Nhất Hanh

As the chaos of our world intensifies, we search for ways to help and bring love, care, and compassion into the world. Some questions that can inform this search include: What is the greatest need in our world today? How do we connect with our inner strength? What service can each of us extend to humanity? How can we restore nature to its rightful beauty and purpose?

We can answer these questions by becoming *master gardeners of the world*. Does this feel like too grand a title for you, or an intimidating premise? Do you wonder if you're up to the task? How we become master gardeners of the world may surprise you. Master gardeners of the world

- ◆ recognize that the greatest need in today's world is that it needs more Light,
- ◆ connect to the Sacred Within, experiencing their inner strength and trusting their willingness and ability to be a Force of Light, and
- ◆ offer their highest service to humanity by breathing Light into the world.

In other words, master gardeners of the world **show another way** by bringing Light onto our planet and into our day-to-day interactions, tasks, doings, and beings. *How do they do this?* Being a master gardener of the world is at once the simplest and most natural role we can possibly play. In fact, it is our *birthright*.

The Gift of the *Hamsa* Mantra

One of the most powerful ways to become a master gardener of the world is to chant the *Hamsa* mantra throughout the day, either silently or aloud. The *Hamsa* mantra is a balance between the out-breath and in-breath of God. Our in-breath is from God; our out-breath (from God) adds to the Light of the world. **We thereby extend God's Life Force into the world with our breath, serving the highest good of humanity and the planet**. *This is true for every breath we take.*

Hamsa means "I am That—That I am." "I" is individual self-awareness. "That" is the unlimited consciousness of the Universal Self, also referred to as the I AM Presence, Divine Source, the God Within, Father-Mother God, the Unknowable Absolute, and the Life Force. The *Hamsa* mantra affirms our connection with the Divine and thus supports our remembering that we are not alone.

The *Hamsa* mantra (also called the natural or *prana* mantra) goes on continually in all living creatures. It is due to the *Hamsa* mantra pulsation that we are alive. In the living human body, the breath comes in and goes out 21,600 times a day. Each time, it repeats this mantra. All living beings breathe the *Hamsa* mantra continuously, day and night—*Ham* on the in-breath, *sa* on the out-breath—again and again: *Ham... sa... Ham... sa...*

In real time, we add to the Light of the world; as we do so, we reflect back to God our gift of life. **By adjusting our awareness about every breath we take**, no matter where we are or what we are doing, thinking, or feeling, we add Light to the world. With our out-breath, we ask that every thought, feeling, and deed be consecrated with Divine Love for the purpose of adding to the Light of the world. In this process, we become Lightbearers, those who **show another way** to serve with love and compassion.

The *Hamsa* Mantra Meditation

The *Hamsa* mantra meditation is a simple technique of quietly watching our breath come in and go out, without doing anything else. As the breath comes in, it makes the sound *Ham* (pronounced *h-ah-m*), meaning **"I breathe in the Light of God."** As the breath goes out, it makes the sound *sa* (pronounced *s-ah*), meaning **"I breathe out God's Light to the world."**

Acknowledge trust in your ability to be a force of Light by affirming from your heart: **"I breathe in the Light of God"** *(on the in-breath)*... **"I breathe out God's Light to the world"** *(on the out-breath)*.

MEDITATION PRACTICE

NOTE: You may use the following practice for either a sitting or a walking meditation, breathing in while saying *Ham* silently and breathing out while saying *sa* silently.

For sitting meditation: Sit upright with a straight spine, but comfortably. Join the index finger and thumb of each hand and rest your hands on your knees with your palms turned upwards.

Close your eyes. Breathe naturally.

Repeat the mantra **silently**: *Ham* on the in-breath, *sa* on the out-breath.

Concentrate on the mantra. Become absorbed in it. Move into meditation, releasing your repetition of the mantra. Bring your attention back to the mantra when you are distracted by thoughts, feelings, or sounds.

Meditate for 20 minutes or for a period of time that is comfortable for you.

Pillars of Light

With every breath we take, we inhale and exhale the breath of God, the breath of Light. When we do this consciously, we become self-responsible for the various roles we were born to play—as master gardeners of our soul, of groups, of nature, and of the world itself.

When we become aware that we are breathing the breath of God, we become pillars of radiant Light for our world: for those we live and work with, for whatever we choose to focus upon—indeed, for everyone and everything that crosses our path. Most importantly, we become pillars of Light who are destined to serve the greater good of our planet and its epochal evolution into the fifth dimension.

By breathing in the Light of God and breathing out God's Light into the world, **we show another way** to learn, heal, and serve at this time of crisis on Planet Earth. It is when we claim our role as pillars of Light in service to the planet that we claim our sacred responsibility—and our Divine birthright—to be master gardeners of the world.

Let every moment be filled with light.
When you know and experience every moment as love, as light,
you preserve your energy, you increase your luster and enthusiasm.

~ Swami Chidvilasananda

To Show Another Way: Applications

◆ Practice the *Hamsa* Mantra as a walking or sitting meditation, especially in the morning and evening or when distraught and seeking peace and calm.

◆ Contemplate thoughts and feelings that arise as you affirm, "My highest service to humanity is to breathe Light into the world. In this way, I am becoming a master gardener of the world."

....

Teetering on the Precipice of Destiny

No precipice can challenge you if you have the ability
to build bridges over any kind of precipice.
The more you fear the precipice,
the [steeper] the precipice will be.

~MEHMET MURAT İLDAN,
TURKISH AUTHOR AND PLAYWRIGHT

Joined as one human race, we find ourselves dangerously teetering on the edge of a precipice. Will we choose to build bridges across the precipice that heal the planet? Or are we destined to plummet into a deep crevice and face further death and devastation? As individuals and as a collective, will we heedlessly allow humanity to bring about its own destruction, or will we choose a destiny that brings humanity and Planet Earth back from the brink of disaster?

For decades, with our fellow countrymen and the rest of the world, we have been leading ourselves to the edge of this precipice, closing our eyes to the reality that our beloved planet is in life-threatening ecological distress. We know that the precipice is steep and hazardous. Yet we continue to perpetuate a world driven by greed and ignorance, a world in which we continue to neglect learning how to care for and cherish Mother Earth. Nature is abused and sobs with pain… as do so many of the world's people, who are suffering from all forms of brutality, inequality, and injustice.

Reader, I invite you to read the following slowly and aloud:

Humanity teeters on the precipice of destiny. Can I recognize the truth in front of me? I stand on the brink of disaster where life on Earth is coming unglued. The truth hits me hard; it nearly knocks me off my feet. With courage and determination, I ask myself: Will I ignore the dangers and fail to build a bridge to safety? Or will I choose to learn how to heal and serve the wellbeing of Planet Earth and all who live upon it? Will I allow myself to continue disregarding the welfare of our world by falling into a chasm of defeat? Or will I remember that it is self-confidence that builds the bridge over which humanity can safely cross the precipice?

*Will **I** make a commitment to do **my** part, joining kindred spirits who are taking action to span the precipice of our destiny to heal our planet and all who make it their Home?*

Enthusiastic Participation

Two options lay before us: resignation or enthusiastic participation. We can either resign ourselves to failure and slowly drain our spirit into denial and complacency, or we can enthusiastically step back from the precipice and find new and creative solutions to rescue ourselves and Planet Earth. If we choose enthusiastic participation, we focus our attention and actions on safety, care, correction, preservation, and a worldview that acknowledges our planet as a living being in crisis. We practice the Chinese translation of crisis—"opportunity"—by viewing teetering on the precipice as an ***opportunity* to show another way to ourselves and others.**

When we engage in enthusiastic participation, we experience a shared vision and a collective will. Our common destiny is an unrealized potential within us that persists in its yearning to be fulfilled. We view Earth as a school, the purpose of which is to learn, heal, and serve. Our lives offer multiple opportunities to "give away" what we have learned… **to show another way** to live and serve at this time of crisis on Planet Earth.

Although redefining ourselves is scary, it is by doing so that we discover who we truly are. We need no longer let separation and hardship define us. Engaged in enthusiastic participation, we are empowered to maintain forward momentum. We keep our internal fire alive. We heal and enjoy the adventure that is our life, regardless of circumstances. We are committed to embrace adventures we have not yet even imagined.

We Become the Mountain

Now is the time to be courageous and open our eyes to the truth of what is happening on our planet. We can no longer afford, as if we were Scarlett O'Hara, to "think about it tomorrow." We can't wait for someone else, or some group that does not include us, to magically swoop in and save our planet. Each of us, not just a select few, is responsible for turning every life event into learning, healing, and service.

Our individual voices can mobilize the hearts and minds of those in our homes, workplaces, communities, states, and countries. Many individuals, groups, and countries are already initiating and supporting projects around the world that address various local and world problems and which offer new ideas for healing Planet Earth. We know now that Earth is a school that teaches us how **to show ourselves and others another way** to live completely and well.

Several years ago, I wrote a poem about the journey of our life on Planet Earth. Recently, I found myself adapting it to reflect the arduous challenges and splendid opportunities of the present moment, unique in the history of our world. May the spirit of its message serve you as you strive **to show yourself and others another way**—today and for years to come.

We Become the Mountain

The spiritual mountain, a steep path to climb.
A journey made alone, though it need not be lonely.
Joined by others, we pass and are passed.
We meet teachers and stop to learn;
We meet students and stop to teach.
If, on the edge of a precipice, we teeter,
Gentle fellow travelers remind us:
"Self-confidence is the bridge to overcoming a precipice."

To extend helping hands is the vow of all.
To save humanity, to rescue Planet Earth.

Passing through the cave of darkness,
Resolving obstacles, progress unhindered,
Ever free to rest and reflect.
Gathering strength, embracing confidence.
Remembering the sun still shines even on a cloudy day.

At last, we stand strong at the top of the mountain.
Embraced by the Light of the Unknowable Absolute,
Grateful we have done our part,
Safe and secure in the knowledge of the True Self,
We save humanity and Planet Earth.

We become the mountain.

APPENDICES

Table of Topics

Cited and Quoted Authors

Table of Practices

Study Guide for Leaders of Support Circles

APPENDIX I

....

TABLE OF TOPICS

Although this book has been structured as a year-long study with the teachings progressing from introductory to more advanced, you might choose instead to focus on a certain teaching or topic that addresses a current and urgent need. This Table of Topics is provided to help you locate teachings that address each of the book's twelve subject areas. A Table of Practices (Appendix II) is also offered for easy access to the various practices, such as meditations and prayers, included throughout the book.

Seeing the Bigger Picture of Life on Earth

Taking Humanity's Next Evolutionary Leap

Honoring Commitment and Self-Responsibility

Knowing What Really Matters in Life

Helping Nature Heal

Radiating Light

Living Our Destiny

Engaging in Personal Healing

Joining Heart and Mind

Loving Our Will

Receiving the Gift of Spirituality

Serving Others and the Planet

TABLE OF PRACTICES

INDEX OF CITED AND QUOTED AUTHORS

TO SHOW ANOTHER WAY
SUPPORT CIRCLES

STUDY GUIDE FOR LEADERS

To Show Another Way can be worked with in Support Circles that study and apply its teachings. This Guide is intended to assist those who wish to lead such a Support Circle with well-tested structures for keeping the group on purpose and maximizing its members' understanding and practice of the book's teachings.

Group Structures

Structures suggested for Support Circles include:

- Group Purpose Statement
- Sample Agenda for Support Circle Meetings
- Group Soul Alignment
- Group Communication Guidelines
- Healthy Boundaries in Groups: Creating a Safe Space
- Meditation Practices

Structures not only keep groups on purpose, they create a sense of safety and trust within the group. Because *To Show Another Way*'s applications require members to do shadow work at a very deep level, it is essential that group members feel safe in the group for the Support Circle to work effectively. As you will have learned from reading this book, groups that come together without an awareness of their vulnerabilities (such as triggers and projections) and without a container for supporting them (such as the above-named structures) can activate in group members past family, school, and other early traumas.

It is recommended that you use all of the structures rather than picking and choosing among them, and use them as written. They have been developed and refined over many years in countless groups and are included here to support you in creating a group that is productive and nurturing for all group members—including the leader.

Preparing to Lead

Before you embark upon leading a Support Circle, you are strongly encouraged to review the teachings on leadership and groups in this book and to work with their applications. The primary teachings on leadership and groups can be found in Chapter Seven:

- ◆ Awakening Leaders and Groups
- ◆ Living the Destiny of Leadership
- ◆ Discovering the Destiny of Groups

Whether leading a country, a corporation, a family, or a Support Circle, any experience in which we serve as a leader is a unique opportunity to learn about our leadership challenges and vulnerabilities and consequently to purify our leadership shadow. These chapters will continue to support you in your growth as a leader if you work with them over time—and what you learn from leading your Support Circle can subsequently be applied to your leadership in any arena. To deepen your awareness of and understanding about your personal leadership challenges, you are encouraged to study *The Soul and Service Trilogy,* which explores in depth our personal shadow of service, the challenges faced by leaders and groups, and ways to grow and evolve as individuals, leaders, and group members.

Why the Group Needs a Leader

In certain groups, in an attempt to be democratic or to share responsibility, the group will try to function by purposely not appointing a leader or by changing the leader at regular intervals so that each group member takes turns serving in the role. **It is vital that a single person serve as the leader of the group.** Without a leader, a void is created into which the strongest personality—though not necessarily the most competent—will rush in. The leader, through preparation and awareness, is a step ahead of group members and as such will keep the group coherent. Through his or her consistent leadership, the group will grow in competence and trust.

Why the Group Should Remain SMALL

The larger a group is, the more variables are involved. All members in a group bring with them a number of variables in addition to their family shadow, including their age/generation, personal biases, past school trauma, personality type, and so forth. The larger the group, the harder it becomes for the leader to manage all these variables. According to research, the perfect size for a group is *eight* members. For your wellbeing as the leader and for the health of the group, a group can be smaller than eight members but should not be larger.

How to Work with this Book in Groups

Some ideas for working with *To Show Another Way* are included in the section "How to Work with this Book" and can be used beneficially in Support Circles. In the first meeting of the Circle, leaders might ask members to take the two inventories listed in this section, which will give group members a starting place to begin applying the teachings to their lives. As group leader, you might also choose to work through the book with your group over the course of one year, as suggested in this section, with the group meeting weekly for review and support.

Also in this section, the subsection entitled "The Power of Commitment: Guiding Principles" will be important for your group to review. You could lead the group to read these principles together in the first meeting, as well as periodically when the group meets. Encouraging and supporting the commitment of group members to stay with the more challenging aspects of this book—which is to say, with the more challenging aspects of their own inner work—will be fundamental to the group's cohesion.

The Sample Agenda included in this Guide suggests a supportive structure for the ongoing work of the group. This method invites the group to read together an individual teaching from the book and to discuss the teaching one section at a time, allowing the group to cover one teaching in any given two-hour session.

Showing Another Way

If you feel called to start a Support Circle or to participate in one, it is a sign that fate has tapped you on the shoulder and called you to action. To study and apply the teachings in this book is to accept the support of **being shown another way** to live and be at this time of crisis on Planet Earth. To do this work as a leader or member of a Support Circle is to rise to another level of commitment and service: as group members commit to themselves and to each other to learn, heal, and serve through the group study and practice of these teachings, they **show another way** to others to learn, heal, and serve.

As leaders and group members ushering in a new era of healing and peace for our planet, I wish you great joy on your destiny journey!

Group Purpose Statement

To study and apply the teachings of *To Show Another Way: How to Learn, Heal, and Serve at a Time of Crisis on Planet Earth* in a safe and nurturing Support Circle.

Sample Agenda for Support Circle Meetings (for a two-hour session)

ESTIMATED
TIME
NEEDED
(IN MINUTES)

10	OPENING—Group Soul Alignment
15	GROUP COMMUNICATION GUIDELINES *Read all guidelines aloud; select one to briefly discuss.*
15	HEALTHY GROUP BOUNDARIES *The leader selects one or two items listed in this Guide and invites group members to share how they can be applied in the group. Do this at each meeting until the group has reviewed all of the boundary items. (Refer to Chapter Seven's teaching "Discovering the Destiny of Groups" for a discussion of healthy boundaries in a group.)*
60	TEACHING

Step One: *Select one teaching to read aloud as a group. Ask someone in the group to read the first section of the teaching aloud. Group members then have an open discussion of the meaning and examples of the first section as it applies to their lives. Once this feels complete, another group member reads the second section, again followed by an open discussion of the meaning and examples as applied to their lives. Continue in this manner until the entire teaching is read aloud and discussed.*

Step Two: *The group explores one or more of the teaching's applications.*

Step Three: *Suggest group members work with the applications between group meetings.*

5   GROUP ACKNOWLEDGMENTS

Each member completes this sentence aloud: "What I appreciate today (this evening) as a member of this group is _____."

15   CLOSING MEDITATION

Choices:

◆ *Prayer for Planet Earth (Chapter 1, Teaching 4)*

◆ *Hamsa Mantra Meditation (Chapter 12, Teaching 4)*

◆ *The Great Invocation (Chapter 9, Teaching 1)*

◆ *Radiating Light to All that Is (Chapter 5, Teaching 4)*

Group Support Structures

GROUP SOUL ALIGNMENT

Purpose: To align each group member with the Group Soul, which protects, guides, teaches, and inspires group members. The alignment allows the individual personalities of group members to receive input and insight from their individual Souls and the Group Soul.

When to Align: Group members can do the alignment before a meeting or class as can the leader. Members can also begin each day with the Group Soul Alignment.

Directions: Explain to those new to this alignment that the human soul (lower case "s") is located in the heart. Therefore, the words "heart" and "human soul," below, are used interchangeably. Each individual's Soul (capital "S") is located about eight inches above the head. The Group Soul can be visualized at an elevated level in the center of the group. *Pause at least 10 seconds between each step.*

1.   Take three deep breaths to calm your physical body. (pause)

2.   Take three deep breaths to calm your emotional body. (pause)

3.   Take three deep breaths to calm your mental body. (pause)

4. Focus your awareness in your heart.

5. Visualize a line of energy extending from your heart down to the heart of the Mother of the Earth.

6. Visualize a line of energy from your heart to your Soul, located above your head.

7. Visualize the energy extending from your Soul to the Group Soul. The Group Soul can be visualized at an elevated level in the center of the group.

8. Visualize the energy extending from each member's Soul, located above the head, to the Group Soul.

9. Visualize the energy extending from the Group Soul to Divine Source.

10. Sit in silence as you hold this alignment from the heart of the Mother of the Earth to Divine Source. See the energy of Source moving down the alignment to the heart of the Mother of the Earth and then back again to Source, creating a circuit of energy carrying the Divine Will for the _To Show Another Way_ Support Circle to all levels of manifestation. (Sit in silence for a few moments.)

GROUP COMMUNICATION GUIDELINES

1. I speak from my own experience, from the "Responsible I." I can only speak for myself. I cannot speak for what is true for someone else.

2. I help to create a safe space by supporting the other members of the group to speak their truth; I do not impose my interpretation on another's sharing.

3. I honor the confidentiality of all sharing by not discussing anyone's sharing outside the group.

4. I am emotionally present with the group and do not interrupt or offer unasked-for advice. This includes not bridging off another person's sharing.

5. I honor using economy of speech as I share, speaking succinctly and allowing time for those to share who have not shared.

6. I value and respect communication, healthy boundaries, and timeliness and apply this understanding in the group.

7. I note whether a group member has completed her/his expression, verbally and emotionally. I wait for the speaker to indicate or say **"I am complete"** before beginning to speak.

8. As a listener, I observe my inner thoughts. Am I really listening? Am I in the present moment? Am I aware of and honoring the person's timing and pacing?

HEALTHY BOUNDARIES IN GROUPS: CREATING A SAFE SPACE

Physical Boundaries

- ◆ Cleanliness, orderliness, pleasantness of physical environment
- ◆ Available supplies and materials
- ◆ Respecting use of private workspace
- ◆ No phone interruptions
- ◆ Respecting use of equipment
- ◆ Awareness of inappropriate physical touching and hugging
- ◆ Time agreements
- ◆ Owning projections and assumptions
- ◆ Safety (doors, awareness of strangers)

Mental/Emotional Boundaries

- ◆ Acknowledging and practicing Group Communication Guidelines
- ◆ Respecting commitments
- ◆ Respecting time agreements
- ◆ Keeping one's word
- ◆ Being self-responsible for projections, attitudes, and behavior
- ◆ Working constructively with differences and conflict
- ◆ Owning age regression, triangling
- ◆ Owning projections; doing inner work
- ◆ Understanding and honoring dual relationships
- ◆ Understanding and honoring group dynamics and group development
- ◆ Willingness to unearth mental models
- ◆ Understanding that "mistakes" are really steps in learning
- ◆ Honoring and staying on course with the group's purpose, vision, and mission
- ◆ Honoring confidentiality

Spiritual Boundaries

- ◆ Acknowledging all paths and traditions
- ◆ Honoring personal choice

Personal Inquiry Questions for Group Members

- ◆ What unhealthy boundaries am I vulnerable to when I am in a group?

- ◆ What tendencies do I have that might invade the boundaries of others in a group? What inner work might I need to do? How can I handle this in a self-responsible way?

- ◆ How do I experience others in a group intruding on my boundaries? Am I triggered? What inner work might I need to do? How can I handle this in a self-responsible way?

Meditation Practices

Choose a practice from one of these teachings:

- ◆ Prayer for Planet Earth, (Chapter 1, Teaching 4)
- ◆ *Hamsa* Mantra Meditation (Chapter 12, Teaching 4)
- ◆ The Great Invocation (Chapter 9, Teaching 1)

Need assistance? Email faculty@showanotherway.org

BIBLIOGRAPHY

Allen, James. *As A Man Thinketh: Original 1902 Edition.* Charles Conrad, editor. Scotts Valley, CA: CreateSpace Independent, 2017.

Andrews, Ted. *Animal Speak: The Spiritual and Magical Powers of Creatures Great and Small.* Woodbury, MN: Llewellyn, 2002.

Andrews, Ted. *Nature-Speak: Signs, Omens and Messages in Nature.* Jackson, TN: Dragonhawk, 2004.

Assagioli, Roberto. *The Act of Will.* Amherst, MA: Synthesis Center, 2010.

Assagioli, Roberto. *Psychosynthesis: A Collection of Basic Writings.* Amherst, MA: Synthesis Center, 2012.

Association for Research and Enlightenment. Edgar Cayce's A.R. E. (website). http://www.edgarcayce.org/ .

Bartocci, Barbara. "I Forgive My Daughter's Killer." *Good Housekeeping,* August 1993.

Bolen, Jean Shinoda. *Goddesses in Everywoman: Powerful Archetypes in Women's Lives.* New York: Harper, 2014.

Bolen, Jean Shinoda. *Gods in Everyman: Archetypes that Shape Men's Lives.* 25th Anniversary ed. New York: Harper, 2014.

Brown, Molly Young. *Unfolding Self: The Practice of Psychosynthesis.* New York: Helios, 2004.

Buonarroti, Michelangelo. *Complete Poems and Selected Letters of Michelangelo.* Trans. Creighton Gilbert. Princeton, NJ: Princeton UP, 1980.

Campbell, Joseph. *Pathways to Bliss: Mythology and Personal Transformation.* The Collected Works of Joseph Campbell, ed. David Kudler. Novato, CA: New World Library, 2004.

Chidvilasananda, Swami. *Enthusiasm.* South Fallsburg, NY: Siddha Yoga, 1997.

Cooper, J.C. *An Illustrated Encyclopaedia of Traditional Symbols.* London: Thames and Hudson, 1987.

A Course in Miracles. Mill Valley, CA: Foundation for Inner Peace, 1976.

DeRohan, Ceanne. *Right Use of Will: Healing and Evolving the Emotional Body.* Santa Fe, NM: Four Winds, 2010.

Drucker, Peter F. *The Practice of Management.* Philadelphia: Routledge, 2017.

Entering the Age of Light. Gathering Wave Press, July 2012. E-book (HTML). http://whenthesoulawakens.org/etaol-unzipped_456.html .

"Eyes are Windows to the Soul." Exploring Your Mind (website). June 30, 2016. http://www.exploringyourmind.com/eyes-windows-soul/ .

Ferrucci, Piero. *What We May Be: Techniques for Psychological and Spiritual Growth through Psychosynthesis.* Los Angeles: Tarcher/Penguin, 2004.

Gordon, Jan. "Top Ten Truths About Commitment." Quality Coaching (website). 2001. www.qualitycoaching.com/Articles/commitment.html .

Greaves, Helen. *Testimony of Light: An Extraordinary Message of Life After Death.* 1st American ed. New York: Penguin, 2009.

Hạnh, Thích Nhất. *Creating True Peace: Ending Conflict in Yourself, Your Family, Your Community, and the World.* New York: Atria, 2004.

Harvey, Andrew. Institute for Sacred Activism (website). www.andrewharvey.net .

Harvey, Andrew, and Carolyn Baker. *Savage Grace: Living Resiliently in the Dark Night of the Globe.* Bloomington, IN: iUniverse, 2017.

Hawkins, David R. *Power vs. Force: The Hidden Determinants of Human Behavior.* Carlsbad, CA: Hay House, 2014.

Higson, Phil, and Anthony Sturgess. "Leadership Quality." The Happy Manager (website). www.the-happy-manager.com/articles/leadership-quality/ .

Hyman, Mark. "Why We All Lie, How It Messes Up Our Lives and How to Fix It, with Lauren Zander." *The Doctor's Farmacy with Mark Hyman, M.D.* (podcast). April 24, 2019. https://podcasts.apple.com/us/podcast/why-we-all-lie-how-it-messes-up-our-lives-how-to-fix/id1382804627?i=1000436260680 .

Johnson, Robert A. *Owning Your Own Shadow: Understanding the Dark Side of the Psyche.* New York: HarperCollins, 1994.

Jung, C.G. "The Fight with the Shadow." *Listener*, November 7, 1946.

Jung, C.G. *Memories, Dreams, Reflections.* Trans. Richard and Clara Winston. London: William Collins, 2019.

Kelly, John, "Chipmunks, dogs and shopping carts: Delving into the reader mail bag," *The Washington Post*, local section, September 16, 2013.

King, Ross. *Michelangelo and the Pope's Ceiling.* New York: Bloomsbury, 2014.

Kubler-Ross, Elisabeth. *The Wheel of Life: A Memoir of Living and Dying.* New York: Simon & Schuster, 1997.

Levine, Stephen. *Becoming Kuan Yin: The Evolution of Compassion*. San Francisco: Red Wheel/Weiser, 2013.

Louv, Richard. *Last Child in the Woods: Saving Our Children from Nature-Deficit Disorder*. Chapel Hill, NC: Algonquin, 2008.

Louv, Richard. "Ten Reasons Why Children and Adults Need Vitamin N." June 24, 2011. *On People and Nature* (blog). http://richardlouv.com/blog/Ten-Reasons-Why-Children-and-Adults-Need-Vitamin-N/ .

Maslow, Abraham H. *The Farther Reaches of Human Nature*. New York: Penguin, 1993.

Muir, John. *Stickeen: The Story of a Dog*. New York: Barnes & Noble, 2011.

Muktananda, Swami. *I AM THAT: The Science of Hamsa from the Vijnana Bhairava*. South Fallsburg, NY: Siddha Yoga, 2015.

Murray, William H. *The Scottish Himalayan Expedition*. London: J.M. Dent & Sons, 1951.

Paddison, Sara. *The Hidden Power of the Heart: Discovering an Unlimited Source of Intelligence*. 2nd ed. Boulder Creek, CA: Planetary Publications, 1998.

Perelandra Center for Nature Research (website). https://www.perelandra-ltd.com/ .

Perkins, John. "Stop Facebook? and Other Questions for the New Year." John Perkins (website). January 1, 2019. https://johnperkins.org/newsletter/stop-facebook-and-other-questions-for-the-new-year .

Redfield, James. *The Twelfth Insight: The Hour of Decision*. Celestine Series. New York: Grand Central Publishing, 2012.

Rinpoche, Tenzin Wangyal. *Awakening the Luminous Mind: Tibetan Meditation for Inner Peace and Joy*. Carlsbad, CA: Hay House, 2015.

Robinson, Phil Alden, dir. *Field of Dreams*. USA: Gordon Co./Universal Pictures, 1989.

Salzberg, Sharon. *Lovingkindness: The Revolutionary Art of Happiness*. Boulder, CO: Shambhala, 2018.

Saraydarian, Torkom. *Cosmos in Man*. Cave Creek, AZ: T.S.G. Publishing, 1973.

Saraydarian, Torkom. *The Flame of the Heart*. Cave Creek, AZ: T.S.G. Publishing, 1991.

Saraydarian, Torkom. *The Solar Angel*. Volume II. Cave Creek, AZ: T.S.G. Publishing, 2004.

Senge, Peter M. *The Fifth Discipline: The Art and Practice of the Learning Organization*. New York: Random House, 2010.

Soames, Mary. *Clementine Churchill: The Biography of a Marriage*. St. Paul, MN: Paragon House, 1987.

Spangler, David. "Our Inner Star." Lorian Association Newsletter (e-newsletter). December 7, 2018.

Spangler, David. "The Light is Here." Lorian Association Newsletter (e-newsletter). December 14, 2018.

Spangler, David. *Views from the Borderland* 2 (December 2018). Issaquah, WA: Lorian Association.

Strauss, Bob. "10 Things You Can Do to Help Wildlife: Ranging from Keeping Cats Indoors to Building Wildlife Shelters." ThoughtCo. (website). November 19, 2019. www.thoughtco.com/things-you-can-do-to-help-wildlife-4110438.

Teresa of Ávila, Saint. *The Interior Castle*. Trans. E. Allison Peers. New York: Doubleday, 1989.

Trout, Susan S. *Born to Serve: The Evolution of the Soul Through Service*. Alexandria, VA: Three Roses Press, 1997.

Trout, Susan S. *The Awakened Leader: Leadership as a Classroom of the Soul*. Alexandria VA: Three Roses Press, 2005.

Trout, Susan S. *The Clarion Call: Leadership and Group Life in the Aquarian Era*. Alexandria, VA: Three Roses Press, 2009.

Tzu, Lao. *Tao Te Ching: The Essential Translation of the Ancient Chinese Book of the Tao*. New York: Penguin, 2018.

Vaughan-Lee, Llewellyn. *Including the Earth in Our Prayers: A Global Dimension to Spiritual Practice*. Point Reyes, CA: The Golden Sufi Center, 2019.

Whitfield, Charles. *Boundaries and Relationships: Knowing, Protecting and Enjoying the Self*. Deerfield Beach, FL: Health Communications, 2010.

Woodman, Marion. *Conscious Femininity: Interviews with Marion Woodman*. Studies in Jungian Psychology by Jungian Analysts. Toronto: Inner City, 1993.

World Goodwill. *The Great Invocation: The Use and Significance of The Great Invocation*. New York, World Goodwill, n.d.

Xavier, Francisco Cândido. *Nosso Lar: Life in the Spirit World*. Trans. Darrel W. Kimble and Marcia M. Saiz. Brasilia, Brazil: International Spiritist Council, 2010.

Zweig, Connie, and Steven Wolf. *Romancing the Shadow: A Guide to Soul Work for a Vital, Authentic Life*. New York: Ballantine, 1997.

APPRECIATION

To Ann Benvenuto, for her high standards and expertise as an editor and her unwavering honor of the book's message. Our writer-editor partnership reflected a joint commitment to practice what the book teaches by placing our working relationship on the altar of devotion. Together, we **showed another way** to engage in a project that has the potential to help others learn, heal, and serve at this time of crisis on Planet Earth. I also appreciate the supportive comments and helpful suggestions from manuscript readers Carolyn Ducca and Peggy Millin.

ACKNOWLEDGMENTS

To Show Another Way is the fruit of words spoken to me and actions taken on my behalf by numerous people throughout my long life. These individuals have guided me toward my destiny and have nudged me back on purpose when I went astray. I have always known that I was born to learn and to view Earth as a school—one in which I was to personally grow, evolve, and learn how to help others and our planet. I have also always known I was to share my learning with others by **showing another way** to live—with understanding, purpose, and integrity. This book shares teachings I have been taught and which I have applied in Earth School "this time around." These teachings are universal and timeless.

I wish to acknowledge the following people who have **shown me another way** by appearing in my life as synchronicities—in unexpected, coincidental, meaningful, and healing ways that could not be explained. Such people do not show up pre-planned and they speak and act in certain ways to shift our thoughts, beliefs, decisions, and actions for the better. Those who **show us another way** can reorient us and even save our life.

The following people—and, not to be forgotten, certain cherished animal beings—have offered such shifts to me during the course of my precious life.

With gratitude, I acknowledge my parents George and Ruth Struve; Mrs. Schnegas, the midwife who helped me into the world; my siblings John Struve and family, Mary Martin and family, and Betty Werner and family; high school classmates and teachers Melvin Taylor and Jane Dittmer; friends Jean Muir Kilroy, Eugene Trout, and Sharon Brown; faculty members at Ball State, Stanford, and Northwestern Universities; Helen Dittman, Peggy Wood, staff, and children and families served at the Anchorage Treatment Center; graduate students and families served at the Department of Learning Disabilities of the University of the Pacific, San Francisco; colleagues Peggy Millin, Molly Whitehouse, Jean and Merrill Whitman, Shirley Fine, and Cornelius Bennhold; Institute for the Advancement of Service participants, volunteers, and staff from its inception in 1980 to today; all past Institute board members; present Institute board members Ann Benvenuto, Maggie Scobie, and Iris Williams; spiritual teachers Michelangelo, Kay Mann, Ken Wapnick, Judith Skutch Whitson, Roberto Assagioli, Torkom Saraydarian, the Dalai Lama, Tenzin Wangyal Rinpoche, and Kempo Konchog Gyaltshen; Swami Muktananda, Swami Chidvilasananda, Swami Ishwarananda, Swami Indirananda, and Panna Hamilton at the Siddha Yoga Ashram; and animal companion laying hens Reddie, Speckie, and Dirty; Husky dog Tok; and cats Cookie, Targie-Miracles, Meara, Clare, and Clare Thomasina.

My heart-filled love to all those who literally saved my life, those who believed in my potential, and those who reminded me of my life's purpose when I had lost my way.

- Written on Thanksgiving Day
November 28, 2019

ABOUT THE AUTHOR

Susan S. Trout, PhD, has focused her life on a single purpose—to practice true service and teach others to do the same. Dedicating her life to teaching about personal healing, service, leadership, soul development, and group life, Susan has served leaders and organizations worldwide. Her training guides them to view and practice their service and leadership as a classroom for spiritual development and self-transformation—a classroom of the soul. Susan's work has been cited in countless publications of various disciplines.

In 1980, Susan cofounded and pioneered an educational and spiritual organization in Washington, DC, which ultimately became the Institute for the Advancement of Service (www.showanotherway.org). The Institute's school of thought is known as **The Clarion Wa**y—the name given to the collective teachings of her seminal work, *The Soul and Service Trilogy. The Trilogy* synthesizes universal psychological and spiritual principles and translates them into practical templates for transforming the lives of individuals and groups. Providing a unique spiritual roadmap to navigate this challenging time in the history of our world, *The Soul and Service Trilogy* includes *Born to Serve: The Evolution of the Soul Through Service*, with a foreword by His Holiness the Dalai Lama (1997); *The Awakened Leader: Leadership as a Classroom of the Soul* (2005); and *The Clarion Call: Leadership and Group Life in the Aquarian Era* (2009).

Subsequent to receiving a bachelor's degree in speech and hearing therapy at Ball State University, Susan earned graduate degrees from Stanford and Northwestern Universities in psychoneurology, speech pathology, audiology, deaf education, and communication disorders. In the 1970s, she cofounded and served as the chair of an innovative, nationally recognized clinical training program in neurological learning disorders at the

University of the Pacific Medical Center in San Francisco. During this decade, she also served as a researcher in neurological learning disorders in children at the San Francisco-based Langley Porter Institute, University of California Medical Center. In the 1960s, Susan was a specialist in communication disorders and a teacher of both deaf and brain-injured children at a children's treatment center in Anchorage, Alaska. She also served as a research audiologist for the Arctic Health Research Center, traveling to numerous Native villages throughout Alaska.

For more information about Susan Trout or **The Clarion Way** programs, visit www.showanotherway.org. To sign up for her blog, visit www.susantroutsblog.com.

ABOUT THE INSTITUTE FOR
THE ADVANCEMENT OF SERVICE

The Institute for the Advancement of Service ("The Institute") is a globally aware service organization that serves as a wayshower for individuals and groups who feel called to bring into manifestation a soul-inspired, holographic model of leadership and group life.

Founded in 1980 as an educational and nonsectarian spiritual organization, the Institute offers classes and trainings in the dynamic relationship between soul development, service, leadership, and group life, providing support and practices that build and sustain humanity's inner strength during this time of crisis on Planet Earth.

The Institute's mission is

◆ to disseminate the teachings and practices of **The Clarion Way**, the psychospiritual path of the Institute, through publications, classes, lectures, and the Institute's teaching website;

◆ to support individuals, groups, and organizations who are ready to recognize Earth as a school in which we learn, grow, and serve, **showing another way** to navigate these challenging times;

◆ to help our planet heal and evolve by radiating Light into the world and guiding others in applying new methods to usher in the new reality of a Planet Earth illuminated with Divine Light.

The Institute's teachings, known as **The Clarion Way,** awaken our inner knowing and guide us in applying that knowing in the world through action. They have been published in four books by Susan S. Trout, PhD: *To Show Another Way: How to Learn, Heal and Serve at a time of Crisis on Planet Earth* and *The Soul and Service Trilogy*. *The Trilogy* consists of three books: *Born to Serve: The Evolution of the Soul Through Service* with a foreword by His Holiness the Dalai Lama; *The Awakened Leader: Leadership as a Classroom of the Soul*; and *The Clarion Call: Leadership and Group Life in the Aquarian Era*. Ten Universal Tributes provide a roadmap for attaining self-transformation through service. Three Roses Press publishes all Institute books and materials. The Institute is a nonprofit 501(c)3 organization.

> *As awakened individuals, leaders, and groups,*
> *we can transform our communities and organizations so that they*
> *truly support their members and those they serve.*
> *We harvest the good from where we have been*
> *and welcome change as new models unfold.*
> *We call on the wisdom of the universe to help us*
> *with the practical application of that knowledge.*
> *We deepen our collective understanding*
> *of what wants to emerge in the world.*
> *Taking a step through the Aquarian doorway,*
> *we move out of the personal into the collective*
> *and out of duality into wholeness.*
> *We choose to articulate a new template for the evolution*
> *of soul-inspired leadership and group consciousness.*

~ FROM *THE CLARION CALL*

CONTACT INFORMATION

Institute for the Advancement of Service
PO Box 320245
Alexandria, VA 22320

www.showanotherway.org
www.susantroutsblog.com

Susan Trout and the Institute's faculty members are dedicating their efforts to supporting those individuals who wish to lead a Support Circle on the teachings of *To Show Another Way*. If we can assist you, please reach out by emailing us at faculty@showanotherway.org.

You may purchase *To Show Another Way* or any of *The Soul and Service Trilogy* books on our website, or order them directly from the Institute by contacting us at info@showanotherway.org.

Ask about our special discount for books ordered for Support Circle members.